Response
to Intervention
the in Core Content Areas
A Practical Approach for Educators

Response
to Intervention
_{the}ⁱⁿ Core Content Areas

A Practical Approach for Educators

Edited by **Jeffrey P. Bakken, Ph.D.**

PRUFROCK PRESS INC.
WACO, TEXAS

Library of Congress Cataloging-in-Publication Data

Response to intervention in the core content areas : a practical approach for educators / edited by Jeffrey P. Bakken.
    p. cm.
  ISBN 978-1-59363-919-8 (pbk.)
  1. Response to intervention (Learning disabled children) 2. Remedial teaching. I. Bakken, Jeffrey P.
  LC4705.R487 2012+
  371.9--dc23

                        2011049730

Edited by Lacy Compton

Cover and layout design by Raquel Trevino

ISBN-13: 978-1-59363-919-8

Printed in the United States of America.

At the time of this book's publication, all facts and figures cited are the most current available. All telephone numbers, addresses, and website URLs are accurate and active. All publications, organizations, websites, and other resources exist as described in the book, and all have been verified. The editor and Prufrock Press Inc. make no warranty or guarantee concerning the information and materials given out by organizations or content found at websites, and we are not responsible for any changes that occur after this book's publication. If you find an error, please contact Prufrock Press Inc.

Prufrock Press Inc.
P.O. Box 8813
Waco, TX 76714-8813
Phone: (800) 998-2208
Fax: (800) 240-0333
http://www.prufrock.com

Table
of Contents

Response
to Intervention in the Core Content Areas: A Practical Approach for Educators

Our school climate has been changing over the last 10 years and this means that our teachers also need to change. The current focus is on educating *all* students to the best of their ability in the general education classroom. Teachers need to find out which students are having problems, provide them support, and keep delivering more intensified supports with hopes the students will then learn the content and be successful. As a last resort, the struggling student may be referred for special education services, but only if all else fails and there is sufficient documentation of what was tried, for how long, and what the outcomes were. It is not to say that special education is a negative or bad thing, but that it should not be the first consideration when students are having academic or social difficulties in the classroom. The familiar term for this new approach is Response to Intervention (RtI). RtI is a school-based, multitiered system that has an academic and social behavior focus. This system utilizes data-based decision making in conjunction with appropriate levels of empirically based interventions. It can be quite a complex system, but if explained in the right way, it is very easy to understand. The purpose of this book is to help you understand what RtI is and how it impacts all kinds of learners in all kinds of environments.

Response to Intervention in the Core Content Areas: A Practical Approach for Educators discusses critical and practical issues related to RtI and how best to deal with all kinds of students in many different content-area classes. This book is comprised of 13 comprehensive and exhaustive chapters addressing important topics related to RtI that teachers will face. In this book, Chapter 1 discusses "What Is RtI?"; Chapter 2 focuses on "Prevention and Early Identification of Students With Academic Difficulties—Tier I"; Chapter 3 addresses "More Intense Instruction—Tiers II and III of RtI"; Chapter 4 explains "Assessment Considerations in Three-Tier Approaches to Academic Instruction"; Chapter 5 provides information on "Making Data-Based Decisions in Tiers I, II, and III"; Chapter 6 explores "English Language Learners and RtI"; Chapter 7 discusses "Culturally and Linguistically Diverse Students and RtI"; Chapter 8 focuses on "Assessment and Instruction in Reading in an RtI Classroom"; Chapter 9 addresses "RtI in Writing: Suggested Screening, Intervention, and Progress Monitoring"; Chapter 10 discusses "Using RtI in the Mathematics Classroom"; Chapter 11 focuses on "Using RtI in the Science Classroom"; Chapter 12 discusses "Using RtI in the Social Studies Classroom"; and Chapter 13 addresses "Data-Based Decision Making Across a Multitiered System of Support." Each chapter gives thorough descriptions and explanations of the topics along with many practical examples that all teachers should find very beneficial. In addition, each chapter has a case study related to real teacher experiences to help you understand the process of RtI.

Chapter 1, "What Is RtI?," discusses what exactly RtI is, why we should do it, and how it works. It also discusses how it is related to the law, the roles of the general and special educator, and resources that might be needed. Lastly, it discusses interventions and how to begin the process.

Chapter 2, "Prevention and Early Identification of Students With Academic Difficulties—Tier I," focuses specifically on early identification and being proactive. Topics include effective teaching, student learning, and formative evaluation. It also explains when teachers should intervene, what criteria they should use, and the use of data to make data-based decisions.

Chapter 3, "More Intense Instruction—Tiers II and III of RtI," deals with the specifics related to interventions in Tiers II and III. It discusses the characteristics of effective interventions and the steps necessary to implement them. Academic and social behavior of students are explained and discussed.

Chapter 4, "Assessment Considerations in Three-Tier Approaches to Academic Instruction," describes the role of assessment as well as decision making in the RtI process. A major focus is on the collection of "good" useable data, where it comes from, and how we interpret it. It also discusses a student's current progress and that progress compared to his or her peers.

Lastly, this chapter discusses obtaining proper documentation and graphing the data results in order to track progress.

Chapter 5, "Making Data-Based Decisions in Tiers I, II, and III," provides specific information on Universal Screening as well as Tiers I, II, and III. The concept of frequent and consistent data collection is further discussed. Steps of assessment are provided, and the concept of decision making based on data is explained. Progress monitoring is also extensively discussed and elaborated on with many examples.

Chapter 6, "English Language Learners and RtI," explores the important topic of serving English language learners. First a breakdown of just how many students fall into this category is described. Then typical models are discussed, as well as effective instruction for these learners. Next implications for RtI are explained and information about Tiers I, II, and III is summarized.

Chapter 7, "Culturally and Linguistically Diverse Students and RtI," discusses how teachers can effectively work with students who are culturally and linguistically diverse. First, problems these learners encounter are discussed, followed by a description of how RtI pertains to these individuals. The process of working with these students in the different tiers is explained, and mistakes to avoid when working with this population are summarized.

Chapter 8, "Assessment and Instruction in Reading in an RtI Classroom," focuses on the content area of reading and RtI. The reading process is discussed, as is data collection. Next, interventions, data collection, and data analysis are explained. Many interventions are highlighted, along with an explanation of how reading comprehension occurs. Finally, the process of learning through reading is highlighted.

Chapter 9, "RtI in Writing: Suggested Screening, Intervention, and Progress Monitoring," touches upon the content area of writing and RtI. First, the act of writing is explained and effective interventions are highlighted. Writing through the three tiers is explained. Next, the implementation steps a teacher can follow are summarized. Finally, how teachers can incorporate writing into their daily lessons and the steps of that process are explained.

Chapter 10, "Using RtI in the Mathematics Classroom," addresses the content area of mathematics and RtI. The chapter opens by discussing mathematics and how it is typically taught. Academic tasks the student must complete to be successful are explained. Then, the chapter focuses on the collection of appropriate data at the different tiers. Progress monitoring is discussed, and effective evidence-based strategies with implementation steps are highlighted.

Chapter 11, "Using RtI in the Science Classroom," discusses the content area of science and RtI. Academic tasks required of students in science classrooms are explained and how RtI works in these environments is highlighted. In addition, what happens in the different tiers is explained and effective teaching methods and evidence-based practices are summarized. Also highlighted are the aspects of effective data collection methods and how to make decisions based on the data.

Chapter 12, "Using RtI in the Social Studies Classroom," focuses on the content area of social studies and RtI. First, social studies is summarized and explained. Academic tasks required of students in social studies classrooms are explained and how RtI works in these environments is highlighted. What happens in Tiers I, II, and III is explained and effective teaching methods and evidence-based practices are summarized. Also highlighted is the aspect of effective data collection methods and making decisions based on the data.

Chapter 13, "Data-Based Decision Making Across a Multitiered System of Support," summarizes the RtI process and is the conclusion chapter of this book. The goal is to help tie everything together and serve as a wrap-up chapter. Issues such as Adequate Yearly Progress, Universal Screening, the core curriculum, effectiveness of Tier II and III support, and effectiveness of special education are addressed. Lastly, the decision-making process is summarized and explained.

The text is written in a style that readers can comprehend and understand and is supported with many examples. In addition, the information can be easily applied by any type of teacher with any type of student in any type of setting. In preparing this book, experts in the field related to RtI were contacted to write meaningful and useful chapters and provide a detailed and comprehensive analysis of all of the different topics a teacher in an RtI environment might experience. On the whole, this book will be an added resource to all teachers working with all types of students in our schools. I am confident that readers will find this book to be helpful and useful regarding all of the aspects associated with teaching in an RtI environment. I think this book is an excellent required or supplementary text for all preservice or experienced teachers regarding the instruction of students in an RtI environment.

CHAPTER 1

What

Is RtI?

Daniel L. Gadke, Gary L. Cates, and Mark E. Swerdlik

Response to Intervention (RtI) is a school-based, multitiered system of academic and social behavior support that utilizes data-based decision making to match students with appropriate levels of empirically based academic and social behavioral support (Cates, Blum, & Swerdlik, 2011; National Association of State Directors of Special Education, 2005). More specifically, RtI emphasizes the systematic collection, analysis, interpretation, and utilization of data to match student levels of academic functioning and social behavior with appropriate instruction and intervention. The primary idea behind RtI is to identify students' needs early to prevent school-based problems from intensifying.

In addition to understanding what RtI is, it is also important to understand what RtI is not. RtI is not a tangible prepackaged program that a school simply implements with its staff and students. RtI is rather a framework of problem solving through data-based decision-making service delivery. Often, RtI is confused with a simple act such as screening using reading fluency probes three times a year or providing a group of students with a math intervention. Although these examples are found within an RtI framework, RtI is much more than any one of them in isolation. Essentially, RtI is a system requiring many components including (but not limited to) screening, diagnostics, intervention implementation, progress monitoring, and evaluation.

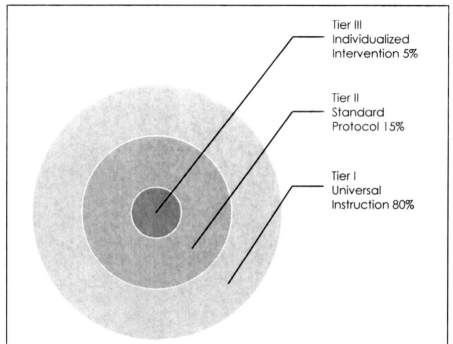

Figure 1.1. A three-tiered Response to Intervention model as presented in Cates, Blum, and Swerdlik (2011).

How Does an RtI Framework Work?

Fortunately, an RtI framework of service delivery is quite user friendly. As mentioned previously, RtI is a multitiered system of support. For the purposes of this chapter, we outline a three-tiered model as described by Cates, Blum, and Swerdlik (2011). Figure 1.1 displays a three-tiered model of student support.

Tier I (Universal Core)

The outer circle represents Tier I. Tier I curriculum, instruction, and assessment should be scientifically based and provided to all students. It is suggested that approximately 80% of the students should sufficiently benefit from Tier I services alone. The level of effectiveness is often determined by the outcome of high-stakes testing typically dictated by the school's state board of education. If the curriculum and/or instruction is not meeting the needs of 80% of the students, changes need to be made to improve either the curriculum, the instruction, or both.

The method of assessment at the Tier I level is simply review of school-level report cards (not the report cards of individual students) and screening. The purpose of assessment at Tier I is to identify (a) areas that need to be targeted at the building level for all students, and (b) students who are at the greatest risk for falling behind their peers and/or not meeting state assessment standards. This universal screening of all students should be conducted three times during the school year (e.g., fall, winter, spring) in the areas of reading, mathematics, writing, and behavior. Those students who do not meet certain predetermined levels of performance are identified as being at risk for failure and are subsequently provided Tier II assessment and intervention.

Tier II (Targeted Group Interventions)

The middle circle in Figure 1.1 represents Tier II. Tier II curriculum and instruction should be delivered to approximately 15% percent of the student population for any given area of academics and behavior. The services at Tier II should be in addition to the core universal Tier I instruction. Typically, Tier II interventions are provided in a small-group format to children who are experiencing similar problems using a scripted standardized protocol or intervention program that is scientifically based.

The goal of Tier II assessment includes minimizing the identification of false positives, or children who were identified as at risk on the screener but who do not actually need additional services. Aside from minimizing the overidentification of children, a primary purpose of Tier II assessment should be to identify the general area of weakness of a particular student. In general, although Tier II assessment reduces the need to do lengthier and in-depth assessments with every child, the assessment measures do require more time and resources to administer than a Tier I screening measure.

Tier III (Individualized Intervention)

The innermost circle represents Tier III. Tier III interventions typically involve approximately 5% of the student population. The services should be provided in addition to Tier I and Tier II services. Intervention should be provided to all students who are not making adequate progress with Tier II levels of support. Evidenced-based Tier III interventions are individualized to meet the unique learning deficits of the student. These unique learning deficits can be identified through the use of methods such as curriculum-based evaluation (Howell & Nolet, 2000) or functional assessment (Steege

3

& Watson, 2009). These types of assessment strategies for Tier III require increased time and resources to deliver than the screeners and diagnostic tools at Tier I and II respectively.

RtI Model as a Whole

Because at each tier both assessment and instruction/intervention change with regard to frequency and intensity, there are four important points to be made with regard to a three-tiered model of RtI. First, tiers are not mutually exclusive from one another (i.e., a child is not placed in one tier or another). That is, if it is determined through assessment that a child requires Tier III intervention, then the child also receives Tier II and Tier I interventions. In the example in Figure 1.2, during Tier III, William receives Tier II with Gary and Tier I with both Gary and Ryan. Second, children receiving services at the same level of intensity (e.g., Tier II) may be provided with different interventions (e.g., different Tier II reading interventions). William, if performing well in math, may have the Think Fast™ program faded to two sessions per week, while Ryan would continue to have a full three sessions per week. Third, students may spend different amounts of time in different tiers depending on their specific need. Similar to the number of sessions, the amount of time in the intervention for William could be faded after 9 weeks, while Ryan may continue to get the intervention for multiple quarters. Finally, students can be at different tiers for different needs. For example, a child may be provided Tier I services for reading, but receive Tier II services for math and Tier III services for writing. This is apparent in Figure 1.2.

When Does One Do RtI?

As the definition suggests, RtI is a perpetual working system; it should be implemented at all times. The same RtI framework should address all of a student's school-based behaviors in the academic, social-emotional, and behavioral domains. In fact, it is suggested that all school improvement plans, as well as staff and teacher professional development, be strategically crafted under the RtI framework.

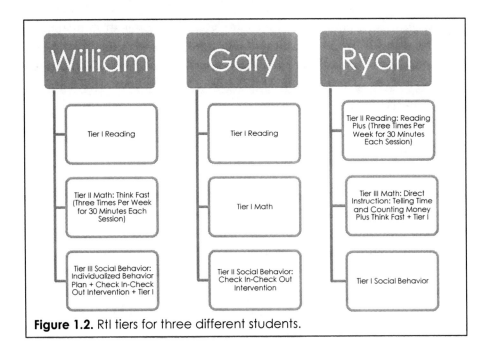

Figure 1.2. RtI tiers for three different students.

Why Do RtI?

There are four major reasons for implementing an RtI framework within schools. First, it emphasizes data-based decision making. It is critical that educators be accustomed to considering a variety of data to make accurate decisions related to their instructional practices (e.g., Cates et al., 2003). Second, an RtI framework emphasizes the importance of evidence-based practice. With increased emphasis on educational accountability through such legislation as the Individuals with Disabilities Education Improvement Act (IDEA) and the No Child Left Behind Act (NCLB), an RtI framework can ensure that schools are adhering to effective instructional practices and appropriately high educational standards. Third, RtI focuses on the performance of all students. Unlike traditional models of school service delivery, RtI does not focus exclusively on specific students such as those entitled to special education. Although a comprehensive RtI model can effectively facilitate the special education entitlement process (Peterson, Prasse, Shinn, & Swerdlik, 2007), it more broadly emphasizes the importance of matching the instructional needs of all students with the available resources in a school (Cates et al., 2011). Fourth, RtI may be required by law. Although no federal mandate (including NCLB or IDEA) currently exists to enforce an RtI model of educational service delivery, all states are implementing some form of RtI policy (Derby, 2011). The most comprehensive report written on a state level mandating an implementation of RtI in July of 2009 indicated that nine states were mandating RtI. However, despite limited state mandates, another survey in 2009 indicated that about 71% of responding districts were at some level of RtI implementation (Pascopella, 2010)

Using Data to Make Decisions

Unfortunately, all too often decisions are made according to anecdotal information, beliefs, feelings of school staff, and arbitrary markers. This method has found a home for itself in the world of education. RtI may help minimize this practice through the use of continuous data collection, analysis, and utilization. Schools implementing RtI continuously screen and monitor student performance across the various tiers in addition to diagnostic data collection and overall program evaluation. See Chapter 5 on data-based decision making in RtI schools for more information.

Evidence-Based Practice

The use of data lends itself to evidence-based practices (EBP). Essentially, EBP is the use of data to make decisions about the educational needs of students. Specifically, EBP involves using effective and efficient educational practices through the provision of services to students based on their respective educational needs, thus minimizing learning and social behavioral concerns. EBPs are implemented in a systematic fashion specifically targeting the learning or behavioral problems that are demonstrated to be problematic (through the collection of data) early on. The level of intensity is also determined through the collection of data and regular progress monitoring during the various stages of intervention implementation.

Legal Basis for RtI

Current legislation is in place that has been designed specifically to target schools and hold them accountable for the educational needs of their students. RtI serves as a vehicle for schools to be accountable for their actions and educational decisions. Such legislation includes the No Child Left Behind Act (2001) and the Individuals with Disabilities Education Improvement Act (2004).

The No Child Left Behind Act of 2001 (NCLB) was signed into law in January 2002. The agenda of NCLB includes closing the achievement gap between the majority and historically lower achieving groups, focusing on student outcomes, using scientifically based methods of instructions, and the implementation and assessment of academic standards. Schools are monitored according to student performance on statewide high-stakes tests mandated by the state board of education. Under NCLB, schools that repeatedly fail to meet minimal annual standards are provided with a series of remedial actions aimed at increasing student performance. The most serious penalties include complete restructuring of a school and its personnel.

The Individuals with Disabilities Education Act (IDEA) was most recently reauthorized in 2004. The intent of the reauthorization was to parallel the mandates put into effect under NCLB. The mandates of IDEA include having all children with disabilities take part in annual state assessments and schools providing evidence that children are being provided with scientifically based instruction. Additionally, if a school does elect to include a particular student with a placement in special education, the school must document that the child has characteristics of a disability, a gap in performance, and a need for additional services (i.e., not responding to current level of services). IDEA allows for educational institutions to use RtI for special education eligibility. Because RtI emphasizes the early identification of students at risk, it may prove helpful in the early identification of students in need of special education services.

Combined mandates of NCLB and IDEA place a demand on schools for increased accountability and the use of high-quality scientifically based instruction. Increased pressure on the school also demands the use of data collection and routine assessment of the students to ensure the educational needs of each child, with or without a disability, are being met. RtI serves as a vehicle for schools to meet these various demands and systematically provide students with the support they need to be successful in meeting educational standards.

Empirical Support for RtI

Unfortunately, the turnaround from research to practice, especially in education, can be upward of 20 years (e.g., Skinner, 1984). That is, heavily explored and empirically supported strategies often take years before they are actually used in the school system. An additional concern is that practices that have little to no empirical support often make their way into the school systems (e.g., focusing on learning styles; see Kavale & Forness,

1987). Fortunately, RtI is rooted in years of empirical research including curriculum-based measurement (CBM; Deno, 1985), behavioral consultation (Bergan & Kratochwill, 1990), and Positive Behavioral Intervention Supports (PBIS; Sugai & Horner, 2006).

CBM, as developed by Deno (1985), is a staple of RtI. The use of these tools allows for all students to be regularly assessed in a fashion that is highly effective, efficient, and representative of the curriculum that a student is exposed to. The benchmarking and progress-monitoring activities prevalent in most RtI models today are based on the idea of CBM. In addition, locating the instructional level of specific students at Tier II in the form of curriculum-based assessment (CBA) and the individual diagnostic assessment that is conducted at Tier III in the form of curriculum-based evaluation (CBE) are also similarly rooted in the CBM framework.

Although CBM, CBA, and CBE are at the heart of RtI, the modern system of RtI is really based on the work of Bergan and Kratochwill (1990), Sugai and Horner (2006), and Gresham (1991). Bergan and Kratochwill outlined a model of a Behavioral Consultation that included the evaluation of the implemented intervention. This process also included modifying the intervention based on the evaluation, if necessary, to meet the needs of the consultee. This adaption of intervention is prevalent in the RtI framework. In addition, Sugai and Horner's Positive Behavior Intervention Supports model was introduced as a systemwide tiered prevention model focusing on intervention supports. This three-tiered system is the general framework for RtI as we know it today. Although Sugai and Horner (2006) may have provided a framework for social behavior in schools specifically, Gresham (1991) pioneered the concept of identifying students for special education based on their responsiveness to intervention.

Best Practices Approach

Although the individual components of RtI as described above have been present in many states for many years, it has only recently started to emerge as a comprehensive model for school systems (Burns & Gibbons, 2008). Prior to using RtI, schools implementing a traditional model of service delivery generally provided services to students who demonstrated a severe discrepancy from their peers on achievement tests or a severe discrepancy between their own cognitive ability and their respective level of academic performance.

Although this may appear to be a reasonable method for allocating services and resources to students, there are a number or inherent problems associated with a traditional method.

First, the traditional model only focused on students who were referred by an adult who suspected the student to be severely struggling. In contrast, a hallmark of RtI is universal screening for academic and social behavioral deficits of all students relative to their respective peers or standards-based criteria. Second, this form of assessment for the allocation of resources involves a tremendous amount of time and resources. In fact, under the traditional model, each individual assessment requires numerous hours of assessment and report writing. This is far from an efficient use of time, especially when there may be any number of children that are in need of assessment. In contrast, an RtI model requires only a few minutes of assessment per student. Moreover, many of the brief screening assessments can be administered in a group format, saving additional time and personnel resources. Third, traditional assessment methods for the allocation of services to students is often conducted with commercial instruments that seek to provide a measurement of student performance relative to a representative national sample with little regard to the actual curriculum a student may be exposed to. In contrast, the RtI framework can be constructed such that a student's actual curriculum is used for the assessment purposes.

Finally, and perhaps the greatest concern related to the traditional model of allocation of services to students is that the traditional model requires waiting for a child to demonstrate significantly discrepant performance. Unfortunately, by the time significantly discrepant performance is obtained, the child may perform lower than his peers by multiple grade levels. Moreover, an isolated academic concern (e.g., reading fluency) may have migrated to negatively impact other areas of learning (e.g., math word problems or social studies). In contrast, the RtI model of assessment requires screenings of academic and social behavior multiple times per year that allows for a detection of performance that is not following an ideal developmental trajectory. Essentially, the data collected through the traditional model are time consuming, lack functional use for interventions, are not representative of what the child is learning, and come too late. In contrast, the RtI model is timelier, can be linked to academic or social-behavioral instruction because it can be constructed from the child's current curriculum, and has a prevention focus. That is, screening for potential problems allows for early intervening steps.

Where Do You Implement RtI— General or Special Education?

General Education Implementation

At the district and building levels, RtI is intended to be integrated into both the general and special education systems. Often RtI is misinterpreted to be a special education initiative, meaning it is primarily part of and implemented by special educators. Assessment and intervention within an effective RtI system should be integrated into all of the tiers discussed previously, which would include both general and special education.

It may be apparent that an RtI model of service delivery focuses on the early detection of students who are at risk for not making adequate progress. By using screening instruments that may predict academic yearly progress (AYP) outcomes, educators can help identify students who may be at risk for not meeting state-level assessment expectations. In doing so, educators can more adequately address instructional needs (through instructional/curriculum modification) and change the educational trajectories of these students through the use of targeted (Tier II) interventions. Tier II interventions can be implemented either within the general education classroom (as part of differentiated instruction), referred to as "push-in" services, or outside of the general education classroom, referred to as "pull-out" services.

Based on the particular students' response to these targeted interventions, the interventions can either be faded (i.e., moving toward Tier I only) or intensified (i.e., moving toward Tier III) seamlessly along a continuum of educational service delivery. Typically Tier III services are more individualized and can be provided either outside (pull-out services) or inside (push-in services) the general education classroom. Although either general or special education personnel can provide these services, most often RtI services are provided as part of general education. In addition to intervention at Tier III, monitoring of student progress continues. The monitoring of progress allows for decisions to be made as to whether or not even more intensive interventions are necessary. If there is a positive response to the intervention, then a determination is made as to whether the intensity of these successful interventions can be maintained within general education or if the student meets eligibility criteria to receive these interventions as part of special education (e.g., Illinois State Board of Education, 2011).

Special Education Implementation

Related more specifically to determining eligibility for special education within an RtI framework, as noted previously, IDEA (2004) permitted the use of a student's response to scientifically based interventions as a method for determining eligibility for special education. When using a student's response to intervention as a basis for special education eligibility and entitlement decisions, the following questions are asked and must be answered by the Individualized Education Program (IEP) team. First, what is the discrepancy of the student's performance with the peer group and/or standard? The focus in responding to this question is on determining if the student is achieving adequately to meet age- or state-approved grade-level standards. If the student is achieving significantly below his grade-level peers or not meeting state-approved grade-level benchmarks, it must be further determined that the student was provided appropriate instruction. For example, if the majority of a student's grade-level peers are also not achieving adequately for their age or fail to meet state-approved grade-level standards, then it would be more difficult to suggest that the lack of achievement is due to a disability rather than the student not being exposed to appropriate/effective core instruction. Second, what is the student's educational progress as measured by rate of improvement? It must be determined whether the progress the student is making in response to scientifically based interventions will allow the student to close the achievement gap with her peers within a reasonable amount of time. Finally, what are the instructional needs of the student? To answer this last question, the focus is on determining that instructional needs have been identified that are beyond what can be met with general education resources alone. This is evident when the curriculum, intensity of instruction (e.g., amount and rate of practice and feedback, how explicit the instruction is, amount of time weekly the intervention is delivered), and/or environmental conditions (e.g., size of the group such as individualized or small group) are more intense as compared to the needs of other students in the general education environment.

What Resources Are Needed?

In order to effectively implement an RtI system a number of resources are needed. These resources include time, space, involvement of key personnel, and funding (Cates et al., 2011).

Time

Time represents a critical resource in effective implementation of an RtI system in two ways. The first is to ensure adequate time is devoted to deliver core instruction to all students. As an example, perhaps a significant number of first-grade students (e.g., more than 20%) are not adequately achieving in reading. An analysis of the core curriculum suggests that there is very limited classroom time devoted to phonics instruction. In order for the students to achieve adequately in reading, a decision is made to increase the amount of time devoted to phonics instruction to all students as part of the core instruction. The second way that time represents a critical resource centers around the need for time to be allotted during the instructional day to deliver interventions either within the classroom (push-in) or outside of the general education class (pull-out). This is typically accomplished by establishing a daily intervention time during which there is flexibility for students to move to appropriate intervention groups without missing out on core instruction.

Space

In addition to time, there must also be space for the various intervention groups to meet. Many schools have limited space. Space needs to be considered when determining the length and time in the scheduling of Tier II and III pull-out intervention groups. Many schools may elect to use space such as the cafeteria, hallways, or music rooms at times when traffic is lower to decrease distractions in those areas.

Person Power

As discussed in this introductory chapter, RtI involves the delivering of effective core instruction and a variety of interventions to address the academic and social-emotional-behavioral needs of students. In addition to having the time and space for these interventions, there must also be the personnel to deliver them. However, with education funding being limited, additional personnel typically cannot be hired but rather the roles and responsibilities of school personnel within an RtI system must change. These personnel include the principal, general education teachers, special education teachers, parents, and other school personnel.

Administrator/Principal. Research on effective RtI implementation (Cates et al., 2011; Peterson et al., 2007) has found that strong leadership by the building principal represents the most important predictor of successful implementation of an RtI system within a building. This leadership includes the principal being knowledgeable about basic RtI principles and providing strong support of the initiative. This support requires providing the critical resources including support for the changing roles and responsibilities of various school personnel, building time into the daily instructional schedule to implement Tier II and III interventions, and allowing space to provide these interventions. Further, principals demonstrate support by building into their budgets funding to purchase a variety of scientifically based standard protocol interventions to target identified academic and social-emotional-behavioral skills. Principals must also function as effective instructional leaders in their buildings to support effective core instruction provided to all students. Strong core instruction is a critical component of any effective RtI system.

Special educator. The special educator is frequently asked to deliver interventions to not only those students who have IEPs, but to integrate into their groups students who are in need of targeted Tier II or more individualized Tier III interventions. In addition, special educators often have a more significant consultation role in an RtI system, serving as members of grade level and/or individual problem-solving teams.

General education teacher. The general education teacher will frequently be involved in data-based decision making by serving as members of the grade-level team. This grade-level team within an RtI system typically determines which students require Tier II intervention and which academic or behavioral skill(s) to target, as well as analyzes progress-monitoring data to assess the student's response to Tier II intervention. Grade-level teams then arrive at decisions based on these data as to whether to continue the Tier II intervention, intensify it, or move the student back to solely core instruction. General education teachers also frequently implement these Tier II interventions through either push-in or pull-out services during a designated intervention time. Further, general education teachers are heavily involved in analyzing their core instruction if more than 20% of their students are not meeting grade-level benchmarks. General education teachers also frequently serve as members of Tier III individual problem-solving teams, either as a building-level teacher representative or as the referring teacher of the student being discussed.

Special service personnel. Special service personnel, who may include the school psychologist, social worker, and guidance counselor, also represent a critical resource for a building implementing an RtI system. For example, school psychologists are experts in data-based decision making including administering, scoring, and interpreting data obtained from universal screening, diagnostic assessment, and progress monitoring. Both school psychologists and social workers serve as consultants to or are members of the building-level RtI implementation team, and grade-level and individual problem-solving teams engaging in data-based decision making. A number of school psychologists, social workers, and guidance counselors also become involved in administering universal screening measures and implementing Tier II and III academic and/or social-emotional-behavioral interventions as part of an RtI system implemented at the building level.

Parents. Parents also function as important resources for implementing an effective RtI system within a district and individual buildings. It is recommended (Cates et al., 2011) that parents be a part of the districtwide and individual building RtI implementation teams. As these RtI teams typically deal with implementation issues at the district or building levels and individual students are not discussed, confidentiality is not violated by having a parent representative involved on these teams. At the individual student level, parent involvement and support, as part of the individual problem-solving process, is critical to developing effective interventions for particular students. Parents frequently provide very useful information that can be part of the various stages of individual problem solving including identifying and analyzing academic and behavioral problems as well as in the development and implementation of various interventions. Research (Christenson & Sheridan, 2001) supports that parent involvement is strongly related to a student's academic achievement and developing social competence. Finally, strong parent support evidenced through an organization such as the building's Parent Teacher Organization (PTO) can provide funding to purchase curricular materials and standard protocol interventions for use at Tiers II and III as well as educate parents as to the goals, various components, and procedures of the RtI system.

Funding

As noted above, it is typically the case that schools do not have additional funding to hire more school personnel, either certified teachers or teacher assistants, to implement interventions as part of a RtI system. However, if funding is available, then this can be a very valuable resource. Teachers and/or teacher assistants hired to assist in the implementation of RtI must be well trained in Tier II and/or III standard protocol interventions and be part of the problem-solving process at each stage such as collecting and analyzing progress-monitoring data. Although many schools are able to effectively implement an RtI system without additional personnel, funding is needed to purchase scientifically based core curricula and standard protocol interventions. The use of an Internet-based data management system such as AIMSweb or DIBELS also contributes to successful RtI implementation but carries a per pupil cost that must be funded by the school district or building.

Where Do I Start When I Am Ready to Implement RtI?

Many schools that are just beginning to implement an RtI system grapple with the question of where to begin. Should the school implement universal screening in each of the basic skill areas or begin with just one area such as reading? Should the school begin by implementing problem solving at all levels including Tier III or begin by focusing on developing strong core instruction so that at least 80% of students at each grade level are meeting benchmarks in the various academic skill areas? We recommend that they begin small, focusing only on one academic area, often reading due to its relationship to success in other academic areas, and then expand the RtI system to include other curricular areas (Cates et al., 2011). Further, we recommend that if universal screening data are indicating that less than 80% of students at particular grade levels are meeting grade-level benchmarks, then the focus of RtI implementation should be on strengthening the core instruction rather than developing Tier III interventions and overloading the system with the number of students who require more individualized interventions.

Related to the need to begin small and to initially focus the building's resources on the tier that will most contribute to effective implementation of the RtI system, a careful analysis of schoolwide assessment data is necessary. These data can include those collected from universal screening, high-stakes testing, discipline records, and other sources. As these data are initially collected, it would also be important to develop an evaluation plan and data collection system based on the vision, objectives, and expected outcomes for the RTI model being implemented in the district or building. The evaluation plan should focus on student outcomes but also include school personnel, parent, and student satisfaction measures. Before evaluating student outcomes, a plan to assess and ensure treatment integrity must be implemented. Treatment integrity focuses on determining that all aspects of the RtI system are being implemented as they are intended prior to assessing outcomes. Often, educational initiatives such as RtI are not found to lead to positive student outcomes—not because they are not good ideas but because they were not implemented as intended.

Example of Meeting the Needs of All Students Through a Multitiered System of Support

Historically, traditional models of special education were designed to identify children who had significantly fallen behind their peers and provide them with special education services. RtI is a system that includes screening of all children's academic and social behaviors relative to one another and/or criterion-based standards multiple times per year such that early detection of potential problems can be identified. Children who do not appear to be benefiting from their current academic or social behavior curriculum are provided supplemental instruction through more intensive interventions. These interventions are typically provided on a continuum within a multitiered system of support (Cates et al., 2011). The following is an example of how an RtI process may look across the tiers.

> Jim is a fourth-grade student enrolled at Lincoln Elementary. During winter benchmarking, Jim was identified as being at risk in mathematics. Specifically, his math computation problem completion rate and accuracy on a universal screening measure was below a predetermined cut-off score. Moreover, his score was also below that of average peer performance. In response, Jim was administered a follow-up diagnostic assessment to ensure that the screening instrument accurately identified Jim as being at risk in addition to isolating what areas of math Jim struggles with. In Jim's case, he was having particular difficulty with his multiplication tables.
>
> Shortly after, Jim was admitted to a small group with four other students that spent additional time focusing on math. The group was using a scientifically based computerized packaged intervention that the school had purchased from a well-known publishing company. The group met for 15 additional minutes per day 3 days per week. The computer program targeted basic math facts. Twice a month, the instructor monitored Jim's and the other students' progress with a curriculum-based measurement probe similar to the universal screening measure. Although after 2 months the other students were progressing, it was clear Jim was not responding to the intervention. In response, Jim was assessed using curriculum-based evaluation procedures (Howell & Nolet, 2000) in order to

develop an individualized Tier III intervention. During the assessment, Jim's previous work was reviewed, his teachers were interviewed, Jim was interviewed, and an error analysis was done on Jim's work.

Following the completion of the error analysis, it was determined that Jim could not accurately complete any problem that involved the subtraction of a double-digit number from a double-digit number that required regrouping from the 10s column. Specifically, Jim was not following the proper procedures for subtracting a double-digit number from a double-digit number that required regrouping. After determining Jim's problem, he was supplied with an evidenced-based intervention in the form of direct instruction. Jim completed the intervention 5 days per week for 10 minutes each time. The instructor met with Jim one-on-one and monitored his progress weekly.

After approximately one month, it was apparent that Jim was responding to the intervention. That is, Jim was starting to get more subtraction problems correct. The data being collected by the Tier II standard protocol computerized packaged intervention corroborated these findings. After completing Tier III intervention for 2 months, it was determined that Jim no longer needed Tier III intervention. Currently, Jim remains in Tier II intervention.

Conclusion

Response to Intervention is a school-based multitiered framework involving the systematic collection, analysis, interpretation, and utilization of data to match students with the appropriate unique academic and behavioral intervention(s) they may need. Overall, RtI is a prevention model aimed at identifying the needs of students early on and addressing those needs before they intensify. RtI is an all-encompassing framework that addresses the academic and social behavior needs of all students (K–12). In essence, RtI is a multitiered data-based decision-making model of service delivery that focuses on the academic and social behavior of all students. Tier I (universal core) should adequately address the needs of at least 80% of the student body; however, curriculum, instruction, and assessment methods used in Tier I should be provided to all students and be scientifically based. Assessment at Tier I has two goals: (1) use screening measures to identify the students who are most likely to fall behind and

(2) examine school- and district-level performance for areas of concern for the majority of students. Tier II (targeted groups intervention) should be delivered to approximately 15% of the student body. Services at this level are provided in a small-group format, usually using a standardized scientifically based protocol. Assessment at Tier II has two goals: (1) minimize the students who were false-positives during Tier I screening (those who appeared not to need screening, but in fact do) and (2) identify general areas of weakness for a student who is in need of further intervention. Finally, Tier III (individualized intervention) usually includes about 5% of the students in a school building. Tier III interventions should be delivered to students not making adequate progress at Tier II. The interventions provided at this level should be evidence-based and delivered more intensively (i.e., more time, smaller group, more narrow curricular focus) to meet the specific needs of a given student. The goal of assessment at Tier III is to address those specific learning needs. It is essential to remember that the tiers are not mutually exclusive of one another; Tier II is provided in addition to Tier I, Tier III is provided in addition to Tiers II and I, and a student can be receiving interventions at different tiers in different skill areas.

There are four major reasons for its implementation. First, RtI utilizes data-based decision making to target the needs of students. Additionally, the framework emphasizes the use of evidenced-based practices. Further, RtI addresses the needs of all students, not just those who have been identified as needing special education services. Finally, although there is currently no federal mandate for RtI, data suggest that all states are implementing the framework in some form or another and a number of states currently mandate its practice.

RtI is a universal framework intended to meet the needs of all students. That being said, RtI should be integrated in both special education and general education settings. In fact, IDEA (2004) now permits the use of data collected using the RtI framework to officially determine eligibility for special education services. Instituting a schoolwide multitiered framework requires certain resources. First and foremost, it requires time. Time is necessary to deliver additional interventions to children. This additional time can be achieved through push-in or pull-out services. Space is also necessary. Most buildings do not have whole rooms they can dedicate to RtI, so using hallways, empty rooms, and isolated classroom areas should be utilized. Additionally, funding is of great importance. Most schools are not afforded additional fiscal resources to allocate toward the hiring of new staff or the purchasing of additional materials. That being said, it is essential for schools to often "work with what they have" and reallocate current staff responsibilities. Finally and perhaps most importantly is person power: Administrators, special and general education teachers, specialists such as school psychologists and social workers, and parents must unite to effectively implement RtI.

Strong leadership is essential for the successful and lasting implementation of RtI. Principals who are knowledgeable about RtI and enthusiastic about the framework play perhaps the most vital role in successful implementation. Special education teachers play an integral role for intervention delivery to students who have IEPs and those who do not but need Tier II and III interventions. General education teachers play an equally important role, especially as members of a grade-level RtI team. General education teachers often determine when students need Tier II interventions and are often heavily involved in data collection at Tier I (i.e., screeners and progress monitoring). Special service personnel such as school psychologists, social workers, and guidance counselors are often readily available to offer their assistance with data analysis/interpretation and intervention delivery. Finally, parents should be recruited as part of a school or district's RtI initiative. Parent support can spread RtI awareness and support and lead to fundraising that can be used to help a school meet the financial demands of initiating RtI.

Knowing where to get started with the implementation of an RtI framework is often perplexing. The general rule is to start small and go slow. A schoolwide needs assessment should be completed to find out specifically where the school should start. Focusing on one academic area at Tier I is often the place to begin; ensure a strong core curriculum and a sound method of data collection (i.e., screening). All too often, schools with the greatest intention and ideal resources struggle with doing too much, leading to the lack of effective implementation of RtI before it is even put in place.

References

Bergan, J. R., & Kratochwill, T. R. (1990). *Behavioral consultation and therapy*. New York, NY: Plenum.

Burns, M. K., & Gibbons, K. (2008). *Response to intervention implementation in elementary and secondary schools: Procedures to assure scientific-based practices*. New York, NY: Routledge.

Cates, G. L., Blum, C., & Swerdlik, M. E. (2011). *Effective RTI training and practices: Helping school and district teams improve academic performance and social behavior.* Champaign, IL: Research Press.

Cates, G. L., Skinner, C. H., Watson, T. S., Smith, T. L., Weaver, A., & Jackson, B. (2003). Instructional effectiveness and instructional efficiency as considerations for data-based decision making: An evaluation of interspersing procedures. *School Psychology Review, 32,* 601–616.

Christenson, S. L., & Sheridan, S. M. (2001). *Schools and families: Creating essential connections for learning.* New York, NY: Guilford Press.

Deno, S. L. (1985). Curriculum-based measurement: The emerging alternative. *Exceptional Children, 52,* 219–232.

Derby, K. (2011). *The status of state-level response to intervention policies and procedures in the west region states and five other states.* Retrieved from http://www.wested.org/cs/we/view/rstudy/56

Gresham, F. M. (1991). Conceptualizing behavior disorders in terms of resistance to intervention. *School Psychology Review, 20*(1), 23–36.

Howell, K. W., & Nolet, V. (2000). *Curriculum-based evaluation: Teaching and decision making* (3rd ed.). Belmont, CA: Wadsworth.

Illinois State Board of Education. (2011). *Special education eligibility and entitlement within an RtI framework.* Retrieved from http://isbe.net/spec-ed/html/rti_speced.htm

Individuals with Disabilities Education Improvement Act, Pub. Law 108-446 (December 3, 2004).

Kavale, K. A., & Forness, S. R. (1987). Substance over style: Assessing the efficacy of modality testing and teaching. *Exceptional Children, 54,* 228–239.

National Association of State Directors of Special Education. (2005). *NASDSE's RtI: Policy considerations and implementation.* Alexandria, VA: NASDSE.

No Child Left Behind Act of 2001, 20 U.S.C § 6301 et seq. (2002).

Pascopella, A. (2010). *RTI goes mainstream. Direct administration solutions for school management.* Retrieved from http://www.districtadministration.com/viewarticle.aspx?articleid=2383

Peterson, D. L., Prasse, D., Shinn, M., & Swerdlik, M. E. (2007). The Illinois flexible service delivery model: A problem solving model initiative. In S. R. Jimerson, M. K. Burns, & A. VanDerHeyden (Eds.), *Handbook of Response to Intervention: The science and practice of assessment and intervention* (pp. 302–320). New York, NY: Springer Science.

Skinner, B. F. (1984). The shame of American education. *American Psychologist, 39,* 947–954.

Steege, M. W., & Watson, T. S. (2009). *Conducting school-based functional behavioral assessments: A practitioner's guide* (2nd ed.). New York, NY: Guilford Press.

Sugai, G., & Horner, R. (2006). A promising approach for expanding and sustaining school-wide positive behavior support. *School Psychology Review, 35,* 245–259.

CHAPTER 2

Prevention

and Early Identification of Students With Academic Difficulties—Tier I

Frederick J. Brigham and Melissa C. Jenkins

A fundamental tenet of any trade or profession is that it is easier, less expensive, and more effective to prevent problems than it is to repair, remediate, or rehabilitate the problems that could have been prevented. The owners' manuals of automobiles specify regular oil changes and other actions to be taken to extend the life of the vehicle. Dentists recommend regular check-ups and cleanings because, left untreated and unmonitored, many people predictably develop preventable dental problems. Medical doctors and insurance companies agree that preventing medical disorders is greatly preferable to treating diseases or conditions that are the result of conditions that predictably lead to unfortunate outcomes. For example, it is better to lower blood pressure and adjust cholesterol levels than it is to deal with the results of a stroke or a heart attack.

Across many trades and professions, good practice related to prevention includes a series of increasingly intensive steps that are recommended in the order of least to most intensive because less intensive interventions are not only associated with avoiding the condition in early stages, but also are often less expensive and associated with collateral benefits in other areas. Controlling one's weight and engaging in regular exercise can avoid the need for expensive medications for blood pressure and other problems. Although medications are remarkably effective in controlling such problems, they are not perfectly effective and also are associated with less desirable side effects. There is more to it than that, however. In addition to the well-known direct benefits of exercise on physical health, there is some evidence that increasing exercise can result in more positive affect—less depression and anxiety (Faulkner & Taylor, 2009)—and some positive aspects of memory and recall (Pesce, Crova, Cereatti, Casella, & Bellucci, 2009). Berk (2007) suggested that the results of physical exercise across a variety of outcomes might occur because physical activity encourages additional behaviors such as organization and being proactive. Like these models of optimal practice from other fields, Response to Intervention emphasizes prevention through the least intrusive intervention that will yield the most positive outcomes.

Brigham and Brigham (2010) noted that RtI was developed through special education research in an effort to (a) increase the accuracy of eligibility decisions for special education, (b) prevent students without disabilities from falling so far behind that they require special education, (c) focus instructional attention on standards-based curricula, and (d) improve the professionalism of educational decision making. The fundamental idea is that by screening every child regularly on simple performance indicators that are critically related to important curricular outcomes, we can catch those students who are showing signs of difficulty and provide them with modest levels of support before their instructional problems become insurmountable. This kind of effort is seen as a proactive approach to instructional issues and is in contrast to the reactive approach that most authors consider to have characterized school responses to underachievement in the past.

Proactive Approach

Leo Tolstoy began his novel *Anna Karenina* with the sentence "Happy families are all alike; every unhappy family is unhappy in its own way." The statement has come to be known as the Anna Karenina Effect. Tolstoy probably overstates the similarity of happy families, but his point serves our discussion well. When things are going well, we usually do not worry too much about what is happening. When things are not working out as we had hoped, we spend a great deal of time and effort to find out why. For the purposes of RtI, the Anna Karenina Effect suggests that we need to find the reasons that children are unsuccessful in their learning and act as quickly as possible to address them. By replacing the word "family" with "child" in Tolstoy's famous statement, we come very close to the fundamental belief underlying special and remedial education. That is, most people respond well to general education instruction, but children can fail to respond well for a wide variety of reasons. Early intervention can address these issues before they become insurmountable.

Early identification and intervention is a familiar topic in general and remedial education, but RtI introduces some new ideas to the concept. First, we should maximize the number of happy families. That is, we should make sure that our general curriculum reaches the maximum number of children possible. Although it is unlikely that we can make every child successful in the general curriculum as presented to all children, we can ensure that our curricula are designed to be effective and are implemented with sufficient intensity and integrity. "Making classroom instruction as effective as possible at Tier 1 minimizes 'curriculum casualties' and reduces over-identification of risk that potentially overwhelms instructional resources at Tiers 2 and 3" (Foorman, Carlson, & Santi, 2007, p. 66).

A second element of RtI is the ubiquity of assessment in monitoring student progress. Rather than doing close scrutiny of only students who have clear and obvious problems, every student in the general education program participates in screening to ensure that he is making sufficient progress in his educational programs (Mellard & Johnson, 2008). By screening *all* children in the early grades, educators are able to detect achievement problems in the early stages, before they lead to outright failure, and before they become more difficult to address.

A third element of RtI is the regularity of measurement that is used to detect academic problems. In Tier I RtI programs, children are monitored much more frequently than in most school programs that preceded RtI initiatives. Typically, Tier I screenings are conducted three times a year, in the fall, winter, and spring (Glover, 2010).

Finally, the assessments used in Tier I RtI screenings are somewhat different than those schools have commonly used. RtI researchers have identified "early warning systems" of simple indicator variables that relate to the more complex outcomes that are the goal of instruction. The area of reading is the most well-developed domain for RtI (Taylor, 2008). Early indicators of reading ability include simple tasks like matching sounds to symbols, rapid letter naming (Brigham & Brigham, 2010), word identification fluency, and passage reading fluency for decoding, with the MAZE fluency task being used to monitor reading comprehension (Fuchs & Fuchs, 2007).

Although reading has received the most attention in RtI, other areas of the curriculum have also been the focus of RtI research. At present, the research in regard to mathematics is generally supportive of RtI for mathematics, but also reveals that our measures are less reliable and predictive of growth over time than are the reading measures (Allsopp, McHatton, & Farmer, 2010; Clarke, Gersten, & Newman-Gonchar, 2010; Foegen, Jiban, & Deno, 2007).

McMaster and Espin (2007) noted that writing indices presently have only moderate relationships to criterion measures of general writing and also have little evidence of sufficient sensitivity for progress and growth in writing, particularly in the early grades. Nevertheless, writing is a skill that, like reading and mathematics, must be practiced to develop proficiency; therefore, it is likely that future research will identify reliable and sensitive indicators of growth. Until such developments are demonstrated, De La Paz, Espin, and McMaster (2010) suggested that teachers select measures relative to how they or their districts define good writing and collect data to develop local growth rates that can be used while more adequate data emerges from the research.

By ensuring that the curriculum in place is implemented with fidelity and sufficient intensity, assessing all students frequently on an "early warning system" of sensitive instructional variables, schools participating in RtI programs have the tools to reach the greatest number of students possible through their general curricula and to find and address the needs of students who are showing signs of inadequate progress before their problems become deeply entrenched and more difficult to address.

Effective Teaching

If one of the outcomes of a well-implemented RtI program is more effective teaching, one must wonder why teaching was not already so effective that there was little room for improvement. There are probably a large number of reasons for this, but we will focus on only two: (a) the political- and philosophy-driven discourse of education and (b) the weak feedback learning model that is in place for most educators.

Politics and Philosophy Versus Achievement

Avoiding the issue. It is difficult to argue that children should be allowed to experience repeated and serious failures needlessly, particularly failures that will create subsequent and larger difficulties in the future. Kauffman (1999) pointed to a number of beliefs that thwart educators' efforts to address and prevent many learning and behavior problems in the early stages. Among these is reluctance to call attention to problems because such attention may somehow set up a self-fulfilling prophecy, leading to even worse issues in the future. Such risk is perhaps most associated with the practice of identifying academic or behavioral difficulties and then doing nothing or very little to address them. By telling a child, "Oh, you are a poor reader right now and you have a disability so there is really very little that we can or will do about that," the mechanism of the self-fulfilling prophecy is clear. Why would a rational person strive if the outcome were predetermined?

Worse, if the parents and teachers of such children come to believe such a thing, they will probably spend more time on seeking accommodations to avoid the areas of poor performance than they will in considering instructional interventions to address the needs. Lovett (2010) noted that very little attention has been directed to providing instruction to offset the conditions that elicited the need for the accommodation. When considered in this manner, it is more likely that the ready provision of accommodations is a self-fulfilling prophecy that could have been mitigated, if not avoided, by early and intensive intervention. By focusing on elements other than providing effective instruction, we diminish the independence of our students in the future.

Irrational optimism. Another issue that limits the effectiveness of educational efforts is an irrational optimism regarding practices that appeal to the emotions but yield little tangible benefit (Kauffman, 1999). The romantic notion that children will unfold naturally to an optimal state stands in opposition to many elements that have been demonstrated to be effective time and time again such as direct and explicit instruction. It is as if we want to believe that what is immediately pleasurable for any individual is always profitable for every individual (Brigham, 2009). Such is clearly not the case, and returning to our exercise metaphor from the introductory paragraphs, one can imagine that people who are in good physical condition and enjoy running or other physical activities may have found them to be less than pleasurable in the early stages. One of the jobs of teachers, parents, and coaches is to get the novice through the less rewarding stages of skill acquisition so that he can enjoy the rewards of proficiency. That suggests that we need to more frequently address academic needs with instruction if we are to be the difference we want to be in the lives of our children.

These are but two elements that undermine the efforts of educators, parents, and policy makers in creating and delivering more effective educational programs. One way of holding these beliefs up to scrutiny is by asking, "How well do the actions that we take based on this belief work out for us in the long run?" One problem that educators regularly face is the absence of a feedback system that can provide them with relevant information in a timely manner. While the state competency tests associated with the federal No Child Left Behind Act (2001) are intended to result in increased feedback for schools about what is working and not working, the tests are given only annually and at the end of the school year. By the time such information is available to the teacher of the individual child, it is probably too late to do much about it. RtI is one way of enhancing the efficacy feedback system for individual teachers, grade-level teams, building administrators, and district-level managers.

Effective Feedback Systems

Many endeavors besides education face the problem of ineffective feedback systems. Additionally, decisions that are clearly foolish in retrospect may have been only calculated risks, given the available knowledge at the moment, or even completely justifiable (Brigham, Gustashaw, & Brigham, 2004). Sometimes, individuals associate a desired outcome with an irrelevant feature of the conditions leading to the outcome. One example is the "cargo cults" that sprang up on South Pacific islands after World War II. Hoping to have the military bases return with their stores of cargo and opportunity, some island residents decided that the cargo was there because of the actions of people speaking into radios. They therefore painted boxes to look like radios and created fake headsets out of shells so that they could call the ships and airplanes back to the island as they had seen others do. Examples of such practices abound in education and other areas, particularly when the action and the outcomes are separated by long periods of time.

The self-correcting nature of science allows misconceptions to be weeded out over long periods of time, but it also requires individuals to be able to read and understand such research findings. Few individuals, particularly teachers, have the time or the training to do so. Something that operates closer to the ground on which they stand is needed to guide their decisions.

Elements of Effective Feedback Systems

Although a great deal of professional attention has been directed at the expertise and competence of teachers in decision making (Kennedy, 2010), a feedback model is probably more appropriate for guiding decisions in teaching and other related areas such as psychotherapy (Bickman, 1999). Bickman (1999) described the model in which "a clinician receives feedback on successes and failures of treatment and improves on the basis of that feedback" (p. 969). He further suggested that in order for the model to work, clinicians must:

1. know outcomes,
2. receive feedback,
3. know their own treatment strategies,
4. connect process with outcome,
5. fit knowledge to individuals,
6. generalize, and
7. apply their knowledge.

According to Bickman (1999), the absence of any single element would lead to difficulty in learning from experience. Bickman further stated that the absence of such complete feedback systems limits the ability of many, if not most, clinicians to benefit from their experience and improve their effectiveness.

The situation described for psychotherapists is actually very similar to that faced by most classroom teachers. Teachers clearly know the outcomes of some of their instructional efforts, but many are loosely coupled to the measurements at hand. That is, some measurements are only tangentially related to instructional outcomes, and therefore teachers may not have as much relevant information as they believe.

The feedback system for teachers and students in No Child Left Behind is annual and also global. Once a year, teachers may learn the outcomes of their instruction on global indicators such as reading, but the feedback is too late to help individual students and too coarse to guide instruction with precision. The unhappy children who fail the test may fail for a variety of reasons, and given the temporal distance between the instruction and the evaluation and the aggregation of skills on the test (e.g., passage reading as opposed to the components that lead to fluent passage reading), it is highly unlikely that educators can determine where to intervene in the curriculum with any precision. Without procedures to promote instructional effectiveness at the individual level in a timely and responsive manner, teachers can hardly be accountable for specific treatments and high outcomes.

RtI promotes effective teaching by linking instructional outcomes to clear measures that are delivered regularly and quickly available to the teachers working with children. Most authorities suggest that Tier I instruction should result in about 80% of the students in the general education program responding acceptably to the instruction. Assessments with lower than 80% pass rates suggest that the curriculum, the teaching, or both are problems that must be resolved before RtI may move to the next stages. In this way, RtI can promote more effective teaching in Tier 1 or general education settings.

When an adequate pass rate has been demonstrated for the school, students who pass screening and exhibit no other problems proceed through the school year to the next screening with no changes. Schools respond to students who do not meet performance expectations at screening by providing clearly defined interventions for limited amounts of time to determine if the student can be brought to the desired level of performance. Tiers II and III are devoted to these interventions.

Student Learning

"No instructional method, even procedures that have been validated using stringent experimental studies, works for all students" (Fuchs & Fuchs, 2008, pp. 44–45). So, what works for *most* students—the 80% or higher who are successful in Tier I—will often fail to meet the needs of *all* students—the 20% or so of students who are involved with Tier II and Tier III interventions. Given that, there will always be a need for some form of special education for a number of learners.

One of the problems that RtI is intended to address is the number of false positive identifications of children as eligible for special education. However, reduction in referrals is a poor indicator of effectiveness *unless* it can be demonstrated that the "unreferred" children are actually making satisfactory progress in the general education curriculum (Scruggs & Mastropieri, 2006; Vaughn & Fuchs, 2006). Much of the debate in the special education literature centers on the appropriateness of using RtI for identification of students with disabilities; however, few can argue that screening all children in general education is a bad idea or that it is likely to depress achievement for any group of students presently in American schools.

Research on Tier I outcomes to date is encouraging. Data regarding the progress of individual students, outcomes of large groups of students, and teacher satisfaction is generally positive; however, the extant literature is derived from program evaluation studies rather than well-controlled scientific research (Kovaleski & Black, 2010). Program evaluations are intended to answer questions about whether a given endeavor attains the goals set for it and avoids undesirable outcomes (McDavid & Hawthorn, 2006). Program evaluations, however, do not conform to the level of proof and certainty required of experimental and quasiexperimental investigations. Better program evaluations are less prone to threats to validity (e.g., the students improved because they were being observed more regularly and not because of the instruction) than are weaker program evaluations, but even so, they are intended to serve a different function and provide information that is not really considered proof in scientific research.

Although the evidence is not yet to a level that supports unrestricted endorsement of RtI programs for Tier I applications, it is consistently positive. Brigham and Brigham (2010) concluded that the most promising applications of RtI programs to date were in regard to the changes it promoted in general education or Tier I.

Formative Evaluation

Four types of assessments are available to measure student progress and guide teachers in designing and implementing their instruction: screening, progress monitoring, diagnosis, and outcome evaluation (Fuchs & Fuchs, 2008). Tier I employs screening procedures. In general, screenings answer the question: "Does this individual need further assessment or attention with regard to the variable of interest?" For individuals who pass the screening, all is considered to be well for the moment. For individuals who fall below a satisfactory cut score on the screening, further assessment or some sort of direct intervention is suggested. Cut scores are addressed in more detail in the next section.

In very general terms, formative evaluation is used to guide instruction, and summative evaluation is used to determine final outcome levels of the instruction. Formative measures are often repeated to determine response to instruction over time, but summative evaluations are rarely administered more than once. Formative evaluation in the context of Tier I RtI programs involves low-risk measures that are efficient (easily and quickly administered), reliable (likely to yield similar scores on closely repeated measures or across raters), valid (measures the right content and matches or predicts other well-established measures), and accurate in classifying students as at risk or not at risk for academic difficulties (Hintze & Marcotte, 2010).

Formative evaluations in RtI are typically fluency tasks. Fluency in responding to early indicators of performance is clearly associated with subsequently acceptable levels of accomplishment. For example, consider the complex relationship between reading comprehension and reading

31

decoding. Reading comprehension, is, of course, the goal of all of reading instruction and the basis for lifelong learning (Taylor, 2008). As one might expect of the capstone achievement of the reading process, comprehension involves a very complex union of decoding written symbols into the sounds that they represent, linking the sounds together into words, linking the words to sentence structure, and then integrating the meaning of the sentences and vocabulary that they contain to the individual's knowledge of the world (Dickinson, Golinkoff, & Hirsh-Pasek, 2010). There is simply no reason to expect good comprehension in the absence of good decoding, so effort in decoding instruction pays dividends in later comprehension abilities.

Formative evaluations are considered to be low-risk in that they are not part of the student's grading system or the school's accountability system. Rather, the information gathered is used to help teachers understand how their instruction is benefitting their students and to suggest ways that instruction can be adjusted for more optimal outcomes.

When Do Teachers Intervene?

RtI is an underspecified construct in the federal regulations (Fuchs, Stecker, & Fuchs, 2008). That means that clear regulatory guidance is unavailable to practitioners with regard to many details of RtI practice, including when to intervene with an individual student. Clearly, students with the lowest scores on their screening measures are most in need of intervention. The problem is rarely the identification of students with extremely low performance as being in need of services; rather, the issue is more often in deciding where to set a boundary between students who do and do not require intervention.

Some measures (e.g., Dynamic Indicators of Basic Early Literacy Skills, DIBELS) come with preestablished cut scores. The DIBELS system suggests that students who fall below the lowest cut score are considered to be at risk for failure, and substantial intervention is recommended for that group. Students who fall between the lowest and highest cut scores are considered to have some risk for failure, and therefore, a more modest level of intervention or academic support is recommended (Fuchs & Fuchs, 2008).

Many measures have yet to be associated with preestablished norms and cut scores. Additionally, some schools may wish to establish local norms to promote greater achievement than would be required to meet norms based on wider populations. For those schools, performance data can be collected during fall, winter, and spring administrations. Typically, the cut score for considering students to be at risk is set at the lowest quartile, or lowest 25%, of the students when their performance data is rank ordered.

Fuchs and Fuchs (2008) suggested conducting screenings to ensure that every student who is at risk for failure is detected and monitored, if not directly supported with additional instruction. To carry out this more expansive screening, they suggested setting the cut score for risk at the 50th percentile. Students between the 50th and 25th percentiles would be termed as "suspected to be at risk" rather than "at risk." Fuchs and Fuchs recommended that these students participate in the progress-monitoring program for students in Tier II for a period of 6–8 weeks to determine whether or not they were improving at a rate similar to their peers or falling further behind. If the progress-monitoring data indicate that the student is making insufficient progress compared to his or her peers, he or she is moved to Tier II interventions. Students making progress at a rate similar to the peer group are considered to be no longer at risk and continue with Tier I monitoring.

Criteria

There are two ways of determining whether or not a student is making adequate progress: the absolute level of performance and the rate of improvement. When cut scores are provided, a student may fall below the score according to his or her absolute level of performance, the score on a given administration. For example, if students at the 25th percentile are able to read 60 words per minute in a given passage, any student who attained a score of 60 or fewer words would meet the criteria for "at risk for failure" under the guidelines described in the previous section.

The previous section contained the recommendation that individuals between the 50th and 25th percentiles participate in the Tier II progress-monitoring system for 6–8 weeks to determine their risk status. Although the absolute (single point measurement) attained by a given student on the date of the screening might have been in the "not at risk" range, it is possible that the student's rate of progress is insufficient and that the student is beginning to fall behind. When the performance data is placed on a graph and compared to rates of improvement expected of most students or compared to the rate of progress needed to reach a preestablished end-of-the-year benchmark goal, one of three situations will exist.

First, the student's rate of improvement might be greater than the rate expected of most children (Figure 2.1). The solid line represents the rate

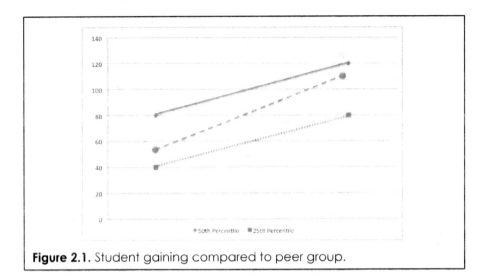

Figure 2.1. Student gaining compared to peer group.

of progress from measure to measure for students at the 50th percentile in the fall and winter screenings. The dotted line at the lower part of the chart represents the rate of progress for children at the 25th percentile on the same measure. The dashed line in the middle represents the observations of a target individual (averaged for clarity) who is making progress at a rate that is faster than the peer group. This individual would be no longer considered to be in need of monitoring.

In Figure 2.2, a different student is showing parallel rates of improvement across the series of measures. Although the individual was below the 50th percentile and considered "suspected to be at risk" on the first measure, subsequent progress monitoring, again smoothed for clarity, shows that the individual is making progress at a rate similar to the peer group and, therefore, no longer considered to be at risk. This individual is making neither gains nor losses compared to the peer group or expected rate of progress but is making progress at a rate similar to the peer group, albeit in the lower range of acceptable performance.

In Figure 2.3, the target individual, represented by the dashed line, is making progress at a rate that is slower than the peer group or expected rate of progress. With such data, promoting this individual to Tier II supports even though the absolute rate of performance is not yet in the unsatisfactory range (≤25th percentile) is justified because the individual is falling further and further behind, and the data suggest that without additional support, the student will soon clearly be at risk for failure.

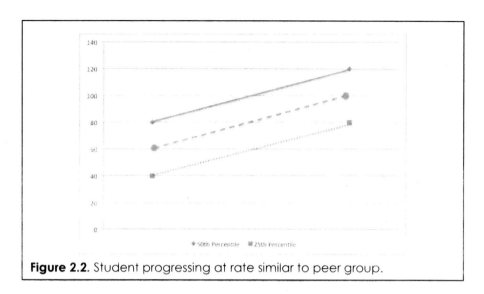

Figure 2.2. Student progressing at rate similar to peer group.

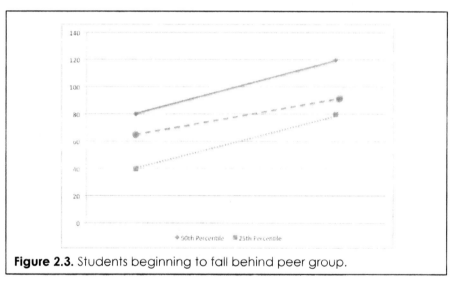

Figure 2.3. Students beginning to fall behind peer group.

Case Study

Faith Mills arrived in Mrs. Simpson's first-grade class in mid-November. It was her third school in less than a year, and the 7-year-old looked shy and uncomfortable as she entered her new classroom for the first time. Her teacher, Mrs. Simpson, seated her next to Rachel, a strong and confident student who would surely help Faith make friends and learn routines

Mrs. Simpson had read Faith's file, and was worried that extra supports might be needed to help the little girl succeed in first grade. Faith had attended two schools for kindergarten, and the second teacher had recommended retention due to "weaknesses in reading readiness and early numeracy skills." There was no other information about her performance level in the file, but Faith's report card for kindergarten in the second school showed marks of "S" and "S-." A note in Faith's folder indicated that the first school she had attended during her kindergarten year had refused to release Faith's record because she owed unpaid fees.

Faith's mother had refused the retention in kindergarten at her previous school so Faith had entered first grade at the beginning of the present school year. She had transferred to her new school as a first-grade student.

Faith's report card for the first semester of first grade indicated borderline satisfactory grades (S-) in reading and writing skills and an N (Needs Improvement) in math. Her teacher requested a conference with Mrs. Mills and explained her concerns about Faith's performance in her class.

"I really want to thank you for coming in to meet with me," Mrs. Simpson began. "It is always good to meet the parents of my students and work with them. I am worried about the marks that Faith earned on her report card, and I wanted to talk with you about what we might be able to do to help her out for the rest of the school year. What did you think about the report card?"

"Well," Mrs. Mills responded, "I think that it's important to realize that kids are sensitive to moving and we have had three moves in a year. I don't think that it's fair to blame Faith for the problems our family has faced. She is just making a slow adjustment to first grade and her new school. I think that she will be just fine if we give her a little more time. I don't want to get her retained like that other school wanted. It would be so hard on her."

"Oh, I don't want to talk about holding Faith back. In our school, we work really hard to make sure that kids move forward. In fact, we check each student's progress with a set of quick measures that we call screenings three times a year," Mrs. Simpson replied.

Before the teacher could continue, Mrs. Mills asked, "Are you talking about special education testing? Because I don't want that."

"I can understand your concern, but we do this with every student in our primary grades three times a year. Most of our children turn out to be doing just fine, and we are always happy when we see that. There are other children who might be doing OK for now but who could be starting to fall behind little by little. Sometimes, when that happens, the kids end up needing special education, but if we catch it early enough, we might be able to get them on track so that they never fall far enough behind that special education becomes necessary," the teacher replied.

Mrs. Mills looked worried. "I think that Faith is afraid of these big tests. You know, she really is shy. Won't she do badly just because she gets scared?"

Mrs. Simpson admitted, "That's always a little bit of a worry for us with big tests." She continued, "The screenings that we use are done individually by teachers who the children see in school all the time. We ask them to name letters, read words, work with numbers, and a few other things that are all based on the materials that we use right in our class. We will be screening each student again in 3 weeks. How about if we schedule another meeting right after that so we can see where Faith stands?"

They agreed to meet in 4 weeks, one week after the screenings had been conducted to examine Faith's performance data. The school conducted screenings in reading and arithmetic for students in first grade. When the meeting began, Mrs. Simpson showed Mrs. Mills the scores from Faith's measures. She began, "We were really happy with how hard Faith worked for us during the screening! She really gave it a great effort and so we are pretty confident that her scores are accurate. Before I show you how Faith did, let me tell you how the scores work.

"Whenever we get scores for our students, the first thing that we do is sort them in rank order. We do not grade these measures or give passing or failing marks on them. Instead, we look for the students who might need a little more help than we have been giving them. Once we put the scores in order from high to low, we look closely at scores in the lowest fourth of the group. We find a score that separates the bottom 25% from the remaining 75% and offer extra help as a part of the regular school day for any student who scores in that range. Sometimes, we watch some of the kids above that 25% mark closely to make sure that they are moving along OK, but we figure most of the kids who score in the higher 75% are doing fine so we keep things as they were for them. The thing to remember is that we are working to make it so kids can do well in our school. This is really about whether or not we are satisfied with how the things we do with them work out. OK?"

Mrs. Mills frowned, but nodded that the teacher should continue.

Mrs. Simpson showed Faith's mother her scores from the reading screening and told her that Faith had done as well as 29 out of 100 students (29th percentile) on one measure and as well as 30 out of 100 students (30th percentile) on the other measure. "You know, I wasn't so sure that Faith would do this well when we spoke back in December," said Mrs. Simpson. "I think that Faith has done very well since then. I think that you were right about her adjusting to her new school. Let's take a look at the arithmetic scores, shall we?"

Mrs. Mills looked relieved and nodded for Mrs. Simpson to continue. "Faith has more trouble in her math work than she does in reading," Mrs. Simpson stated. "Her scores on the arithmetic measures that we used are all around the sixth percentile. That suggests that we should give her some more help in that area. I would like to recommend that our Response to Intervention team take a look at Faith's scores and make some recommendations for us and maybe another teacher or teacher assistant to help her with this area. What do you think?"

Mrs. Mills asked if Faith would stay in her present class and if the school thought that she would be embarrassed to need to have a tutor. Mrs. Simpson responded that the kinds of things they were talking about were called Tier II interventions and that about 15% or close to 120 of the nearly 850 students in the school worked with the Tier II program. It was just part of the school day. Mrs. Simpson offered to put Mrs. Mills in touch with some of the parents of students in the Tier II intervention. She said that parents had been part of the school's advisory board for the RtI program from the beginning and they were very helpful. Mrs. Mills said that she was willing to give it a try.

The RtI team met and examined the data from Faith's screening. They concluded that Mrs. Simpson's class was, on the whole, making good progress in the curriculum. In fact, 89% of her students were above the school's 25th percentile. That suggested that they should work with Faith directly instead of examining the classroom instruction further.

The team agreed that Faith's math skills were becoming increasingly problematic for her and needed improvement. Faith was only able to count to 20 and had difficulty recognizing written numerals beyond 10. She seemed to have great difficulty matching a quantity of items with a numeral. They suggested that Faith and several other students in her grade would benefit from some extra attention to arithmetic instruction. They decided to incorporate a daily counting activity into her arithmetic class and to increase the use of student sets of manipulatives for all instruction. Mrs. Simpson also set up center-based math activities that emphasized counting and number recognition for early finishers, indoor recess, and other free periods. During a scheduled intervention period, Mrs. Simpson or one of the teacher assistants would work with Faith and the other students in the math center to focus specifically on the skills she needed to develop.

The RtI team also noted that even though Faith's reading skills seemed to be emerging at a rate that was within the range of typical development, she should have more regular monitoring of her performance than the three-times-a-year screening. They suggested that she should complete a reading measure once a week in addition to the weekly arithmetic measures that she was completing in her Tier II program.

The team set a review date for her Tier II interventions. They had read the research that suggested that 8–10 data points are a good number to show stable trends in performance. They had also read the complaints of some RtI critics who worried that RtI, when carried on for too long without review, might actually delay the provision of special education services for some students with disabilities. The team decided that in order to ensure good measurement data and protect Faith's interests, they would meet to review her data in 8 weeks.

Conclusion

Tier I intervention is carried out in general education settings by general education teachers. The intention of Tier I is to ensure that the general education program is conceived and delivered in a manner that enables about 80% of the students to make adequate progress in the curriculum. When fewer than 80% of the students make adequate progress, schools are advised to address the curriculum and teaching. When schools can demonstrate that a sufficient number of children perform well in the curriculum, they are able to rule out adequacy of instruction as the root of student problems.

Most schools monitor all students in Tier I at least three times a year. In addition to verifying the overall quality of instruction, this systematic screening allows for early identification of students who show signs of achievement problems. Typically, students who fall in the lowest quartile or below a preestablished cut score move into Tier II interventions. Successful Tier II interventions bring those students to a level of academic achievement commensurate with their adequately performing peers, thereby preventing a widening of the achievement gap and unnecessary referral for special education evaluation. Successful intervention in Tier II hopefully results in returning those students to Tier I.

[Handwritten margin notes: "1x a week progress mo..."]

[Handwritten notes at bottom: "Tier I – classroom 80% progress [3x a year] or teacher/curr review Tier II – tutor of low performer."]

39

References

Allsopp, D. H., McHatton, P. A., & Farmer, J. L. (2010). *Technology, mathematics PS/RTI, and students with LD: What do we know, what have we tried, and what can we do to improve outcomes now and in the future?* Retrieved from http://www.thefreelibrary.com/Technology,+m athematics+PS%2FRTI,+and+students+with+LD%3A+what+do+we. ..-a0242754547

Berk, M. (2007). Should we be targeting exercise as a routine mental health intervention? *Acta Neuropsychiatrica, 19,* 217–218. doi: 10.1111/j. 1601-5215.2007.00201.x

Bickman, L. (1999). Practice makes perfect and other myths about mental health services. *American Psychologist, 54,* 965–978. doi: 10.1037/ h0088206

Brigham, F. J. (2009). Confusing the momentary and the monumental. *Focus on Research, 22*(2), 1–2.

Brigham, F. J., & Brigham, M. S. P. (2010). Preventive instruction: Response to intervention can catch students before their problems become insurmountable. *The American School Board Journal, 197*(6), 32–33.

Brigham, F. J., Gustashaw, W. E., III, & Brigham, M. S. P. (2004). Scientific practice and the tradition of advocacy in special education. *Journal of Learning Disabilities, 37,* 200–206. doi: 10.1177/ 00222194040370030301

Clarke, B., Gersten, R., & Newman-Gonchar, R. (2010). RTI in mathematics: Beginnings of a knowledge base. In T. A. Glover & S. Vaughn (Eds.), *The promise of Response to Intervention: Evaluating current science and practice* (pp. 187–203). New York, NY: Guilford Press.

De La Paz, S., Espin, C., & McMaster, K. L. (2010). RTI in writing instruction: Implementing evidence-based interventions and evaluating the effects for individual students. In T. A. Glover & S. Vaughn (Eds.), *The promise of Response to Intervention: Evaluating current science and practice* (pp. 204–238). New York, NY: Guilford Press.

Dickinson, D. K., Golinkoff, R. M., & Hirsh-Pasek, K. (2010). Speaking out for language. *Educational Researcher, 39,* 305–310. doi: 10.3102/ 0013189x10370204

Faulkner, G., & Taylor, A. (2009). Promoting physical activity for mental health: A complex intervention? *Mental Health and Physical Activity, 2*(1), 1–3. doi: 10.1016/j.mhpa.2009.04.001

Foegen, A., Jiban, C., & Deno, S. (2007). Progress monitoring measuring in mathematics: A review of the literature. *The Journal of Special Education, 41,* 121–139. doi: 10.1177/00224669070410020101

Foorman, B. R., Carlson, C. D., & Santi, K. L. (2007). Classroom reading instruction and teacher knowledge in the primary grades. In D. Haager, J. K. Klingner, & S. Vaughn (Eds.), *Evidence-based reading practices for Response to Intervention* (pp. 45–71). Baltimore, MD: Brookes.

Fuchs, D., Stecker, P. M., & Fuchs, L. S. (2008). Tier 3: Why special education must be the most intensive tier in a standards-driven, No Child Left Behind world. In D. Fuchs, L. Fuchs, & S. Vaughn (Eds.), *Response to Intervention: A framework for reading educators* (pp. 71–104). Newark, DE: International Reading Association.

Fuchs, L. S., & Fuchs, D. (2007). The role of assessment in the three-tier approach to reading instruction. In D. Haager, J. K. Klingner, & S. Vaughn (Eds.), *Evidence-based reading practices for Response to Intervention* (pp. 29–42). Baltimore, MD: Brookes.

Fuchs, L. S., & Fuchs, D. (2008). The role of assessment within the RTI framework. In D. Fuchs, L. Fuchs, & S. Vaughn (Eds.), *Response to Intervention: A framework for reading educators* (pp. 27–49). Newark, DE: International Reading Association.

Glover, T. A. (2010). Key RTI service delivery components: Considerations for research-informed practice. In T. A. Glover & S. Vaughn (Eds.), *The promise of Response to Intervention: Evaluating current science and practice* (pp. 7–22). New York, NY: Guilford Press.

Hintze, J. M., & Marcotte, A. M. (2010). Student assessment and data-based decision making. In T. A. Glover & S. Vaughn (Eds.), *The promise of Response to Intervention: Evaluating current science and practice* (pp. 57–77). New York, NY: Guilford Press.

Kauffman, J. M. (1999). How we prevent the prevention of emotional and behavioral disorders. *Exceptional Children, 65,* 448–468.

Kennedy, M. M. (2010). Attribution error and the quest for teacher quality. *Educational Researcher, 39,* 591–598. doi: 10.3102/00 13189X I 0390804

Kovaleski, J. F., & Black, L. (2010). Multi-tier service delivery: Current status and future directions. In T. A. Glover & S. Vaughn (Eds.), *The promise of Response to Intervention: Evaluating current science and practice* (pp. 23–56). New York, NY: Guilford Press.

Lovett, B. J. (2010). Extended time testing accommodations for students with disabilities: Answers to five fundamental questions. *Review of Educational Research, 80,* 611–638. doi: 10.3102/0034654310364063

McDavid, J. C., & Hawthorn, L. R. L. (2006). *Program evaluation & performance measurement: An introduction to practice.* Thousand Oaks, CA: Sage.

McMaster, K., & Espin, C. (2007). Technical features of curriculum-based measurement in writing: A literature review. *The Journal of Special Education, 42,* 68–84.

Mellard, D. F., & Johnson, E. (2008). *RTI : A practitioner's guide to implementing Response to Intervention.* Thousand Oaks, CA: Corwin Press.

No Child Left Behind Act of 2001, 20 U.S.C § 6301 et seq. (2002).

Pesce, C., Crova, C., Cereatti, L., Casella, R., & Bellucci, M. (2009). Physical activity and mental performance in preadolescents: Effects of acute exercise on free-recall memory. *Mental Health and Physical Activity, 2*(1), 16–22. doi: 10.1016/j.mhpa.2009.02.001

Scruggs, T. E., & Mastropieri, M. A. (2006). Response to "Competing views: A dialogue on Response to Intervention." *Assessment for Effective Intervention, 32*(1), 62–64. doi: 10.1177/15345084060320010901

Taylor, B. M. (2008). Tier 1: Effective classroom reading instruction in the elementary grades. In D. Fuchs, L. Fuchs, & S. Vaughn (Eds.), *Response to Intervention: A framework for reading educators* (pp. 5–25). Newark, DE: International Reading Association.

Vaughn, S., & Fuchs, L. S. (2006). A response to "Competing views: A dialogue on Response to Intervention." *Assessment for Effective Intervention, 32*(1), 58–61. doi: 10.1177/15345084060320010801

More
Intense Instruction—
Tiers II and III of RtI

April L. Mustian and Valerie L. Mazzotti

Picture this: As a classroom teacher, you have been implementing a core research-based reading program daily for 90 minutes as part of Tier I of the RtI model your school has recently adopted. For *most* of your students, this core reading instruction is exactly what they need to develop critical early literacy skills such as phonemic awareness and reading fluency. Through weeks of progress monitoring, however, your data indicate that four of your students are not making sufficient progress with this method of instruction alone.

Perhaps your classroom scenario doesn't quite fit the one just described. Maybe you have issues in your classroom related to the inappropriate behavior some of your students have exhibited throughout the school day despite the supports you have in place. For instance, you may have Schoolwide Positive Behavior Support (PBS) procedures in place for your students as well as rules and procedures within your own classroom. You reward students' appropriate behavior daily with "cool cash" or some other incentive, and for *most* of your students, this approach to behavior management works great. But you have one or two students who continue to act out or are socially withdrawn and require more support.

The resulting question in both of these scenarios is the same: What are your next steps in providing effective instruction that reaches *all* of your students? The answer lies in the next tiers of instruction within the RtI framework (see Figure 3.1). For the 15% to 20% of students who continue to struggle academically or socially despite solid Tier I instruction,

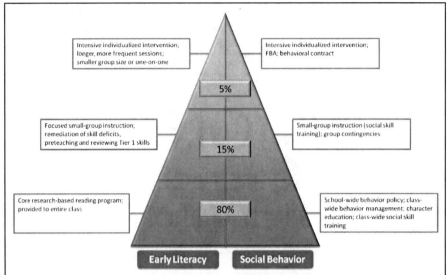

Figure 3.1. Three-tier RtI model reflecting support in early literacy and social behavior. Adapted from "Increasing social and academic success: Positive Behavior Support meets Response to Intervention," by T. Lewis, n.d. Retrieved from http://www.pbis.org/common/pbisresources/presentations/lewis_pbs_rti.ppt

the supplemental teaching provided through Tier II and, in some cases, Tier III interventions are the next step(s) of increasing support for these learners (Vaughn & Roberts, 2007). The sections below provide teachers with knowledge of the characteristics of Tier II and Tier III interventions and practical implementation and data collection suggestions in the areas of early literacy *and* social behavior.

Tier II Interventions in Early Literacy

The number-one skill area to which the RtI model has been applied is reading. This comes as no surprise considering that reading is a fundamental skill required for success in all other content areas. There is also a plethora of empirical support indicating that when children become efficient readers early, they are much more likely to experience better educational outcomes (Armbruster, Lehr, & Osborn, 2001; Bursuck & Damer, 2011). For those students in need of more support, interventions in Tiers II and III of RtI become critical stages in improving their trajectory for successful outcomes during their school years (Fuchs & Fuchs, 2005).

Early Literacy Case Study: Xavier

Xavier has been receiving core daily reading instruction for 90 minutes each day in his kindergarten classroom as part of Tier I of RtI. His teacher, Mrs. Starnes, with the help of her aide, uses the Dynamic Indicators of Basic Early Literacy Skills (DIBELS; Good & Kaminski, 2002) progress monitoring probes to assess her students weekly on initial sound fluency (ISF), letter naming fluency (LNF), and phoneme segmentation fluency (PSF). After 8 weeks of progress monitoring, Mrs. Starnes sees that Xavier's PSF scores are still falling in the at-risk range (<7 phonemes per minute) and determines that Xavier is in need of more intensive small-group support that can be provided through Tier II of RtI.

Characteristics of Tier II Interventions

Interventions within the second tier of RtI provide additional support to struggling learners in a variety of ways. During this phase, a teacher's goals should be to: (a) remediate skill deficits, (b) preteach or review skills taught during Tier I instruction, (c) provide multiple opportunities to practice target skills, and/or (d) provide immediate corrective feedback. Just as in Tier I reading instruction, Tier II interventions should also reflect research-based reading practices. Specifically, effective reading instruction across *all* tiers of RtI should include one or more of the "Big 5" in reading: (a) phonemic awareness, (b) phonics, (c) fluency, (d) vocabulary, and (e) comprehension (National Reading Panel [NRP], 2000). Figure 3.2 provides more information on the major areas of reading instruction and suggested Tier II interventions to support those students, such as Xavier, in need of supplemental reading support.

Implementing Tier II Interventions

One of the struggles for classroom teachers is working within the instructional time allowed each school day to determine the best way to provide effective instruction to the entire class *and* find time to provide more intensive support through Tier II instruction to targeted students. Unfortunately, there is no cookie-cutter answer to this dilemma. In many schools and classrooms, the classroom teacher must also provide Tier II instruction. In other schools, a reading specialist or other professional provides the interventions that occur as a part of the secondary tier of RtI. Schools must work together to determine how best to designate this responsibility, and those taking part in the implementation of Tier II inter-

45

Reading Area	Defined	Tiers II and III Intervention Suggestions
Phonemic awareness	Understanding and manipulating the smallest units of sound in spoken language	➤ Use explicit instruction • Teacher-directed (Bursuck & Damer, 2011) • Reciprocal peer tutoring with computer-assisted instruction (Wood, Mustian, & Lo, 2010) ➤ Limit instruction to two types of phoneme manipulation (e.g., segmenting and blending) rather than multiple types of phoneme manipulations (NRP, 2000) ➤ Make an explicit connection between phonemic awareness and reading during instruction (i.e., connecting sounds to letters; NRP, 2000)
Phonics	Knowledge of the relationships between sounds and written letters	➤ Use explicit instruction (Bursuck & Damer, 2011) • Teacher explains and models • Students receive multiple opportunities to practice • Corrective feedback is provided ➤ Use a systematic, preplanned skill sequence that follows the core reading program during Tier I (Bursuck & Damer, 2011) • Progresses from easier sounds to more difficult sounds • High-utility sounds and letters taught first • Letters with similar shapes and sounds are separated • Vowels are separated in sequence of alphabetic instruction
Fluency	Reading accurately and with sufficient speed and expression	➤ Practice repeated reading • Choral reading, paired reading, technology (e.g., CDs, computers) ➤ Implement Classwide Peer Tutoring (CWPT; see http://www.jgcp.ku.edu/projects/Grants_Completed/Begin_Read.shtml)
Vocabulary	Understanding the meanings of new words	➤ Preteach critical terms ➤ Teach morphographs (i.e., prefixes, suffixes, roots; Wood, Mustian, & Cooke, 2010) ➤ Create word awareness by calling attention to words and playing with words (Armbruster et al., 2001) ➤ Teach the use of context clues ➤ Use "read alouds" to build listening vocabulary ➤ Use "Text Talk"
Comprehension	Understanding what is read	➤ Use prereading strategies • Activate prior knowledge • Preteach critical vocabulary terms ➤ Provide explicit (or direct) instruction: direct explanation, modeling, guided practice, application ➤ Use text enhancements such as graphic and semantic organizers ➤ Teach imagery ➤ Reread ➤ Use adjunct aids such as guided notes ➤ Teach specific questioning strategies ➤ Use reciprocal teaching

Figure 3.2. Examples of Tier II and III reading interventions.

ventions should be trained on how to do so. By revisiting the example of Xavier, we can see how Tier II of RtI is applied in Mrs. Starnes' classroom:

As part of Tier II, Xavier and three of his classmates also in need of additional support based on Tier I data, now receive small-group instruction focusing on the "Big 5" (i.e., phonemic awareness, phonics, fluency, vocabulary, comprehension) in reading. In addition to this small-group instruction, Xavier and his three classmates continue to receive the 90-minute core reading instruction provided to the entire class through Tier I. Mrs. Starnes' aide, Ms. Jimenez, provides this instruction during 20-minute sessions each day for approximately 10–12 weeks. During these 20-minute sessions, Ms. Jimenez uses a direct instruction, model-lead-test approach to remediate skill deficits and preteach skills to be learned during Tier I core reading instruction. An example of a teacher-student interaction during Tier II instruction is provided below:

Ms. Jimenez: "Tell me the sounds in *frog*."
Xavier and rest of small group: "/f/ /r/ /o/ /g/"
Ms. Jimenez: "Good job! The sounds in frog are "/f/ /r/ /o/ /g/."

During this particular preteaching session, Xavier's group is provided with multiple opportunities to practice critical phonemic awareness skills. As shown above, Ms. Jimenez offers immediate corrective feedback. Because phoneme segmentation was a designated area of need for Xavier, Mrs. Starnes and Ms. Jimenez will continue working together to conduct curriculum-based measurements (CBMs) on Xavier's phoneme segmentation fluency for approximately 10–12 more weeks while Ms. Jimenez provides Tier II instruction. Providing Tier II instruction for anywhere from 8–12 weeks is typical in many RtI classrooms. Providing instruction for this long can be beneficial because it allows enough time for learning changes to be observable, and the data collection is frequent enough that the most optimal educational decisions can be made.

Tier III Interventions in Early Literacy

Most students who require Tier II instruction in an RtI model are able to make the progress necessary to discontinue Tier II interventions and move back into the primary tier of RtI. For these students, 8–12 weeks of additional support were all that they needed to catch up to their typically developing peers. A small percentage, however, still do not make adequate progress in Tier II. Classroom teachers must then use progress monitoring data on each student to determine whether or not he or she would benefit from an additional round of Tier II instruction or if more intensive support is needed. Students who are making steady progress in Tier II but need more time to reach benchmark expectations may simply need 8–12 more weeks of Tier II intervention. If a teacher determines that increased intensity of the intervention is the answer, the student then enters the third and most intensive tier of support in the RtI model. Let's revisit Xavier's scenario to learn how decisions are made to determine the need for Tier III interventions.

It is now the end of January, and at the end of 10 weeks of Tier II instruction, Xavier has made some gains in his ability to blend and segment phonemes. The PSF benchmark for midkindergarten is 18 or higher; however, Xavier's average over the last three PSF probes was just over 13 phonemes per minute. Mrs. Starnes must decide how best to support Xavier's reading needs. After looking at his data and speaking more in depth with Ms. Jimenez, Mrs. Starnes believes Xavier is not making sufficient progress in Tier II and would benefit from Tier III instruction, specifically with phonemic awareness.

Characteristics of Tier III Interventions

The third tier of RtI is highly individualized based on each student's progress-monitoring data. These data are used to set realistic yet achievable goals for each student. For instance, based on Xavier's PSF data, a specific and individual goal will be set during Tier III instruction. Xavier's goal may be different than any other student's goal in Tier III. In Tier III interventions, students may be grouped according to skill need. For example, Xavier may be grouped with one or two other students also in need of phonemic awareness instruction.

Characteristics of Tier III reading interventions are very similar to those provided in Tier II (see Figure 3.2). In Xavier's case, the focus is still on the five areas of effective reading instruction, but instruction is more intense and more explicitly focused on a specific skill area (e.g., phoneme segmentation and blending). Tier III interventions are delivered more frequently and through smaller group sizes, sometimes even in one-to-one situations. This phase of RtI typically occurs five times per week for 30–40 minutes *in*

48

addition to the 90-minute core reading instruction that takes place as part of Tier I instruction.

Implementing Tier III Interventions

Once a student reaches Tier III instruction, it may seem almost impossible for the general education teacher to provide all tiers of instruction in his or her classroom without support from other school personnel. For this reason, Tier III intervention is often provided outside the general education setting by someone who specializes in providing and designing individualized interventions. In some schools, special education personnel are highly involved in implementation during this tier of instruction. In others, a reading specialist or other trained professional is responsible for implementation of these Tier III interventions. Just as with Tier II, how implementation looks during the second tier of RtI depends on the district's or school's resources.

By revisiting the example of Xavier, we can see how Tier III of RtI is applied:

> Xavier is soon to begin Tier III of RtI. His school has one reading specialist and two paraprofessionals who have been specifically trained on delivering intensive reading interventions during Tier III of RtI. Xavier already receives 90 minutes of core reading instruction in his general education setting. The multidisciplinary team, which guides classroom teachers in making RtI decisions (including scheduling of interventions), has helped Mrs. Starnes determine when best to pull Xavier out of the classroom to provide this Tier III instruction. Rather than removing Xavier from content-area instruction or taking him out of his special areas (e.g., art, music, physical education), one of the paraprofessionals, Mrs. Costner, will work with Xavier from 8 a.m.–8:35 a.m. in the conference room. During this time in his classroom, Xavier and his classmates get unpacked and settled, complete morning seatwork, and recite the pledge, and Mrs. Starnes takes attendance and lunch counts.
>
> During Tier III instruction, Mrs. Costner specifically works with Xavier and another student, Nicholas, who both need intensive support with segmenting and blending phonemes. She works with both students each morning by providing explicit instruction using PowerPoint presentations. Mrs. Costner uses the audio input

feature before each session to record individual phonemes or phonemes comprised to make a word onto a PowerPoint slide to provide the additional support Xavier and Nicholas require. See Figure 3.3 for an example application of this tool.

In this example, each slide allows Xavier and Nicholas to listen to a word, break the word apart (i.e., segment), and say it fast (i.e., blend). By using this approach, Mrs. Costner and the computer provide explicit instruction, modeling, multiple opportunities to practice, and immediate feedback. After 10 weeks of providing this intervention and collecting weekly progress monitoring data on Xavier's PSF, Xavier is now segmenting 65 phonemes per minute! His progress places him well above the "Established" level of performance (i.e., >35) according to DIBELS scoring guidelines (Good & Kaminski, 2002). Mrs. Starnes and Mrs. Costner meet to examine Xavier's data and determine that he is ready to discontinue Tier III interventions. He will now only be receiving the 90-minute core reading instruction, and his progress will continue to be frequently monitored.

Although Tier III interventions were successful in Xavier's case, this is not true for *every* student receiving Tier III support. Some students still do not make sufficient growth despite the extensive efforts provided throughout all three tiers of RtI. It is at this point (when a student fails to respond to intervention efforts), that the classroom teacher or a designated RtI team determines that a formal referral for special education services is warranted. The special education or IEP team is then able to use the data collected throughout the RtI process to determine how best to evaluate a student for eligibility in special education.

Tier II Interventions in Social Behavior

In addition to applying RtI to reading, the RtI model has been applied to social behavior. The RtI social behavior model is also known as Schoolwide Positive Behavior Supports (PBS) and has been implemented in schools across the country. Social behavior is an important component of the RtI model, because students' appropriate social behavior at school has been empirically linked to behavioral and academic success (Alberto & Troutman, 2009; Walker, Cheney, Stage, & Blum, 2005). Tier I of the RtI social behavior model addresses behaviors of all students at the schoolwide

Figure 3.3. Sample PowerPoint slide used during Tier III to teach phonemic awareness.

level. For students in need of additional support, Tier II addresses social behavior via small-group instruction, and Tier III addresses social behavior at the individual student level to ensure that all students are successful both socially and academically. See Figure 3.1 for a three-tier RtI model reflecting social behavior.

Social Behavior Case Study: Landry

Landry is a second grader at Estes Elementary School. The school uses a schoolwide model of RtI to address students' social behavior. Landry's teacher, Ms. Hernandez, has worked hard to teach her students the class expectations and procedures that align with the school's RtI social behavior model. She spent the first week of school practicing behavior expectations with her students, has systematically arranged her classroom to meet her students' social and academic needs, and has a token reinforcement system in place to reward appropriate social behavior. Additionally, she uses role-play to practice class behavior rules and social skills. Although these steps have been successful for the majority of students in her classroom, Landry is still struggling socially in that she constantly gets out of her seat and interrupts during instruction, can be defiant when spoken to, and does not consistently complete her assignments. Ms. Hernandez has determined that Landry is in need of more intensive small-group support that can be provided through Tier II of RtI to help improve her social behavior.

Characteristics of Tier II Interventions

Tier II of the RtI social behavior model provides support to students struggling with social behavior in several ways. Students participating in Tier II are often considered at-risk for school failure due to poor academic performance and behavior problems and need more focused support, which is delivered via small-group instruction (Morrissey, Bohanon, & Fenning, 2010). Examples of interventions provided to students at this level include social skills group instruction, peer mentors, check-in/check-out systems, and mentoring programs. Similar to RtI Tier II for early literacy, teachers have several goals: (a) address social behavior deficits, (b) review schoolwide and classroom social behavior expectations and procedures, (c) provide opportunities to practice social behavior skills, (d) provide positive reinforcement and corrective feedback for appropriate social behaviors, and (e) use ongoing progress monitoring to ensure students have the appropriate social behavior skills to succeed in school.

Implementing Tier II Interventions

Oftentimes, interventions at this level are provided to students in pull-out social skills groups. Instruction may be provided by a variety of school personnel such as a school guidance counselor, school psychologist, special education teacher, teacher assistant, or even an administrator (Sandomierski, Kincaid, & Algozzine, 2010). Instructional lessons might include revisiting school and classroom behavior expectations, developing group contingency contracts, and role-playing appropriate social behavior skills with the group of students (Miller, 2009). Other methods that can be used in addition to the pull-out social skills group include setting students up with an adult mentor who can help them cope with behavior issues, providing positive reinforcement, and serving as someone the student can talk to about problems he or she might face throughout the school day. Peer mentors can also be an effective method for enhancing social behavior deficits in students. By providing students at Tier II with peer mentors that are close in age to the student, students can begin to recognize what appropriate social behavior looks like and begin to understand social behavior expectations and skills. The peer mentor serves as a role model who interacts socially with others in a positive way. Another method that might be used is a check-in/check-out program. Check-in/check-out programs can provide students in Tier II with a mechanism for talking to someone about his or her school day prior to the ringing of the first bell and at the end of the school day to discuss how the day went, including all positive and negative aspects of the school day.

Finally, teachers should use progress monitoring to determine if students are gaining the appropriate social behavior skills. If the interventions are effective for improving social behavior skills, teachers should begin to see positive changes in student behavior and academic performance across the school environment. Just like RtI Tier II for early literacy, school personnel have to collaborate to determine how to designate responsibility for providing Tier II RtI social behavior support to students at this level. One key element in this process is to ensure that regardless of who is providing the Tier II interventions, he or she is trained to implement the interventions effectively.

Let's revisit the example of Landry to see how Tier II of the RtI social behavior model works:

> As part of Tier II, Landry and four other students in need of additional support at the Tier II level are receiving small-group instruction that focuses on social skills training. Mr. Torino, the assistant principal in charge of behavior at Estes Elementary, pulls students out of Ms. Hernandez's class for 30 minutes a day for approximately 10–12 weeks. During this time, Mr. Torino reteaches school and classroom behavior expectations, rules, and procedures. He also uses the time to discuss various topics, including setting behavior goals, study skills, solving conflicts, developing positive peer relationships, and using self-control. The students, along with Mr. Torino, use role-play to practice various skills and expectations. In addition, Mr. Torino, with input from the students, has set up a group contingency system. Together, the group has established a written agreement between Mr. Torino and themselves regarding expected classroom behavior. The contingency contract includes a statement of the desired behavior(s), terms and conditions of the agreement, reinforcers or rewards the students will be given based on meeting the requirements of the contract, and signatures of each student and Mr. Torino.

During these pull-out social skills sessions, Landry and the other students are given opportunities to discuss behavior goals, practice critical social behavior skills, and receive both positive reinforcement and corrective feedback from Mr. Torino regarding appropriate social behavior. Figure 3.4 provides an example of a group contingency contract that can be used during Tier II to address social behavior and establish expected classroom behavior with a group of students.

Tier III Interventions in Social Behavior

Although the majority of students participating in Tier II of the RtI social behavior model will be successful, there is still a possibility that a few students may not be successful at the Tier II level. Therefore, it may be necessary for students who are unsuccessful at Tier II to move into Tier III of the RtI social behavior model. At this level, social behavior is addressed with each individual student. During Tier III, the classroom teacher, along with the support of other school personnel, begins to conduct Functional Behavior Assessments (FBA), develop Behavior Intervention Plans (BIP), and implement intensive individualized interventions to meet the student's behavioral and academic needs (Alberto & Troutman, 2009; Miller, 2009).

Social Behavior Case Study: Landry

After participating in Tier II of RtI for social behavior, four of the students in Landry's group were successful and moved back into Tier I. Unfortunately, Landry's behavior did not improve. She still exhibited disruptive classroom behaviors and was struggling socially. She continued to get out of her seat and interrupt during instruction, showed defiance when spoken to, and was not completing her assignments. Based on progress monitoring, Ms. Hernandez did not see positive changes in Landry's behavior; therefore, Ms. Hernandez determined that Landry was in need of individualized intensive interventions that could be provided through Tier III of RtI. By moving Landry into Tier III, Ms. Hernandez and the support team can determine the function of her problematic behavior and identify specific individualized interventions to help her be successful socially and academically.

My Contract

Student Name: _____

Date: _____

These are my goals:

1. _____
2. _____
3. _____

These are my consequences if I don't meet my goals:

_____

_____

_____

These are my rewards/reinforcers if I meet my goals:

_____

_____

_____

_____

My contract will be reviewed on: _____

Signatures: _____

_____

_____

Figure 3.4. Contingency contract.

Characteristics of Tier III Interventions

Tier III of the RtI social behavior model provides support to individual students who have been unsuccessful at the Tier I and Tier II levels and need individualized support. Students who require Tier III interventions have exhibited ongoing behavior problems that have affected their learning and the learning of other students in the classroom (Morrissey et al., 2010). Students at the Tier III level may also be referred to and qualify for special education services to address problem behaviors (Miller, 2009; Walker et al., 2005). During Tier III, classroom teachers work with parents and school personnel, such as special education teachers, school psychologists, and behavior specialists, to address the student's problem behaviors. This process includes several steps. First, the team conducts an FBA to investigate and gain information to determine the function of the student's problem behavior(s). Next, based on results of the FBA, the team begins to develop a BIP that includes specific interventions to address the student's problem behavior(s). Once the BIP has been developed, the team determines the most effective methods for implementation (Alberto & Troutman, 2009; Sandomierski et al., 2010; Miller, 2009).

Implementing Tier III Interventions

The first step in the process for determining appropriate interventions for students in Tier III of RtI for social behavior is to conduct an FBA to determine the function of the student's problematic behavior(s). The FBA process consists of gathering information related to the student's academic and functional performance. Specifically, an FBA includes interviewing the student and anyone who is involved with the student (e.g., teachers, parents, teacher assistants, bus drivers) and direct observations of the student in the classroom setting (Alberto & Troutman, 2009; Miller, 2009). The interviews should directly relate to the student's problematic behaviors and should provide useful information that can help develop the BIP. Direct observations should investigate antecedents (i.e., what happens before the problem behavior is exhibited) and consequences (i.e., what happens after the problem behavior has occurred; Alberto & Troutman, 2009; Miller, 2009). One method for conducting direct observations is to use what is called a three-term contingency model to record the antecedents, behavior, and consequences (A-B-C) of the problem behavior. Figure 3.5 provides an example of an A-B-C observation form that relates to Landry and can be used to identify Landry's pattern of problem behavior.

After interviews and direct observations have been conducted to determine the function of the student's problem behavior, the next step in the process is to develop the BIP. The BIP should be developed as a team and should be based on the findings of the interview and direct observations. In developing the BIP, the team should ask the following questions regarding environmental changes, persons implementing the intervention(s), data collection, and progress monitoring:

> ‣ What changes to the environment should be made regarding alterations to the antecedents?
> ‣ What is an appropriate replacement behavior?
> ‣ What specific evidence-based interventions are we going to use to reduce the problem behavior and increase the appropriate replacement behavior?
> ‣ What types of reinforcements and contingencies should be in place prior to implementing the intervention?
> ‣ Who will implement the intervention?

A-B-C Observation Form

Student Name: Landry
Date: January 18, 2011
Observer: Ms. Hernandez
Location: Ms. Hernandez' class
Length of observation period: 8:30 – 8:45 AM

8:30–8:35	Ms. H explains assignment and tells students to begin work	L gets out of her seat and walks around the room	Ms. H asks her if there is something she needs
8:35 – 8:40	Ms. H asks her if there is something she needs	L says she doesn't like the assignment	Students laugh at her response
8:40 – 8:45	Ms. H tells her to sit down and get to work	L goes to her desk and puts her head down	Ms. H sends her to the principal's office

Figure 3.5. Antecedent-behavior-consequence (A-B-C) observation form.

> What type of data will be collected to monitor the student's progress?
> How will we fade the intervention and ensure the student can generalize the appropriate behavior across school settings?

After the plan has been developed and all questions have been answered, implementation of the intensive intervention begins. At this point, it is the responsibility of the team to conduct ongoing progress monitoring to ensure the intervention is effective in reducing the problem behavior, make changes to the intervention if the student is not making progress, and deliver the appropriate reinforcement and contingencies as the student moves through the intervention process.

Let's revisit the example of Landry to see how Tier III of the RtI social behavior model works:

Moving into Tier III is an important step in reducing Landry's problem behavior. Landry is receiving intensive individualized instruction to help her gain the appropriate social behavior skills. Ms. Hernandez began the FBA process by interviewing Landry and her parents. She gathered information from them regarding Landry's behavior at school and at home. She also conducted interviews with Mr. Torino (assistant principal), Mrs. Goforth (music teacher), Ms. Easler (physical education teacher), and Mr. Johnson (guidance counselor). Because all of these people work with Landry in some way, this allowed Ms. Hernandez to get a well-rounded picture of Landry across the school environment. For the direct observations of Landry's behavior, Ms. Hernandez used an A-B-C observation form to record what happened before and after the problem behavior occurred. See Figure 3.5 for the A-B-C observation form documenting the occurrences of Landry's problem behavior.

Once the FBA process was completed, Ms. Hernandez called a meeting with the team to discuss development of the BIP for Landry. The team consisted of Ms. Hernandez, Ms. Miekler (school psychologist), Mr. Watson (special education teacher), Mr. Torino (assistant principal), Landry, and Landry's parents. Together the team worked to answer all of the questions regarding environmental changes, persons implementing the intervention, data collection, and progress monitoring. The final step in the process was implementation of the intervention. It was determined that Ms. Hernandez would be responsible for implementing the intervention since Landry spent the majority of her day in Ms. Hernandez's classroom. The intervention that the team decided to use with Landry was a self-management intervention that required Landry to monitor her behavior throughout the school day. She was given a self-monitoring checklist to use and also was given the opportunity to set her behavior goals. Based on the first week of progress monitoring by Ms. Hernandez, Landry is showing progress in that she is not interrupting the class as often and has begun to complete assignments. Although it is a work in progress, Ms. Hernandez feels positive that they have found an intervention that is working to help Landry improve her social behavior skills.

Conclusion

Tiers II and III of RtI are designed to provide research-based interventions to students who are academically and/or behaviorally at risk. RtI should be viewed as a preventive and proactive approach to intervening efficiently, effectively, and early. Many factors contribute to the success of RtI interventions in the school setting such as (a) quality of interventions chosen, (b) scheduling of instructional time, (c) quality and frequency of data collection, (d) school or district resources to support the RtI model, (e) school personnel buy-in, and (f) fidelity of implementation. No matter who has been designated as responsible for implementing Tier II and III interventions, RtI should be viewed as a team effort. Additionally, training of those individuals is essential for ensuring RtI is implemented successfully and optimal student outcomes are achieved. Tiers II and III of RtI, if delivered effectively, can provide the support that many students need to catch up to their peers and experience academic and behavioral success throughout their school years.

References

Alberto, P. A., & Troutman, A. C. (2009). *Applied behavior analysis for teachers* (8th ed.). Upper Saddle River, NJ: Pearson.

Armbruster, B. B., Lehr, F., & Osborn, J. (2001). *Put reading first: The research building blocks for teaching children to read.* Jessup, MD: National Institute for Literacy.

Bursuck, W. D., & Damer, M. (2011). *Teaching reading to students who are at risk or have disabilities.* Upper Saddle River, NJ: Pearson.

Fuchs, D., & Fuchs, L. S. (2005). Responsiveness-to-Intervention: A blueprint for practitioners, policymakers, and parents. *TEACHING Exceptional Children, 38*(1), 57–61.

Good, R. H., & Kaminski, R. A. (2002). *Dynamic Indicators of Basic Early Literacy Skills* (6th ed.). Eugene, OR: Institute for the Development of Educational Achievement.

Lewis, T. (n.d.). *Increasing social and academic success: Positive Behavior Support meets Response to Intervention.* Retrieved from http://www.pbis.org/common/pbisresources/presentations/lewis_pbs_rti.pdf

Miller, S. P. (2009). *Validated practices for teaching students with diverse needs and abilities* (2nd ed.). Upper Saddle River, NJ: Pearson.

Morrissey, K. L., Bohanon, H., & Fenning, P. (2010). Positive behavior support: Teaching and acknowledging expected behaviors in an urban high school. *Teaching Exceptional Children, 42*(5), 26–35.

National Reading Panel. (2000). *Teaching children to read: An evidence-based assessment of the scientific research literature on reading and its implications for reading instruction.* Washington, DC: National Institute of Child Health and Human Development.

Sandomierski, T., Kincaid, D., & Algozzine, B. (2010). *Response to Intervention and Positive Behavior Support: Brothers from different mothers and sisters from different misters.* Retrieved from http://flpbs.fmhi.usf.edu/FLPBS and RtI article.pdf

Vaughn, S., & Roberts, G. (2007). Secondary interventions in reading: Providing additional instruction for students at risk. *TEACHING Exceptional Children, 39*(5), 40–46.

Walker, B., Cheney, D., Stage, S., & Blum, C. (2005). Schoolwide screening and Positive Behavior Supports: Identifying and supporting students at risk for school failure. *Journal of Positive Behavior Interventions, 7,* 194–204.

Wood, C. L., Mustian, A. L., & Cooke, N. L. (2010). Comparing whole word and morphograph instruction during computer-assisted peer tutoring on students' acquisition and generalization of vocabulary. *Remedial and Special Education.* Advance online publication. doi:10.1177/0741932510362515

Wood, C. L., Mustian, A. L., & Lo, Y-y. (2010). *Effects of supplemental computer-assisted reciprocal peer tutoring on kindergarteners' phoneme segmentation fluency.* Manuscript submitted for publication.

Assessment
Considerations in Three-Tier Approaches to Academic Instruction

Frederick J. Brigham, Nancy Johnson Emanuel, and Jennifer Walker

This chapter is about ensuring that the data used in RtI programs are adequate unto the magnitude of the task RtI addresses—guiding decisions about curriculum, instruction, and students in schools. One of the most important elements of any RtI program is data-based decision making. In fact, some authors (e.g., Taylor, 2008) have suggested that the hallmark of RtI is the constant use of data. It is possible that many educators and laypersons considering the impact of RtI on their school may wonder what's new. We've had prereferral activity requirements in place for years, and schools are awash in data. Besides that, teachers have been making decisions about students for as long as there have been schools.

Other chapters have described how RtI is different than the older prereferral requirements and how the use of data as universal screening outcomes can guide program decisions. However, the reasons that the data-based decision-making procedures involved in RtI are a step forward are rarely described in the literature. Before turning to the kinds of data that are collected and the requirements of adequate measurement within RtI programs, we will first describe how RtI data dramatically change the model of decision making used by practitioners.

Approaches to Decision Making

There are a number of general models of decision making (Goldstein & Hogarth, 1997). Most can be grouped according to one of the two major distinctions among approaches to decision making: clinical judgment and actuarial judgment. Although professionals who engage in decision making collect and interpret data to plan and carry out their treatments, the issue at question in regard to clinical versus actuarial judgment is more about interpretation than data collection. Collecting data and using data are actually quite different processes. We will briefly describe the distinctions between clinical and actuarial models of interpretation and then show how RtI relates to each of them.

Clinical judgment is based on the individual's intuition and professional experience and seeks to develop a unique understanding of the individual within the relevant context (Bell & Mellor, 2009). Actuarial judgment is based on making comparisons of the individual to groups of individuals with known characteristics about whom statistical generalizations can be made with relative certainty (Dawes, 1994). Given these descriptions, readers might recoil from the actuarial model simply because it sounds cold, impersonal, and mechanical. Conversely, readers may wonder when subjective judgment should replace more objective measures. Others might ask how we can decide between relying on our judgment and relying on our data.

The answer depends on whether or not a well-developed and applicable actuarial method is available. When such a method is present, the actuarial method is well supported and thoroughly justified. Across dozens of studies since the original analysis (Meehl, 1954), actuarial methods have yielded superior results to clinical judgment. One of the benefits of the heavy reliance on assessment in RtI is that it promotes the actuarial approach to making decisions about individual students. The problem is that we do not yet have sufficient actuarial data in all areas where we must make decisions. In such cases, educators must rely on their judgment (Brigham, Gustashaw, & Brigham, 2004).

Data-driven judgment methods, when available, should take precedence over clinical judgment methods. Dawes, Faust, and Meehl (1989) described a variety of reasons that the actuarial model yields superior results to clinical judgment. Among these are:

> Clinicians tend to identify too many "exceptions" to the rule, thus inflating the rate of false positives and false negatives rather than increasing the accuracy of the decisions being made.

‣ Actuarial methods can discriminate between relevant and irrelevant data sources, but in clinical judgment, it is often difficult to determine which sources of information are relevant or irrelevant.

‣ Along with the preceding point, actuarial methods have been shown to reach the same conclusion on repeated analyses of the same case data, while presenting the same case repeatedly to different sets of clinical judges very often yields different determinations.

Dawes et al. (1989) concluded that although actuarial methods are superior to clinical judgment, they are far from infallible and need to be reevaluated periodically to ensure that they are optimal. Additionally, actuarial decisions are only as good as the models on which they rest. The watchwords "garbage in—garbage out" that apply to computer analysis can apply to actuarial models supporting RtI. Therefore, it is essential that RtI practitioners employ sound measures that yield reliable and valid indicators of performance. In the next section, we turn to the general requirements of good data for RtI. Although our case study deals with a student who has difficulties in reading, we deal with data as a general construct rather than subject-specific data. A discussion of what variables should be measured, how they should be measured, and how they should be weighted in making decisions within any given domain is beyond the scope of the present chapter.

Collecting Appropriate Data

The importance and difficulty of developing measures in education and professional evaluation is underscored by the length of volumes such as the *Handbook of Test Development* (Downing & Haladyna, 2006). The recentness and difference of RtI and its component curriculum-based measures are indicated in that, across the more than 750 pages of dense text in that handbook, neither topic is addressed in the table of contents, index, or as a major subject heading within the component chapters. This suggests no deficiency in the 2006 *Handbook of Test Development*, but rather that the approaches to measurement used in RtI are, in many ways, different than those pursued by other test and measurement producers.

One of the biggest differences between measures in RtI and more traditional measures is in their intended frequency of administration. Individual and group achievement tests, as well as other measures such as IQ tests, are intended for infrequent administration. Some measures used in RtI can be administered frequently and repeatedly, even daily. That is because items that are selected for RtI assessments are small tasks that must be conducted with great fluency (the union of accuracy and rate) in order to carry out other, more sophisticated tasks that are of greater importance. For example, rapid letter naming and syllabication predict later word reading, which in turn predicts passage reading. Fluent passage reading, with other elements such as vocabulary and background knowledge, predicts comprehension (Denton & Vaughn, 2010).

Requirements of Good Measurements

Regardless of the particular element selected for measurement, certain characteristics of good assessment apply. Four of the most important aspects of any measurement system are (a) reliability, (b) validity, (c) sensitivity, and (d) specificity (Jimerson, Burns, & VanDerHeyden, 2007).

Reliability. "Reliability refers to the consistency of the relationship between observed values and the events that actually occurred" (Johnston & Pennypacker, 2009, p. 143). Reliability is a particularly important element of any assessment. In the absence of consistent measures of a phenomenon that is itself relatively stable, it is difficult to defend the claim that one is measuring much of anything. Reliability has several specific meanings, all of which are related to the consistency of the measures across time, raters, or items purported to measure the same construct.

Stability across time. Demonstrating reliability of the phenomenon across time is usually carried out with test-retest procedures in which the same test is given to the same test takers more than once in a relatively short time. If the total scores are highly correlated, the test is considered to have adequate test-retest reliability. We can be confident in measures that yield similar scores on repeated administrations that occur within a short time period. The time period should be short enough that we would expect no substantial change in the scores. For example, a thermometer should give roughly similar measures of atmospheric temperature at 6 a.m. and 6:15 a.m., but we would expect the measures taken at 6 a.m. and noon to be quite different under typical conditions.

Test-retest correlations exceeding 0.80 are desirable, but in cases where no more stable measures are available or where the research is in its early stages, measures with coefficients as low as .60 may be used with great caution (Salvia, Ysseldyke, & Bolt, 2010). Measures with stability coefficients that fall below .60 should be avoided, as they possess insufficient test-retest reliability (Hintze & Marcotte, 2010). Nunnally (1978) suggested that, in the initial stages of research, coefficients below .80 are quite acceptable, but in applied settings, particularly applied settings with important consequences tied to the decisions, correlation coefficients of .90 and higher may be needed. Thus, practitioners are wise to consider the stability indicators of the measures they select, and use the ones associated with the strongest test-retest correlations. Decisions in RtI, however, are fluid and can be changed quickly depending on the individual's performance. Therefore, most RtI decisions carry less severe consequences than do decisions regarding eligibility for special education or admission to a college, because they can quickly be detected and reversed.

Stability across raters. Demonstrating stability across raters (i.e., interrater or interobserver reliability) is done by presenting the same observations of behavior or responses to multiple individuals and obtaining their ratings. In some cases, the same observer may rate the same behavior multiple times in order to demonstrate consistency of scoring (Johnston & Pennypacker, 2009). Traditionally, interrater reliability coefficients are considered to be adequate when they meet or exceed 80% agreement (Kazdin, 1982). As with measures of stability across time, measures with greater reliability are more desirable than are less reliable measures. Training in the method of obtaining and scoring the observations is an important part of obtaining stability across raters in RtI as well as in other areas of assessment and behavioral observation.

Stability across items and forms. Two additional considerations of score stability are also important. Stability across items, or internal consistency, is important because it suggests that the items all sample the same construct. One example of an assessment where the items often sample more than one construct is scales of mathematical word problems. For students with adequate reading ability, the measure is a relatively clear measure of their mathematical ability; however, for students with reading difficulties, the mathematical measure is contaminated by the influence of reading skills. Most violations of internal consistency are less obvious than the word problem example; therefore, educators should examine the internal consistency of their RtI measures to ensure that the measures are truly measuring the skills they purport to measure.

Cronbach's alpha is the most common measure of internal consistency (Hintze & Marcotte, 2010). Although other measures exist, they are primarily adaptations for specific statistical purposes. The general idea behind these statistics is the measurement of the correlation between one half of the test items and the other. This is also called a "split-half" reliability. The Cronbach's alpha statistic represents the correlations among all of the possible split-half coefficients (e.g., first half of the test compared to the second half, even items compared to the odd items, etc.). Nunnally (1978) suggested that the major source of measurement error for most situations is content sampling. Internal consistency measures of .70 are the minimum acceptable for use in RtI programs (Gersten et al., 2009).

RtI measures often use different measures or probes to assess the same skills. These are essentially alternate forms of the same test and therefore must also possess high levels of correlation with one another. Alternate form reliability is established by administering different forms of the same measure to the same student and then correlating the scores. In the absence of instruction or practice, one would expect measures of the same construct administered in very close succession to yield very similar scores. If measures of the same skill with different versions of the test are similar to each other when given close together but become less similar when administered further apart, the most likely conclusion is that the measures are consistent and that people are changing over time. If the measures yield low correlations when given close together and also when given far apart, the logical conclusion is that they are measuring different constructs or different types of content (Nunnally, 1978). One of the uses of measures in RtI is to show growth over time; therefore, high levels of alternate form reliability are necessary in order to remove the score variability associated with different and noncomparable assessment versions from student performance measures.

Considerations in continuous progress monitoring. In continuous progress measures associated with RtI and curriculum-based measurement (CBM), reliability over time is demonstrated with slightly different procedures than described in the previous sections. Measurement in RtI and CBM is intended to demonstrate progress and also to be quite sensitive to changes in performance. Therefore, measures of stability across short time periods are important for establishing the utility of the assessments, but we also must ensure that the assessments track progress over time. Statistical procedures for showing reliability of repeated measures are rarely discussed in the RtI literature. One reason is that the statistical procedures for such determinations are complex. Another reason is that the conventions for graphic display of performance data are associated with single-subject research designs. Single-subject research designs tend to rely on visual inspection of the data display (graph) rather than statistical analysis to determine whether or not a clear trend with reliable measurement properties exists.

Kratochwill et al. (2010) concluded that six features are used to examine within- and between-phase data patterns in single-case research designs:

(1) level, (2) trend, (3) variability, (4) immediacy of the effect, (5) overlap, and (6) consistency of data patterns across similar phases. Three of these features, level, trend, and variability, are useful in evaluating individual response to the measures used in Tiers II and III:

> "Level" refers to the mean score for the data within a phase. "Trend" refers to the slope of the best-fitting straight line for the data within a phase and "variability" refers to the range or standard deviation of data about the best-fitting straight line. (Kratochwill et al., 2010, p. 18)

The concept of level suggests that scores of desirable performance should increase with intervention. Failure to detect increases in level suggests (a) that the measures are unreliable or (b) that the intervention is ineffective, improperly executed, or being carried out with insufficient intensity. Figure 4.1 shows a simplified diagram in which no change in level is detected from the points on the left side of the chart and those on the right side of the chart. Figure 4.2 shows a chart with a notable change in level between the points on the left side of the chart and those on the right side of the chart. Clearly, if one were seeking to increase the behavior shown on the chart, the response in Figure 4.2 suggests that the treatment is far more effective than the one used in Figure 4.1.

The concept of trend or slope refers to the rate in which the behavior is changing. Steeper slopes suggest a more rapid response to the intervention. Figure 4.3 shows a simplified diagram in which no change in slope is detected from the points on the left side of the chart and those on the right side of the chart. Figure 4.4 shows a chart with a notable change in level between the points on the left side of the chart and those on the right side of the chart. Clearly, if one were seeking to increase the behavior shown on the chart, the response in Figure 4.4 suggests that the treatment is far more effective than the one used in Figure 4.3. Failure to detect increases in slope suggests that the measures are unreliable or that the intervention is ineffective, improperly executed, or being carried out with insufficient intensity.

The variability of the data is quite important for considering the reliability of the measurement. Figure 4.5 shows a simplified diagram in which little variability around the line of best fit for the chart data is observed. Figure 4.6 shows a chart in which far greater variability around the line of best fit for the chart data is observed. It is unrealistic to expect children with learning problems to progress in an even and consistently upward

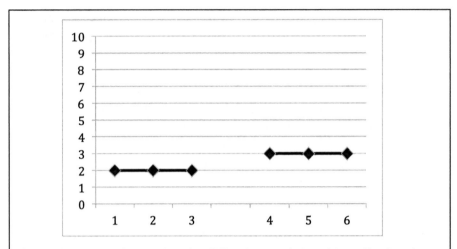

Figure 4.1. Data display showing little change in level from the treatments on the left and right sides of the chart.

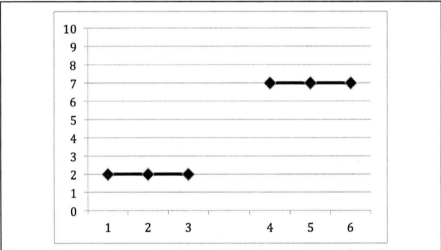

Figure 4.2. Data display showing notable change in level from the treatments on the left and right sides of the chart.

trend. Factors such as fatigue or even changes in the time of day when the measure is given can, along with simple random measurement error, yield small changes in performance from day to day. Wide variability in data points across a measure suggests that the measures are unreliable or that the intervention is ineffective, improperly executed, or being carried out with insufficient intensity. It can also indicate that the student is making better efforts on some occasions than others.

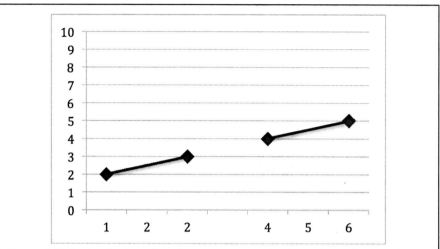

Figure 4.3. Data display showing no change in slope from the treatments on the left and right sides of the chart.

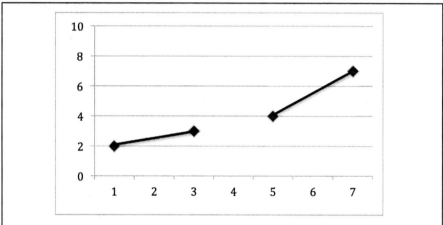

Figure 4.4. Data display showing notable change in trend (slope) from the treatments on the left and right sides of the chart.

The rules for visual inspection of data are stated only in general terms so no precise indications of the necessary changes in level or slope or of acceptable variability in the measures around a trend line are available. Even so, comparisons of these features across students, across teachers, or across time can suggest whether or not the measures possess sufficient reliability and are being implemented properly. When the measures are adequate and being implemented properly, the next most logical source of variability is in the child. In some cases, educators may need to target consistent performance as well as the target skill they are teaching.

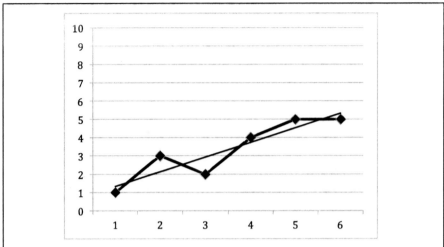

Figure 4.5. Data display showing little variability around the line of best fit for the chart data.

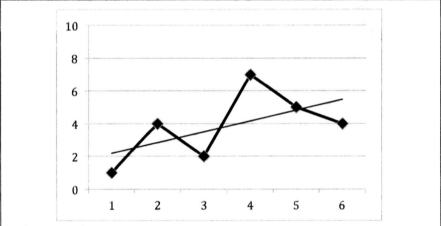

Figure 4.6. Data display showing greater variability around the line of best fit for the chart data.

Validity. Convergent validity refers to the degree to which a given measure correlates with other measures believed to be capturing the same construct. Discriminant validity refers to the degree to which a measure departs from other assessments believed to be measuring different constructs (Greiffenstein, Fox, & Lees-Haley, 2007).

In order to demonstrate convergent validity, measures used in RtI should rank students in a manner similar to other measures of the same skill. For example, measures of phonology in RtI should yield similar rankings of students as measures of phonology on norm-referenced scales. Thus, educators are justified in using the simpler and more efficient measures associated with RtI in place of the more complicated and time-consuming scales.

In order to demonstrate discriminant validity, measures used in RtI should tap into skills that are distinct from other measures. One indication that the probes used in CBM and RtI possess discriminant validity is in their reduction in disproportional identification of students from African American and Latino/Latina backgrounds (Hosp & Madyun, 2007). The reductions in referrals and placement noted in previous studies suggest that the instruction provided is more likely to be effective and that the skills being taught are more adequately discriminated from the culture of the school. In that way, these measures may be more likely to target the skills being taught, as opposed to the skills of what some have referred to as the "hidden curriculum." The hidden curriculum is mostly involved in learning to navigate the differences between the school and one's home (Hosp & Madyun, 2007). For some children, the difference can be quite challenging. Measures with adequate discriminant validity help ensure that educators are measuring the acquisition of skills instead of the understanding of particular contextual information in which the skill is embedded.

Sensitivity. "Sensitivity is defined as a scale's ability to detect conditions or traits known to be present" (Greiffenstein et al., 2007, p. 217). Any measure that is used in RtI must identify the children who have actually failed or who are at risk for failure. In other words, we want to avoid false negatives (i.e., the measure indicates that the child is doing well, but the child is actually at risk for failure). Brigham and Jenkins (Chapter 2, this volume) recommended that children who are not quite in the "at risk range," usually the bottom quartile of the distribution, should be monitored more frequently to ensure that they do not unnecessarily fall behind. This is a way of ensuring that we identify all children who need assistance while there is time to help them. Avoiding false negatives means tolerating false positives (Hammond, 1996). False positives are the assessment equivalent of false alarms. Although it is important to reduce false alarms, it is better to be safe than sorry when the cost of the false alarm, providing Tier II or III intervention, is less dramatic than the cost of the false negative (allowing the child to fail when it could be prevented).

Sensitivity also refers to the potential of the variable of interest to respond to treatment (Johnston & Pennypacker, 2009). Table 4.1 presents a set of variables associated with early reading that are known to be sensitive to treatment. Early treatment also tends to be more effective and efficient than does intervention with older students who have fallen further

Table 4.1
Recommended Target Areas for Early Screening and Progress Monitoring

Measures	Recommended grade levels	Proficiencies assessed	Purpose	Limitations
Letter naming fluency	K–1	Letter name identification and the ability to rapidly retrieve abstract information	Screening	Poor for progress monitoring because students begin to learn to associate letters with sounds. It is not valid for English learners in kindergarten, but seems valid for grade 1.
Phoneme segmentation	K–1	Phonemic awareness	Screening and progress monitoring	Problematic for measuring progress in the second semester of grade 1. As students learn to read, they seem to focus less on phonemic skills and more on decoding strategies.
Nonsense word fluency	1	Proficiency and automaticity with basic phonics rule	Screening and progress monitoring	Limited to only very simple words and does not tap the ability to read irregular words or multisyllabic words.
Word identification	1–2	Word reading	Screening and progress monitoring	Addresses many of the limitations of nonsense word fluency by including multisyllabic and irregular words.
Oral reading fluency (also called passage reading fluency)	1–2	Reading connected text accurately and fluently	Screening and progress monitoring	This measure has moderately strong criterion-related validity, but cannot give a full picture of students' reading proficiency. Many students will score close to zero at the beginning of grade 1. The measure still is a reasonable predictor of end-of-year reading performance.

Note. Adapted from "Assessing students struggling with reading: Response to Intervention and multi-tier intervention for reading in the primary grades. A practical guide" by R. Gersten, D. Compton, C. M. Connor, J. Dimino, L. Santoro, S. Linan-Thompson, and W. D. Tilly, 2009. Retrieved from http://ies.ed.gov/ncee/wwc/publications/practiceguides

behind in the curriculum (Denton & Vaughn, 2010). Remedial efforts can pay off for older students, but the intensity and duration of the treatment needed is often much greater.

Specificity. Specificity refers to a scale's ability to rule out conditions or traits known to be absent" (Greiffenstein et al., 2007, p. 219). In other words, measures with adequate specificity separate the responses from the rest of the individual's repertoire of behaviors (Johnston & Pennypacker, 2009). Ruling out false alarms is one way of reducing the number of children who are *misidentified* as requiring services from special education programs. It is also a way of maximizing the efficiency of the instructional program. Once students have acquired the target skill(s), they should move on to other skills or return to less intensive levels of intervention. Measures with adequate specificity allow educators to have greater confidence that they are responding to the minimum number of false alarms to ensure the stability of their educational communities.

Current Progress

Current progress is assessed only periodically in Tier I during triannual screenings. These single-point measures provide a snapshot of the students at the specific points in time that the assessments are administered. Several sets of simple assessments paired with norms for a variety of skills, particularly in reading, are available. For example, Virginia's Phonological Awareness Literacy Screening (PALS; Invernezzi, Juel, Swank, & Mier, 2007) provides brief assessments for group administration and also for individual administration, if needed, on skills such as rhyme awareness, beginning sound awareness, alphabet knowledge, letter sounds, spelling, and word concepts for PreK and early kindergarten students. The measures require approximately 30–45 minutes to complete and the results are then compared to fall and spring norms. Students with adequate scores on these measures in turn are likely to do well on state tests for measuring educational progress such as Virginia's Standards of Learning (SOL). A large-scale factor analytic study was recently conducted with the PALS-PreK modules. The results across more than 4,500 children suggested that PALS-PreK effectively measures the most important precursors to successful literacy acquisition—alphabet knowledge, phonological awareness, and print concepts—with generally the same degree of accuracy for boys and girls (Townsend & Konold, 2010).

There are several other popular tools for evaluating student performance and planning instruction based on the data obtained for their screenings. Two very prominent web-based evaluation and planning tools are Dynamic Indicators of Basic Early Literacy Skills (DIBELS; Good & Kaminski, 2002) and AIMSweb. Both tools provide indicators of adequate performance (at or above a benchmark for the time of year) as well as indicators of students who are at risk for failure, the lowest performers, and students who are possibly at risk for failure, the group of students performing just above the cut score for "at-risk."

Progress Compared to Peers

Progress at any single point in time is important, but the peer group is a moving target. With each subsequent administration of the measures used, the peer group will be performing at a higher level. The performance of individual students needs to be considered in terms of where they stand on a particular measure and also on the rate of improvement that they demonstrate across repeated measures.

Tools for Determining Progress

Three tools are available for comparing an individual to his relevant peer group. The first is a single-point comparison of the individual to a measure of central tendency and its accompanying measure of dispersion. The second is comparing the individual's rate of change to that expected of the peer group. The third combines data from both the individual's standing relative to the peer group and also the individual's rate of change compared to the peer group. This third method is called a dual-discrepancy approach (Fuchs, 2003).

Single-point comparisons. Single-point comparisons compare the individual to a measure of relative standing within the group or to a preestablished benchmark for performance at a given time during the year. Measures of relative standing are usually computed in one of two ways: using the mean and standard deviation, or using the median and interquartile ranges. The benchmarks to which students can be compared are often constructed in methods that are based on these approaches as well.

In a normal distribution, the mean will split the group into two halves, each with 50% of the population. The measure of dispersion associated with the mean is the standard deviation (SD). The SD literally is the average of the distance of the scores from the mean. Statistically, the first SD on each side of the mean accounts for the expected range of variability of any given phenomenon. Scores lying outside of the mean $\pm 1SD$ are considered to be unusual in the sample of data collected. Thus, when considering adequacy of progress, scores within the first standard deviation around the mean can be considered to represent typical variability in the population, and scores below the first standard deviation represent less than adequate performance.

With a large data sample that conforms to normal distribution properties, the first SD on either side of the mean accounts for 34% of the population. Subtracting 34% from the 50% of the population lying below the mean leaves 16%. Thus, the mean minus one SD model will identify 16% of the population as at risk for failure or demonstrating inadequate performance. Schools wishing to create local norms can easily calculate mean and SD statistics with spreadsheet applications available on almost all computers.

There are some concerns to bear in mind using the mean and SD. School populations may not conform to normal distribution characteristics. For example, as children master rapid letter naming, the distribution becomes skewed, with the scores stacking up at the high end. Also, extreme values can influence the mean, causing it to move from the middle of the distribution toward the extreme value. Additionally, the mean and SD comparison will identify only 16% of the population as at risk. In some cases, particularly in screening, it is wise to identify a larger proportion of the population for additional attention. In cases where these concerns apply, comparisons may better be made using the median and interquartile ranges.

The median is the score that divides the top 50% of the scores from the bottom 50% of the scores. It has the advantage of being resistant to extreme values and also working within nonnormal distributions. As with the mean and SD, most computer spreadsheets allow easy calculation of the median and interquartile ranges. By selecting the lowest quartile, 25% of the population is identified as at risk or at least needing additional monitoring of their status.

Schools are actually able to set "cut scores" for adequate performance anywhere that they choose. Methods using mean and SD comparisons or selecting the lowest quartile are simple and can readily be explained using their underlying statistics. In some cases, however, schools may wish to establish higher cut scores than would be suggested by either of these methods. Officials establishing high cut scores will identify more students as being in need of services. That increases the rate of false positives. Educators must bear in mind that consideration of statistics such as mean and SD as well as medians and quartiles will always show a proportion of the population in the lowest range. It is simply impossible for all children to score in the above-average range on every measure (Kauffman & Konold, 2007).

Single-point comparisons are conducted infrequently, most often at the end of an instructional unit or end of an intervention period. Such comparisons fail to consider how much learning has actually taken place during the instructional period (Fuchs, 2003). Rate of change comparisons provide an index of learning across the intervention period.

Rate of change comparisons. Rate of change comparisons are made with graphic displays of data. Recall the difference in Figure 4.4 between the data on the left side and the data on the right side of the graph. There is a clear improvement in the rate of performance in the data on the right side of the graph. Many of the teachers and parents with whom we work respond positively to the increase in rate, noting that the individual is improving faster and doing better than before the intervention change. The problem with settling for simple improvement is that it ignores the probability of attaining the final achievement level within the time available (Fuchs, 2003).

One way of accounting for final achievement level is by adding a goal line (also called an aim line) to the graph. A goal line traces the rate of progress needed from the student's baseline or current level of performance to the level desired by the end of treatment. Figure 4.7 shows the same data with and without a goal line. Without the goal line connecting current level to desired end of treatment levels, the data actually look encouraging to most educators and parents. When the goal line is added, it is clear that the individual is making insufficient progress and additional considerations of the instruction (e.g., more time, additional redundancy or clarity) are needed. As time goes on, the trend will diverge from the goal line, and although the individual is performing at a higher level than before, the level will not be the one desired.

The goal line provides a useful reference to the desired end state. Adding a goal line alone, however, gives no guidance about how far the data points should deviate from the goal line or how different the slopes of the goal line and actual data should be before the data suggest the need for altering the intervention or suggesting the presence of a disability. The dual-discrepancy method is one way of dealing with these issues.

Dual-discrepancy approaches. A dual-discrepancy (DD) approach considers both the individual's level of performance and rate of change over the time of the intervention (Fuchs, 2003). Burns, Scholin, Kosciolek, and

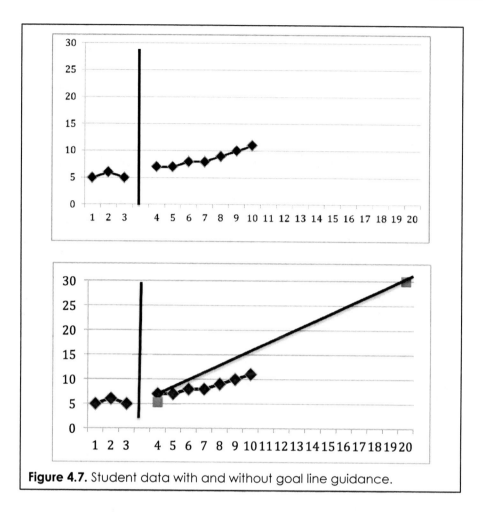

Figure 4.7. Student data with and without goal line guidance.

Livingston (2010) operationalized DD as being present when the median score from the final three data points of an intervention period was below the criterion for "low risk" set for the DIBELS measure they employed *and* when the rate of growth fell more than one standard deviation below the mean of the other students in the class. The DD method of identifying students in need of services proved to be far more reliable and accurate than using simple goal line comparisons.

By having two indices on which to compare data, level, and rate of change, educators can, perhaps, be more certain of the decisions that they make. Factors such as administration accuracy and uniformity of probes will affect the decisions made regarding the data that they yield. Additional research is needed regarding the manner in which progress in RtI is evaluated (Burns et al., 2010; Fuchs, 2003).

Documentation

Regardless of the measures and decision rules selected, RtI programs must provide adequate documentation of (a) what was done, (b) how often it was done, (c) how long it was done, (d) the way it was carried out, and (e) the deliberations and decisions regarding the individual from whom the data was collected. A good RtI program will result in a paper trail, even if it is stored electronically, that will allow others to retrace the entire process of screening, decision making, intervention, assessment, and so forth. Another important aspect of documentation is the way that the data and decision options are communicated to parents. All stakeholders need to be able to understand the principles and procedures of the RtI program in order for it to yield optimal benefits.

Many schools create forms that allow RtI teachers and interveners to record and track data across screenings, assessments, intervention sessions, and decision-making meetings. Chapter 4, Appendix A contains a form developed by one of the schools in the Virginia RtI project for planning and monitoring student performance. In addition to collecting demographic data describing the student, class, and teacher, team members record their participation in the meeting and then describe the target behavior for intervention, their goal for the intervention, and the intervention method to be employed. They then record the date that the intervention will begin and the date that they will meet to review the individual's progress with the intervention program. Additionally, they record the frequency and length (duration) of the intervention sessions. Finally, they identify the progress-monitoring data they will collect and use to make subsequent decisions about the individual student and the interventions.

The school where this form was developed uses a standard protocol model for interventions. The interventions that are available for use with any individual student have been screened for their efficacy by the school's RtI steering committee and assembled into an intervention manual that is available schoolwide. Additionally, teachers in the school receive regular training on the interventions and are periodically observed delivering instruction to ensure treatment integrity. Schools using a problem-solving model may find a form referring to the steps of the problem-solving model to have great utility.

All RtI programs and decisions are predicated upon the assumption that the interventions selected are based on solid research evidence and carried out with fidelity. The form developed by this school requires that the intervener or her supervisor attest to the fidelity of treatment by signing the form. Although this is far from a guarantee that the fidelity of treatment was acceptable, it is yet another way of calling attention to its importance.

By recording the kinds of information specified on the form, school officials and parents can easily retrace the steps in any decision regarding an individual student. Also, the amount of support a student is receiving in any grade or skill area is documented with regard to what is needed to attain satisfactory performance of the student. An additional benefit is in including such data in student records. Although it is not common to place RtI records in cumulative folders, if such forms are included when students transfer from one school to another, then it is likely that the instructional efforts can be carried on without delay or without reimplementing interventions that may have already been attempted.

Many online tools for RtI contain sophisticated reporting systems for collecting and reporting RtI data. Along with schoolwide data, RtI reports can be disaggregated by skill area, grade level, classroom, and individual students. Some sites also produce preformatted letters that can be distributed to parents of participating students. Our purpose is not to endorse or evaluate any specific commercial vendor, so school officials should investigate the available options and select the one that meets their needs with the greatest economy of cost and also of time required for teachers to learn how to use the system, enter data into the system, and create and produce necessary reports.

Graphing Results/Pictorial Display

Spatial representation of performance data is a large part of the measurement element of RtI. Placing information in graphic forms allows users to more quickly interpret students' performance. Although there are several methods for representing data in RtI programs, two (box and whisker plots and line graphs) have particular utility for monitoring and interpreting the progress of individual students. We described single-point and rate of change procedures in an earlier section. Each of these procedures is associated with a different form of graphic representation.

Box and Whisker Plots

Single-point comparisons contrast the performance of a given individual with variability of the group. A box and whisker plot provides a simple and straightforward graphic method for making this comparison.

The first step in creating a box and whisker plot is to obtain a five number summary of the data. A five number summary contains the: (1) minimum, (2) first quartile, (3) median (or second quartile), (4) third quartile, and (5) maximum. Next, draw the box to represent the middle 50% of the scores, from the first to the third quartiles. A horizontal line is then inserted to show the median or middle point of the distribution. Vertical lines are added to represent the upper and lower quartiles of the distribution, and then horizontal caps on the vertical lines are provided to represent the maximum and minimum values of the distribution.

In addition to representing the overall distribution, a box and whisker plot can display an individual score superimposed upon it as a single point. In that way, the single-point performance of an individual student can be plotted relative to the group. Box plots can also be placed on a scale to show repeated measures of the group and also individual students at different points in time (e.g., fall and winter screenings).

Figure 4.8 shows the hypothetical distribution of a screening conducted in October and again in late January of the same school year. The data point on each distribution represents the score of the same student relative to the distribution on each administration. The student performed well into the lowest quartile during the October administration but had risen to the low end of the second quartile by the time of the January administration.

Box and whisker plots are ideal for portraying an individual's performance relative to a distribution, but they are too cumbersome for showing small changes in trends over time. Additionally, collections of data for the entire distribution are unlikely to be available for more than a few specified points across the school year. It is possible, however, to establish desirable levels of performance at the end of a grade level or for particular skills and to compare the individual's progress from a current level toward the target level. Line graphs are the tool for portraying this kind of data.

Line Graphs

Line graphs are useful for showing continuous progress-monitoring data over time. The point of reference in a box and whisker plot is the five number summary of the group. The point of reference for a line graph is called a goal line. The left anchor for the goal line is determined by the individual's level of performance in baseline conditions or before the current intervention began. Estimates of desirable performance for a given skill can be used to establish the right anchor for the goal line.

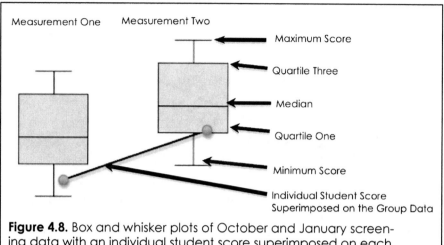

Figure 4.8. Box and whisker plots of October and January screening data with an individual student score superimposed on each distribution.

The graph shown in Figure 4.9 displays the performance of a single individual relative to a goal line. The data at points one, two, and three on the x-axis represent the individual's performance on three separate occasions before the current intervention began. In behavioral terms, points one, two, and three represent the baseline condition. The vertical line between points three and four is called a phase line and represents a major change in the instructional program (e.g., a new intervention or movement to a new tier of instruction). Phase lines can appear in more than one place in a graph. The aim line appears as a straight line between the individual's baseline level of performance and the preexisting goal—in this case, 30 responses in a given time interval. The individual data points make up the remainder of the image.

Selecting the proper display can increase the clarity of communication regarding the individual's performance. Many schools include data displays such as these in their reports to parents. Considering the data displays shown in Figures 4.8 and 4.9 together suggests that the individual has made substantial progress from the fall to winter screenings, but still needs additional support because the rate of progress suggests that he or she is still not keeping pace with the peer group.

In the case study that accompanies this chapter, Ellie, a child from an elementary school, is followed across each of the tiers of instruction, and the decision processes are traced back to the data that the schools collect to guide their decisions. The individual in this case was ultimately found to be eligible for special education services. In many other cases, individuals who come into the second and third tiers of the RtI process are supported

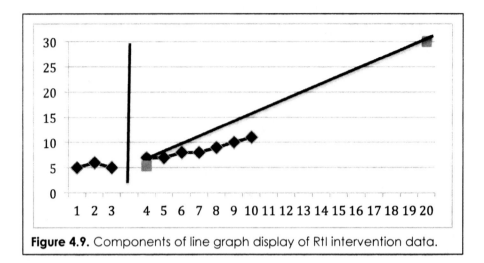

Figure 4.9. Components of line graph display of RtI intervention data.

adequately and returned to the general education program. It should be noted, however, that it is unknown whether individuals who were successful in the second and third tiers in the early grades and returned to Tier I will maintain continued successful performance without referral for special education services in the future.

Preventing a child from *ever* requiring special education services is a different mission than ensuring that children are as successful as possible in their studies and development. RtI is intended to promote success, not to delay needed services for students with disabilities. Using an RtI program to delay needed services is unethical, as is avoiding methods that reliably promote success for large numbers of children. RtI has the potential for misuse in delaying services and also the potential to enhance the educational services provided to many children, particularly those in the general education program (Brigham & Brigham, 2010).

Case Study

Green Valley Elementary School had long been recognized as the premier elementary school in the Valley Spring community—so much so that potential real estate purchases were often based on living in this school district. Eleanor "Ellie" Anderson and her family had moved to Valley Spring 2 years ago, and Ellie attended preschool at the neighborhood church-affiliated preschool for 4-year-olds. Ellie struggled to name the letters of the alphabet and match numbers to objects like her peers, but Ellie's parents knew that she would be attending the best elementary school in the community and were certain she would catch up in no time.

Early the next year, Ellie became known as the "quiet little angel" of Mrs. Wilson's kindergarten class. Ellie was polite and complied with every request made by the teacher and instructional assistant. She went to her seat when directed, threw her trash away after snack time without having to be asked, and sat quietly in her seat waiting to be told what to do next. Unlike the other rambunctious 5-year-olds in the class, Ellie followed directions and never misbehaved.

In many ways, Ellie was the perfect kindergarten student! But Ellie also sat quietly during instructional time, only smiling when asked to answer a math question, write her name, or count the objects on the table. Teachers were concerned, but when they discussed her performance, they all agreed that she was such a kind and loving child that they wouldn't worry about her yet. Kids like that, they thought, pretty much turned out OK.

In November, while the other students moved on to writing three-word sentences, Ellie was still working on forming letters correctly for her first name. Mrs. Wilson worked diligently with Ellie and often asked her instructional assistant to work with Ellie when she was busy with the other children. Ellie continued to be the only student in her class unable to routinely write her name. During the fall PALS (Phonemic Awareness Literary Screening) evaluation phase, Ellie scored below expectations in the areas of oral language, phonological awareness, print awareness, and alphabetic knowledge. Mrs. Wilson discussed the results of this assessment with Ellie's parents during the fall parent conference meeting.

"I want you to know how adorable Ellie is—she is the sweetest kindergarten student I have worked with in years," Mrs. Wilson gushed. "I am somewhat concerned, however, that Ellie has not progressed more with her literacy and numeracy ability. Let me show you a picture of the scores for our kindergarten children and also where Ellie falls in comparison to them."

Mrs. Wilson suggested that the Andersons encourage Ellie to practice writing her name at home and count toys or coins as well as any other objects they encountered. She also encouraged the parents to read to Ellie as much as possible. The Andersons were quite agreeable and comfortable with all of the suggestions and assured Mrs. Wilson that they would work with Ellie. Mrs. Wilson then explained the school's tiered intervention system to Ellie's parents and told them that she would like to move Ellie to Tier II interventions so that the school staff could work with her more closely.

Mrs. Wilson explained that the Tier II program used the same instructional materials and measures as Ellie had encountered in Tier I, but that she would receive additional instruction from her teacher or some of the other school staff who worked with early reading. She also explained that the measures would be administered more frequently in Tier II, weekly or biweekly instead of the three times per year provided for most of the other students. The additional measures were to help the teachers know if what they were doing was working.

Ellie's parents looked at each other and whispered between themselves a few times. Her father then said, "You know, we want our daughter to do well in school. Won't this make her feel like she is failing?"

"Well," replied the teacher, "that is always a risk when we provide extra support for students. I used to worry about it much more, but we do this kind of thing, and actually another level of support beyond this, so regularly that nobody seems to think anything about it anymore. It's just another part of the school day."

The Andersons agreed to the program, and although Ellie continued to charm her teachers in kindergarten and the Tier II interveners, she made little to no progress during subsequent phonemic evaluations. The school had collected data on Ellie's progress for 8 weeks and noted that she was still not approaching proficiency on her performance. Another meeting was scheduled with Ellie's parents.

Ellie was achieving in the lowest quartile for letter naming fluency, phoneme segregation, nonsense word fluency, word identification, and passage reading fluency. In spite of center-based arithmetic activities emphasizing counting, number recognition, and numeral-item matching, Ellie's math skills were not improving. Ellie's parents were notified that she was considered to be at risk for failure and that she would be receiving intensive interventions for the next marking period. The RtI team proposed moving Ellie to Tier III services for the next 8 weeks. The Andersons were in full agreement with the RtI team, as they recognized that Ellie struggled with basic skills.

Despite intensive interventions and the best efforts of several professional educators, Ellie was beginning to stand out as a student who no longer blended in with her peer group. CBM data was collected for Tier III interventions three times per week, and Ellie received daily intervention services in a group of three students using direct instruction procedures and several other specially designed curriculum materials for 30 minutes per day. After 8 weeks, the team reviewed the data for the group. One student had made substantial progress and was moved back to Tier II interventions so he could continue to consolidate his gains. Ellie and the other student were still performing substantially below proficiency levels, so the team decided to revise the interventions and add other measures from DIBELS and AIMSweb to be sure that they were obtaining accurate data. They agreed to meet again in 5 weeks, late in the month of April.

When the RtI Tier III team met in late April, they reviewed all of the data from the Tier III interventions over the past 5 weeks. Ellie's classmate was beginning to respond positively to the intervention but was not yet proficient. The team decided that this student should remain in Tier III interventions for another 5-week session. The data for Ellie were less encouraging. Although everyone continued to remark about her pleasant disposition, the data suggested that she was still making only small gains on most of her areas of instruction. Her parents were clearly distressed by this news.

"I'm so frustrated," began Mrs. Anderson. "We have worked and worked with her, and it looks like you have too. What else can we do? Is there something wrong with my daughter?"

The principal and the RtI team leader explained that some children have a great deal of difficulty in acquiring school skills and for a few of them, the reason is because they have a disability that requires specially designed instruction. They continued that before they reached any major conclusions, they would like to have Ellie undergo an evaluation to determine the presence or absence of a disability. Ellie would remain in her current program while the evaluation was being conducted, and a meeting with the school personnel and the Andersons would take place before any further decisions regarding special education services would be made.

Ellie's parents agreed to the recommendation, and after being briefed on their parental rights and the rest of the procedural issues related to referral for evaluation, they signed the referral form.

Conclusion

RtI programs must employ high-quality assessments that are reliable, valid, and able to identify individuals who are and are not at risk for failure in a given target skill. The method of continuous progress measurement used in the CBM component of RtI also requires consideration of the data in their visual form. As schools collect data and make decisions about students, the quality of the records that they keep can do much to support further analysis of the educational program and guide program development for individual students. Selecting adequate methods for guiding decisions and creating clear and effective displays of the data further enhance the effectiveness of the RtI program as well as the school that conducts it. Many issues surrounding RtI have not yet received adequate research attention; therefore, practitioners are required to fill in the gaps between what we know and what we need to know. Such will always be the case in considering the scientific basis for educational activities, and practitioners must be alert so that their actions reflect newly developed science (Brigham et al., 2004). Nevertheless, the practices associated with RtI appear to be more than the latest fad that will soon disappear. Rather, they represent a potential union between our goals for our children and our understanding of how to reach them.

Chapter 4, Appendix A
Intervention Strategies Recording Form

Date: _____ Referred by: _____

Student:_____ Date of Birth: _____ Age: _____

School: _____ Grade: _____ Teacher: _____

Parent(s): Father: _____ Mother:_____
Mailing Address(es):

Father: _____ Mother: _____

_____ _____

Phone(s): Father: _____ Mother:_____

Intervention Team Members:
Current Tier: I   II   III

Interventions: (Suggested Minimum, 6 Weeks)

Target Behavior 1: _____

Intervention Goal: _____

Intervention Utilized: _____

Beginning Date   Scheduled
of Intervention: _____   Review Date: _____

Frequency: _____   Duration: _____

Progress Monitoring Data:_____

Target Behavior 2: _____

Intervention Goal: _____

Intervention Utilized: _____

Beginning Date   Scheduled
of Intervention: _____   Review Date: _____

Frequency: _____   Duration: _____

Progress Monitoring Data:_____

Validity Statement: I certify that the interventions were conducted as described above.

Signature:_____   Date:_____

Status: (choose one)
Problem resolved; exit to Tier ❏ I   ❏ II
Problem not resolved; redesign or modify intervention at Tier ❏ II   ❏ III

References

Bell, I., & Mellor, D. (2009). Clinical judgements: Research and practice. *Australian Psychologist, 44*(2), 112–121. doi: 10.1080/0005006 0802550023

Brigham, F. J., & Brigham, M. S. P. (2010). Preventive instruction: Response to Intervention can catch students before their problems become insurmountable. *The American School Board Journal, 197*(6), 32–33.

Brigham, F. J., Gustashaw, W. E., III, & Brigham, M. S. P. (2004). Scientific practice and the tradition of advocacy in special education. *Journal of Learning Disabilities, 37*(3), 200–206. doi: 10.1177/00222194040370030301

Burns, M. K., Scholin, S. E., Kosciolek, S., & Livingston, J. (2010). Reliability of decision-making frameworks for Response to Intervention for reading. *Journal of Psychoeducational Assessment, 28*(2), 102–114. doi: 10.1177/0734282909342374

Dawes, R. M. (1994). *House of cards: Psychology and psychotherapy built on myth.* New York, NY: Free Press.

Dawes, R. M., Faust, D., & Meehl, P. E. (1989). Clinical versus actuarial judgment. *Science, 243*(4899), 1668–1674.

Denton, C. A., & Vaughn, S. (2010). Preventing and remediating reading difficulties: Perspectives from research. In T. A. Glover & S. Vaughn (Eds.), *The promise of response to intervention : Evaluating current science and practice* (pp. 78–112). New York, NY: Guilford Press.

Downing, S. M., & Haladyna, T. M. (2006). *Handbook of test development.* Mahwah, NJ: Lawrence Erlbaum.

Fuchs, L. (2003). Assessing intervention responsiveness. *Learning Disability Research & Practice, 18,* 172–186.

Gersten, R., Compton, D., Connor, C. M., Dimino, J., Santoro, L., Linan-Thompson, S., & Tilly, W. D. (2009). *Assisting students struggling with reading: Response to Intervention and multi-tier intervention for reading in the primary grades. A practice guide* (NCEE 2009-4045). Retrieved from http://ies.ed.gov/ncee/wwc/publications/practiceguides

Goldstein, W. M., & Hogarth, R. M. (1997). Judgment and decision research: Some historical context. In W. M. Goldstein & R. M. Hogarth (Eds.), *Research on judgment and decision making: Currents, connections, and controversies* (pp. 3–65). New York, NY: Cambridge University Press.

Good, R. H., & Kaminski, R. A. (2002). *Dynamic Indicators of Basic Early Literacy Skills* (6th ed.). Eugene, OR: Institute for the Development of Educational Achievement. Retrieved from http://dibels.uoregon.edu

Greiffenstein, M. F., Fox, D., & Lees-Haley, P. R. (2007). The MMPI-2 fake bad scale in detection of noncredible brain injury claims. In K. B. Boone (Ed.), *Assessment of feigned cognitive impairment: A neuropsychological perspective* (pp. 210–235). New York, NY: Guilford Press.

Hammond, K. R. (1996). *Human judgment and social policy: Irreducible uncertainty, inevitable error, unavoidable injustice.* New York, NY: Oxford University Press.

Hintze, J. M., & Marcotte, A. M. (2010). Student assessment and data-based decision making. In T. A. Glover & S. Vaughn (Eds.), *The promise of Response to Intervention: Evaluating current science and practice* (pp. 57–77). New York, NY: Guilford Press.

Hosp, J. L., & Madyun, N. I. H. (2007). Addressing disproportionality with Response to Intervention. In S. R. Jimerson, M. K. Burns, & A. M. VanDerHeyden (Eds.), *Handbook of Response to Intervention: The science and practice of assessment and intervention* (pp. 172–181). New York, NY: Springer.

Invernezzi, M., Juel, C., Swank, L., & Mier, J. (2007). *Phonological Awareness Literacy Screening* (PALS). Retrieved from http://pals.virginia.edu

Jimerson, S. R., Burns, M. K., & VanDerHeyden, A. M. (2007). Response to Intervention at school: The science and practice of assessment and intervention. In S. R. Jimerson, M. K. Burns, & A. M. VanDerHeyden (Eds.), *Handbook of Response to Intervention: The science and practice of assessment and intervention* (pp. 3–9). New York, NY: Springer.

Johnston, J. M., & Pennypacker, H. S. (2009). *Strategies and tactics of behavioral research* (3rd ed.). New York, NY: Routledge.

Kauffman, J. M., & Konold, T. R. (2007). Making sense in education: Pretense (including No Child Left Behind) and realities in rhetoric and policy about schools and schooling. *Exceptionality, 15*(2), 75–96.

Kazdin, A. E. (1982). *Single case research design: Methods for applied and clinical settings.* Columbus, OH: Oxford Press.

Kratochwill, T. R., Hitchcock, J., Horner, R. H., Levin, J. R., Odom, S. L., Rindskopf, D. M., & Shadish, W. R. (2010). *Single-case designs technical documentation.* Retrieved from http://ies.ed.gov/ncee/wwc/pdf/wwc_scd.pdf.

Meehl, P. E. (1954). *Clinical versus statistical prediction: A theoretical analysis and a review of the evidence.* Minneapolis: University of Minnesota Press.

Nunnally, J. C. (1978). *Psychometric theory* (2nd ed.). New York, NY: McGraw-Hill.

Salvia, J., Ysseldyke, J. E., & Bolt, S. (2010). *Assessment in special and inclusive education* (11th ed.). Belmont, CA: Wadsworth/Cencage Learning.

Taylor, B. M. (2008). Tier 1: Effective classroom reading instruction in the elementary grades. In D. Fuchs, L. Fuchs, & S. Vaughn (Eds.), *Response to Intervention: A framework for reading educators* (pp. 5–25). Newark, DE: International Reading Association.

Townsend, M., & Konold, T. R. (2010). Measuring early literacy skills: A latent variable investigation of the Phonological Awareness Literacy Screening for Preschool. *Journal of Psychoeducational Assessment, 28*(2), 115–128. doi: 10.1177/0734282909336277

Making
Data-Based Decisions in Tiers I, II, and III

Yojanna Cuenca-Sanchez, Karen H. Douglas,
and Jeffrey P. Bakken

For Response to Intervention (RtI) to be successful with all students, it is critical that data are collected and evaluated continuously over time. Not only should schools be looking at the progress (or lack thereof) being made by students, but also at the effectiveness of their teachers and interventions/strategies being implemented. In order to effectively implement RtI, data-based decisions need to be made at all levels (Tiers I, II, and III) and in a timely fashion. When should assessment take place? What should assessment look like? How often should assessment be implemented? What decisions should be made based on the data? This chapter will address all of these questions and more through description and the use of a specific case study.

Universal Screening

The first component of the RtI framework is universal screening. Universal screening refers to the assessment of all students in the classroom with the purpose of identifying those students who are struggling in reading. There are a variety of already available measures that schools and teachers can employ to conduct these screenings. For example, some schools might use a criterion-referenced measure such as Dynamic Indicators of Basic Literacy Skills (DIBELS) or use a norm-referenced test such as the Woodcock Reading Mastery-Test Revised. Regardless of the measure being used, data collected on all students are used to evaluate where they stand in relation to meeting the established benchmarks (if using a criterion-referenced test) or the established standard score (if using a norm-referenced test). Students' scores are compared against the established benchmark (i.e., student measure below the benchmark) or standard score, and students who are struggling are identified. Universal screenings might be administered between two and three times per year, but it is always recommended to administer these screenings at the beginning of the school year so that teachers can identify struggling readers early on and monitor their progress. The following case study will illustrate the RtI framework. We will discuss the RtI process and refer back to it throughout the rest of this chapter.

Case Study: Ms. Noland's Second-Grade Class

It is the beginning of the school year, and Ms. Noland has a second-grade class of 21 students. She is excited about the new school year and her new group of students. She is preparing her lesson plans that focus on reading, but she knows that it is important to first assess each student's current reading level. Prior to school starting, she takes time to review previous school records, teacher notes, and assessments conducted with her students last year in order to have a better understanding of the students who will be in her class this year.

During the first weeks of school, she conducts universal screening assessments that give her an idea of the students' current reading level. These assessments help her make data-based decisions and identify students who might be struggling with reading. She decides to use the DIBELS as her assessment tool because it includes an oral reading fluency (ORF) measure, which is the measure to assess how accurately and fluently second graders can read connected text in grade-level materials. Ms. Noland knows that when students are able to read fluently they can decode letters into sounds, blend sounds together to read words, recognize words without thinking, use their background knowledge, make inferences to find information, and make connections within and between sentences. Over the next 8 weeks, she conducts 1-minute oral reading fluency assessments with each student while the rest of class reads silently. After completing the assessments, Ms. Noland compiles the data for each student into a table (see Table 5.1) so she can evaluate the progress of the entire class against the DIBELS second-grade benchmark (see Table 5.2). She also wants to identify the students

Table 5.1
DIBELS Oral Reading Fluency (ORF) for Ms. Noland's Class

Student Name	Oral Reading Fluency (ORF) Week 1
Luis	67
Mark	65
Jenna	60
Brittany	59
Brad	58
Scott	56
Jeff	67
April	65
Nichole	60
Anna	59
Suzanne	58
Kyrie	56
Olga	53
Robin	50
Rodney	50
Lisa	47
Soni	36
Nina	35
Jake	30
Josh	23
Lauren	20

Table 5.2
DIBELS Second-Grade Benchmark

Fall	Winter	Spring
0–25: High risk 26–43: Moderate 44 and above: Low risk	0–51: High risk 52–67: Moderate 68 and above: Low risk	0–69: High risk 70–89: Moderate 90 and above: Low risk

who do not meet the benchmark level for the beginning of their second-grade year.

After analyzing the data for her entire class, Ms. Noland realized that five of her students (Soni, Nina, Jake, Josh, and Lauren) were at high risk for struggling with reading. She knew this because the ORF for these five students was below 44, showing some risk for reading difficulties. She realized she had to monitor their reading progress more closely over the next few weeks while receiving Tier I instruction.

Tier I

Tier I is the first level within the RtI framework. Within this level, three steps must be followed: (a) provision of high-quality instruction, (b) frequent monitoring of students' performance, and (c) data-based decision making. The following is a description of each.

High-quality instruction. All students, regardless of their ability level, should receive high quality, research-based instruction in the general education setting. High-quality instruction in the area of reading should be delivered via comprehensive core reading programs. Core reading programs usually organize and sequence the lessons by the specific skills that should be taught. In addition, they should reflect state standards and identify benchmarks for targeted instruction at each grade level. According to the National Reading Panel (NRP, 2000), in Tier I students should receive at least a 90-minute core reading block that should target the five comprehensive reading components: (a) phonemic awareness, (b) phonics and word study, (c) fluency, (d) vocabulary, and (e) reading comprehension.

Phonemic awareness is usually taught in kindergarten and first grade. It is in these grades that students learn to identify and manipulate phonemes (units of sounds) in spoken language. There are a variety of skills taught as part of phonemic awareness, but two skills that are said to be of great importance are segmenting (breaking apart words into their individual sounds) and blending (combining single sounds into new words). Students who are at risk of reading problems will typically struggle to develop these skills naturally (Armbruster, Lehr, & Osborn, 2001).

Phonics and word study instruction typically begins by kindergarten or early first grade and continues through third grade and the years following. In phonics instruction, students learn the alphabetic principle, which is the relationship between sounds and written letters. They also receive word study instruction in which they learn to decode words by identifying word parts such as affixes and root words. The NRP (2000) has recommended the use of systematic and explicit phonics programs for teaching students who are at risk.

Reading fluency is the ability to read with accuracy, speed, and expression. Fluency develops over time and with extensive practice. The more students practice reading fluently, the more their decoding and word-recognition skills will increase up to the point of automaticity (Chard, Vaughn, &

Tyler, 2002). When students are able to read fluently, they can focus more on the meaning of what they read, rather than on trying to decipher the words they are reading.

Vocabulary refers to the ability of students to understand the meaning of words by recognizing words they hear, read, or write. Research has shown that vocabulary and reading comprehension are strongly correlated (Armbruster et al., 2001); thus, vocabulary instruction should begin in kindergarten and continue in all grades. Students at risk for reading difficulties usually have a more limited vocabulary when compared to their peers (Hart & Risley, 1995). These students might benefit from direct vocabulary instruction and strategy instruction that teach them how to use context clues, words parts, and dictionaries to find the meanings of words (Stahl & Nagy, 2006).

Finally, reading comprehension is a complex cognitive process that refers to the ability to understand written text by identifying simple facts in readings, making judgments with regard to the content being read, and making associations between the reading and other situations. According to the NRP (2000), reading comprehension is the ultimate goal of reading, and it is strongly linked to students' overall academic success and continued learning. Students who are successful comprehending text are able to use their background knowledge to make meaning out of text, use questioning while reading, summarize and make conclusions of what they read, and monitor their comprehension. For students who are at risk, the development of these skills might not occur naturally so they need direct and explicit instruction on reading comprehension strategies. All five of these reading components should be taught and assessed on a regular basis to determine whether progress is being made and instruction is effective.

Frequent and consistent progress monitoring. In addition to providing research-based instruction, another component of the RtI model is the need to frequently monitor progress of all students, but especially those students who were identified as struggling learners based on universal screening results. Students' progress should be assessed at least one time each week for a minimum of 8 weeks (and up to 12 weeks), and the data collected will serve to identify students who are not meeting given benchmarks despite receiving high-quality instruction through the core reading program. Data collected will help teachers make more accurate instructional decisions (Johnson, Mellard, Fuchs, & McKnight, 2006).

To monitor progress, the use of curriculum-based measurements (CBM) is recommended. CBM is an effective assessment approach that is directly linked to instruction and is an effective tool that directly and consistently monitors student progress (Cohen & Spenciner, 2011). CBMs are criterion-referenced measures where students are assessed on the curriculum being taught. The skills assessed are selected from all of the skills that should be learned by the end of the year and provide recommended performance levels multiple times throughout the school year (Deno, 2003). CBMs are conducted on a regular basis (e.g., once a week), and all skills in the instructional curriculum are assessed by each test or probe across the year. The probes include items that cover skills the students are expected to master by the end of the school year.

When using these probe measures, the administration and procedures have been standardized so the results are reliable and valid (Hosp, Hosp, & Howell, 2007). Results from CBMs are useful for observing trends, as each score is graphed and the teacher can easily determine if the student is making progress or not. There are several benefits associated with the use of CBMs. Research has shown that when teachers use CBMs student achievement increases, teachers are more structured in their teaching, and students become more self-regulated, as they are more aware of their learning goals and progress (Davis, Fuchs, Fuchs, & Whinnery, 1995; Fuchs, Butterworth, & Fuchs, 1989).

In order to see the abovementioned benefits and to effectively monitor progress, teachers must follow the multistep CBM process (Fuchs, Fuchs, & Powell, 2004; Fuchs & Fuchs, 2004):

1. **Select appropriate tests (probes).** Teachers should select probes according to the student's grade and skill level. Each probe will have different test items, but the probes are similar in that they assess the same skills and level of difficulty and include all skills taught throughout the year (Fuchs & Fuchs, 2009).

2. **Administer and score probes.** It is recommended that teachers administer probes on a weekly basis and strictly follow administration and scoring procedures to ensure the reliability of the scores and the validity of the tests.

3. **Set performance goals.** It is imperative that teachers establish in advance the expected amount of growth on a weekly basis and the expected performance level at the end of the year.

4. **Graph the probe data.** Graphs provide a visual representation of the data that helps teachers have a better understanding of students' progress and how they are benefiting from instruction. By graphing scores, teachers can make instructional decisions and compare individual student growth with the established weekly goals and expected proficiency level by the end of the year.

5. **Make instructional decisions**. Once the sufficient amount of data is collected for several weeks, teachers have enough data to make instructional decisions to determine if instruction is being effective or if the student is not responding to instruction and might be in need of more targeted or intensive intervention.

6. **Communicate progress**. Graphs are a very useful and effective way for communicating progress to parents and students. It is important to keep all parties informed throughout the RtI process. Parents should be made aware of current performance level, future goals, and strategies to use at home with their student. When data are shared with students, they are able to visually see their own performance level, which can motivate them to work harder or to see that their hard work pays off.

CBMs in reading cover early and grade-level reading skills. The administration of probes is usually timed, and scores on each probe will be determined based on the amount of items the student got correct. Scores obtained provide information about a student's accuracy and fluency on each reading skill (Hosp et al., 2007). Table 5.3 provides information about the recommended reading CBM tasks by grade level.

There are a variety of CBMs in reading already available that provide a fast and accurate way to collect data (see Table 5.4). For example, a useful and popular CBM for assessing reading skills is the Dynamic Indicators of Basic Early Literacy Skills (DIBELS; http://DIBELS.uoregon.edu). This tool can be used for screening and progress monitoring in the elementary grades. Other useful assessments are the AIMSweb and the Phonological Awareness Literacy Screening (PALS). For other information about progress-monitoring tools, we recommend visiting the National Center on Response to Intervention website at http://www.rti4success.org/tools_charts/progress.php.

Data-based decision making. Student progress is determined by two measures—rate of growth and performance level. The rate of growth (slope) provides information about how the student's reading skills have improved over time and will help predict if a student will be able to meet the established goal or benchmark (e.g., an end-of-year goal; Vaughn & Chard, 2006). Teachers should collect data for a minimum of 8 weeks (and up to 12 weeks) using CBMs and then graph each student's scores.

The rate of growth is calculated by determining the average performance across several weeks of data collection and the slope. Teachers will first establish a goal line, which is the ideal performance level students

Table 5.3
Recommended Reading CBM Tasks by Grade Level (Fuchs & Fuchs, 2009)

Grade	CBM Task	Purpose and Procedure
Kindergarten	Letter sound fluency (LSF)	Student is given a sheet of randomized letters and asked to say as many sounds corresponding to the letters as possible in one minute.
Grade 1	Word identification fluency (WIF)	Student is asked to read as many words as possible in one minute. Words are randomly selected from a list of the 500 most frequent sight words with 10 words randomly selected from each hundred (Zeno, Ivens, Millard, & Duvvuri, 1995)
Mid-first grade to grade 3	Passage reading fluency (PRF)	The student reads a passage for one minute. The passage's difficulty is based on the student's expected end-of-year reading competence. The score is the number of words he or she read correctly per minute.
Grade 4+	Maze passages	The student reads a passage for 2.5 minutes. In the passage, every seventh word has been deleted and three possible choices offered. The score is the number of correct replacements circled in 2.5 minutes.

should meet. The criteria against which students' progress will be compared will depend on the type of measure being used (Fuchs, Fuchs, Hintze, & Lembke, 2007). This information can be found by looking at the benchmarks the measure has established according to the type of probe and grade level.

While providing instruction and collecting data for several weeks, the teacher should be simultaneously graphing the data to see how it compares to the goal line. When graphing students' scores, teachers can examine the slopes of each student in comparison with the expectations of growth (i.e., goal line). This information is useful in determining which students are responding to instruction and which students are not (McMaster, Fuchs, Fuchs, & Compton, 2005). Teachers will calculate the slope (growth rate) to visually see the difference from the goal line. The slope formula is:

Table 5.4
Reading CBMs

Assessment	Publisher	Grade	Phonemic Awareness	Phonics	Fluency	Vocabulary	Comprehension
AISM/CBM	Ed-formation	K–12	YES	YES	YES	NO	YES
CORE assessments	CORE	K–8	YES	YES	YES	YES	YES
CTOPP (Comprehensive Test of Phonological Processing)	PRO-ED	K–3	YES	NO	NO	NO	NO
DIBELS (Dynamic Indicators of Basic Early Literacy Skills)	Sopris West	K–3 4–6	YES	YES	YES	NO	NO
DRA (Developmental Reading Assessment)	Pearson/Scott Foresman Addison Wesley	K–3 4–8	NO	YES	YES	YES	YES
DRP (Degree of Reading Power)	TASA	K–12	NO	NO	NO	NO	YES
QRI (Qualitative Reading Inventory)	Addison-Wesley Longman	K–12	YES	NO	YES	NO	YES
SRI (Scholastic Reading Inventory)	Scholastic	K–12	NO	NO	NO	NO	YES
TPRI (Texas Primary Reading Inventory)	McGraw-Hill	K–3	YES	YES	YES	YES	YES
Woodcock Reading Mastery	American Guidance	K–12	YES	NO	NO	YES	YES
Woodcock–Johnson III	Riverside	K–3	YES	YES	YES	YES	YES

Adapted from "Tools charts" by National Center on Response to Intervention, 2010. Retrieved from http://rti4success.org/node/699

$$\text{Slope} = \frac{(y2-y1)}{(x2-x1)}$$

with

$y1$ = score of the first probe

$y2$ = score of the last probe

$x1$ = first administration time period

$x2$ = last administration time period

Here is an example for calculating slope: A student was probed every Thursday for 4 consecutive weeks resulting in the scores 5, 10, 15, and 20, respectively. To determine the slope, first determine the values of the x and y variables. So $y1$ = 5, $y2$ = 20, $x1$ = 1 (week 1), and $x2$ = 4 (week 4). Then divide (20–5) by (4–1) to get a slope of 5. Finally compare the slope to the benchmarks provided by the assessment manual.

An alternative to determining growth rate is determining students' performance level. Performance level is calculated by averaging the last three data probes. So for the example given in the prior paragraph, the performance level would be 15. If the performance average is equal to or greater than the established benchmark, then the student is making progress and instruction is effective for that student. However, if the student's performance average is less than the established goal line, then this is an indication that more intensive instruction is required (Fuchs & Fuchs, 2006).

Ms. Noland's classroom. In returning to the case study, Soni, Nina, Blake, Josh, and Lauren were identified as struggling readers because their data were below the universal screening benchmark. Since then, Ms. Noland has been providing Tier I instruction to all students through 90-minutes of core reading instruction. To monitor her struggling students' progress, she has been administering DIBELS CBMs on a weekly basis for approximately 8 weeks (see Table 5.5) and has been graphing students' scores (see Figure 5.1). After the 8 weeks, Ms. Noland needed to make some decisions with regard to the reading progress of Soni, Nina, Blake, Josh, and Lauren.

By looking at the graphs (see Figure 5.1), Ms. Noland determines that Nina is making progress according to her rate of growth and performance level according to the second-grade fall benchmark of 44. However, the other four students are not meeting the goal line, so they move into Tier II. Visually, there is a discrepancy between the goal line and slope (actual student data). This indicates that instruction needs to change, which is why they need supplemental instruction (i.e., Tier II) in addition to Tier I instruction. This information provided by the data and graphs for each

Table 5.5
First 8 Weeks of Probe Data for Ms. Noland's Struggling Readers

	Week 1	Week 2	Week 3	Week 4	Week 5	Week 6	Week 7	Week 8
Soni	36	36	35	39	35	35	36	36
Nina	35	40	45	48	52	52	54	56
Blake	30	35	30	34	36	34	32	31
Josh	23	26	23	25	26	24	27	27
Lauren	20	22	20	23	22	20	24	22

individual student, whether looking at growth rate or performance level, will help teachers make instructional decisions for each student.

Tier II

The focus of Tier II intervention is to provide small-group instruction to students who did not respond to instruction in Tier I. Between 15% and 20% of students receive Tier II intervention (Murray, Woodruff, & Vaughn, 2010). These students will continue to receive Tier I high-quality instruction, and they will receive three to four 30-minute sessions per week of targeted intervention in the areas with which they struggle. Tier II explicit interventions should also reflect research-based reading practices that match the students' needs. It is recommended that students with the same difficulties are grouped together (teacher/student ratio of 1:3 or 1:5) to receive additional instruction from qualified professionals such as reading specialists (Bender & Shores, 2007). However, in some cases where a specialist may not be available, then the general education teacher is responsible for providing Tier II intervention. It is important to remember that Tier II is defined by the targeted instruction and not by the location (general or special education classroom) or person delivering instruction (reading specialist, general or special education teachers; Basham, Israel, Graden, Poth, & Winston, 2010). However, it is important to recognize that in order for RtI to be successful, collaboration between general and special education teachers as well as other specialists (e.g., reading coaches, Title I teachers, special service providers) is imperative. Typically, special education teachers are the ones who have been trained on how to individualize instruction, assess, differentiate, and monitor progress. Thus, through collaboration and teaming with each other, special education teachers can share their knowledge and make sure these strategies are being implemented with fidelity in general education classrooms (Murawski & Hughes, 2009).

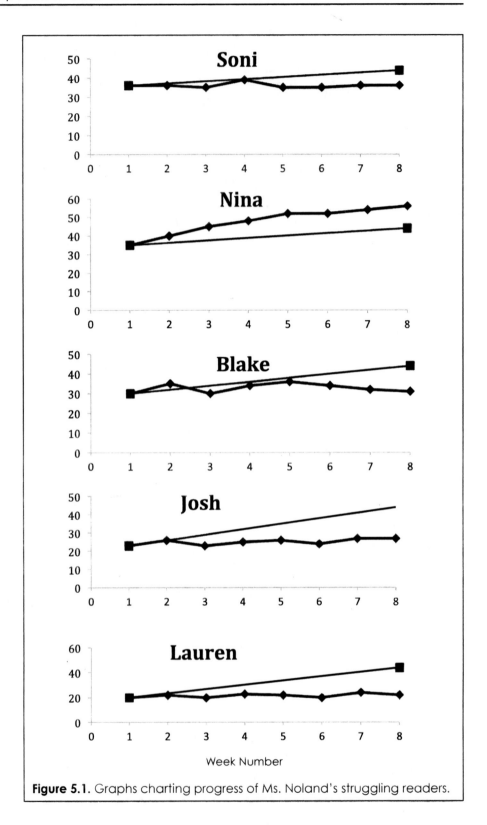

Figure 5.1. Graphs charting progress of Ms. Noland's struggling readers.

Targeted intervention. The purpose of targeted intervention in Tier II is to help students: (a) remediate skill deficit areas, (b) preteach or review skills taught during Tier I instruction, (c) provide multiple opportunities to practice target skills, and (d) provide immediate corrective feedback on performance. For example, students who are receiving Tier II intervention in a second-grade classroom might be grouped together in small groups to get more opportunities to practice reading fluency by rereading stories or by participating in partner reading (Bursuck & Dammer, 2011).

Progress monitoring. Progress should be monitored between one and two times a week (Foorman, 2003) over a minimum of 8 weeks (and up to 12 weeks) using the same CBMs as in Tier I. The data can also be illustrated on the same graph that was started in Tier I. This will show the student's continued performance in the different tiers. In Tier II, educators need to look at both performance level and rate of growth to determine progress. Together they offer the most reliable information about the student responding to instruction (McMaster et al., 2005).

Data-based decision making. When making decisions in Tier II, there are three options: (a) going back to Tier I, (b) staying in Tier II, or (c) going on to Tier III. In order to return to Tier I, the student has to be consistently performing at or above the goal line. Once having returned to Tier I, performance will still need to be carefully monitored to ensure that the student continues to make progress (Justice, 2006). Some students will stay in Tier II when the data shows growth but they have not consistently been at or above the goal line. They will continue to need Tier I core instruction in addition to the 30-minute supplemental support with weekly progress monitoring for another 8 weeks. This additional instruction in Tier II should show continued progress and confirm that the student is ready to return to Tier I. Students will move into Tier III if the slope of their data falls below the goal line.

Ms. Noland's classroom. After 8 weeks of supplemental instruction in a small-group setting for the identified four students, Ms. Noland needs to make some more decisions based on the collected CBM data. Soni's graph shows that she is above the goal line so she can return to receiving only Tier I instruction (see Figure 5.2). Blake's performance level of 44.33 shows progress is being made by meeting the benchmark of 44; however his rate of growth as illustrated by the graph (see Figure 5.2) does not show consistent progress for an extended period of time. He needs to remain in Tier II for another 8 weeks to ensure that he has learned the skills. Josh's and Lauren's graphs (see Figure 5.3) show that progress is not being made based on both performance level (28.6 and 24.6, respectively) and rate of

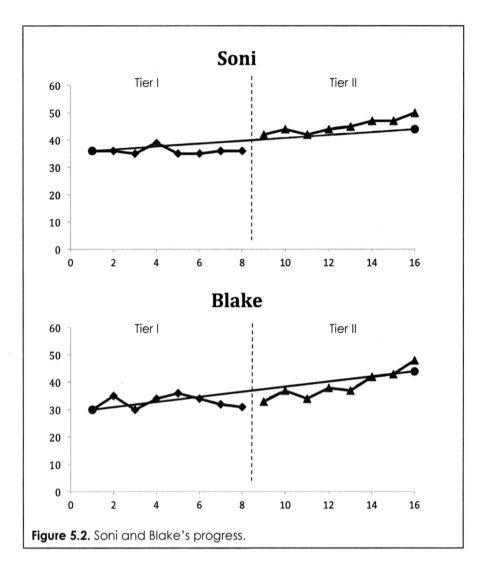

Figure 5.2. Soni and Blake's progress.

growth factors therefore they will move into Tier III for more intensive interventions.

Tier III

Typically a small percentage (5%–10%) of students will be placed in Tier III (Murray et al., 2010), where they will receive Tier I instruction in addition to intensive individualized instruction using research-based strategies. These strategies need to meet the specific needs of the student in order to accelerate student progress. The strategies will be delivered in a one-on-one manner or with no more than three other students. Students will receive 40–60 minutes of daily intensive instruction in addition to

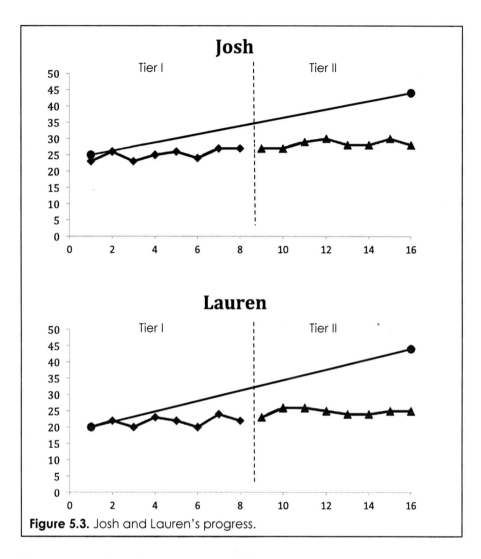

Figure 5.3. Josh and Lauren's progress.

Tier I instruction. If students are being served in a three-tier model, then students might be referred to the formal process for determining eligibility for special education services. However, if students are served under a four-tier model, Tier IV might mean special education (Bursuck & Dammer, 2011).

Intensive intervention. Students placed in Tier III intervention typically have difficulties with decoding, fluency, and comprehension; thus, at this point instruction is very intensive, explicit, and should focus on teaching specific skills that will cover the five reading components. High-quality instruction in Tier III should be research based and include key instructional principles (i.e., systematic and direct instruction, corrective feedback, constant review, opportunities to practice, scaffolded instruction; The IRIS Center for Training Enhancements, 2008a).

Progress monitoring. Weekly progress monitoring is needed in this tier along with the other tiers. Decisions should be made about the data every 8 weeks, but data should be collected on a weekly basis. When making decisions in Tier III, there are four options: (a) continuing in Tier III for another round of intervention, (b) going back to Tier II with the goal of eventually transitioning to Tier I, (c) going back to Tier I, or (d) initiating the special education referral process (The IRIS Center for Training Enhancements, 2008b).

Data-based decision making. The amount of time in this tier varies across students and on the multitier model being used. If students are receiving services in a Tier IV model, teachers can provide students with multiple opportunities of intensive intervention while constantly collecting data on students' progress. If the student's last four data points are above the goal line, then the student is responding to instruction and the student might be sent back to receiving Tier II support. If the last four data points are below the goal line, teachers might consider trying another type of intervention because the student is not responding to one intervention after 8 weeks. If the last four data points are around the goal line, the student is on target and making progress. However, if, after several interventions are provided, the student is still not making progress, then he or she would be referred for special education evaluation (The IRIS Center for Training Enhancements, 2005).

Ms. Noland's Classroom. Josh and Lauren have now been receiving Tier III intensive instruction for 8 weeks in addition to receiving Tier I instruction with their classmates (see Figure 5.4). Both students still have not met or exceeded the goal line so Ms. Noland will try another intervention for 8 weeks. Figure 5.5 displays the data after the second intervention. Josh has now exceeded the goal line and can return to Tier II. Lauren still is not making progress after multiple interventions so she needs to be referred to special education.

Conclusion

For Response to Intervention (RtI) to be successful with all students, it is critical that data are collected and evaluated continuously over time. For RtI to be successful, teachers and schools need to constantly monitor the performance of their students and make decisions based on their

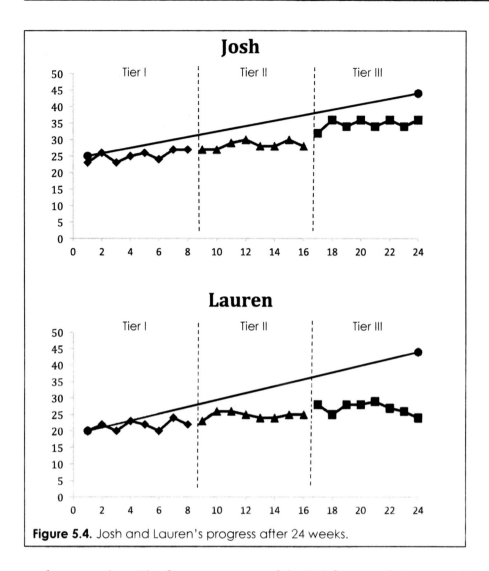

Figure 5.4. Josh and Lauren's progress after 24 weeks.

performance data. The first component of the RtI framework is universal screening. Universal screening refers to the assessment of all students in the classroom with the purpose of identifying those students who are struggling in reading. If there are some students who are struggling, then they would be involved with Tier I instruction in addition to their normal classroom reading instruction where the focus is on high-quality instruction with research-based interventions. If the students are still not successful (as indicated by progress monitoring), then they would move into Tier II instruction. In Tier II, the focus of instruction is on small groups with targeted research-based interventions in addition to Tier I interventions. If not done so already, this is where the general educator should be collaborating with the special educator. It is important to recognize that in order for

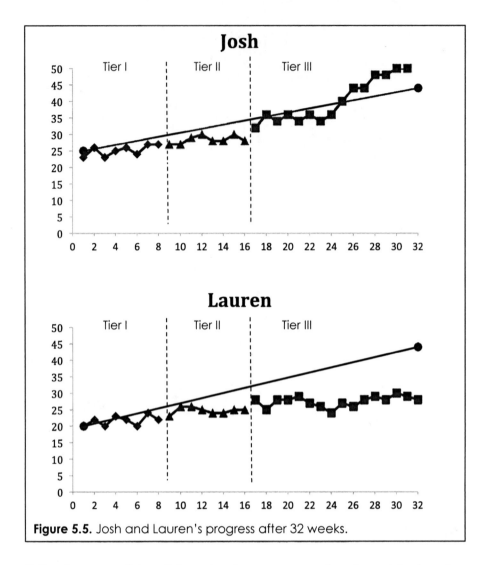

Figure 5.5. Josh and Lauren's progress after 32 weeks.

RtI to be successful, collaboration between general and special education teachers as well as other specialists (e.g., reading coaches, Title I teachers, special service providers) is imperative. Through collaboration and teaming with each other, special education teachers can share their knowledge and make sure these strategies are being implemented with fidelity in general education classrooms (Murawski & Hughes, 2009). Finally, if not successful there, the student would move to Tier III, where instruction is typically one-to-one with intensive intervention. Data are continuously collected and monitored so that decisions can be made. No data, no decisions. It is crucial that all students participate in progress monitoring to investigate student and teacher progress.

References

Armbruster, B. B., Lehr, F., & Osborn, J. (2001). *Put reading first: The research building blocks for teaching children to read.* Jessup, MD: National Institute for Literacy.

Basham, J. D., Israel, M., Graden, J., Poth, R., & Winston, M. (2010). A comprehensive approach to RTI: Embedding universal design for learning and technology. *Learning Disability Quarterly, 33,* 243–255.

Bender, W. N., & Shores, C. (2007). *Response to Intervention: A practical guide for every teacher.* Thousand Oaks, CA: Corwin Press.

Bursuck, W. D., & Dammer, M. (2011). *Teaching reading to students who are at risk or have disabilities.* Upper Saddle River, NJ: Pearson.

Chard, D. J., Vaughn S., & Tyler, B. J. (2002). A synthesis of research on effective interventions for building reading fluency with elementary students with learning disabilities. *Journal of Learning Disabilities, 35*(5), 389–406.

Cohen, L. G., & Spenciner, L. J. (2011). *Assessment of children and youth with special needs* (4th ed.). Boston, MA: Pearson.

Davis, L. B., Fuchs, L., Fuchs, D., & Whinnery, K. (1995). Will CBM help me learn? Students' perception of the benefits of curriculum-based measurement. *Education and Treatment of Children, 18,* 19–32.

Deno, S. L. (2003). Developments in curriculum-based measurement. *Remedial and Special Education, 37,* 184–192.

Foorman, B. R. (Ed.) (2003). *Preventing and remediating reading difficulties: Bringing science to scale.* Austin, TX: Pro-Ed.

Fuchs, D., & Fuchs, L. S. (2006). Introduction to Response to Intervention: What, why, and how valid is it? *Reading Research Quarterly, 41,* 93–99.

Fuchs, D., Fuchs, L., Hintze, J., & Lembke, E. (2007). *Using curriculum-based measurement to determine Response to Intervention (RTI).* Retrieved from http://www.studentprogress.org/summer_institute/default.asp#RTI

Fuchs, L., Fuchs, D., & Powell, S. (2004). *Using CBM for progress monitoring.* Washington, DC: American Institutes for Research.

Fuchs, L. S., Butterworth, J. R., & Fuchs, D. (1989). Effects of ongoing curriculum-based measurement on student awareness of goals and progress. *Education & Treatment of Children, 12,* 63–72.

Fuchs, L. S., & Fuchs, D. (2004) *Using CBM for progress monitoring.* Retrieved from http://www.studentprogress.org

Fuchs, L. S., & Fuchs, D. (2009). *Using curriculum based measurements in Response to Intervention framework: Introduction to using CBM.* Retrieved from http://www.rti4success.org/index.php?option=com_content&task=view&id=1172&Itemid=150#cbmReading

Hart, B., & Risley, T. (1995). *Meaningful differences.* Baltimore, MD: Brookes.

Hosp, M., Hosp, J., & Howell, K. (2007). *The ABCs of CBM: A practical guide to curriculum-based measurement.* New York, NY: The Guilford Press.

The IRIS Center for Training Enhancements. (2005). *Classroom assessment (part 2): Evaluating reading progress.* Retrieved from http://iris.peabody.vanderbilt.edu/rpm/chalcycle.htm

The IRIS Center for Training Enhancements. (2008a). *RTI (part 4): Putting it all together.* Retrieved from http://iris.peabody.vanderbilt.edu/rti04_alltogether/chalcycle.htm

The IRIS Center for Training Enhancements. (2008b). *RTI (part 5): A closer look at tier 3.* Retrieved from http://iris.peabody.vanderbilt.edu/rti05_tier3/chalcycle.htm

Johnson, E., Mellard, D. F., Fuchs, D., & McKnight, M.A. (2006). *Responsiveness to Intervention (RTI): How to do it.* Lawrence, KS: National Research Center on Learning Disabilities.

Justice, L. M. (2006). Evidence-based practice, Response to Intervention, and the prevention of reading difficulties. *Language, Speech, and Hearing Services in Schools, 37,* 284–297.

McMaster, K. N., Fuchs, D., Fuchs, L. S., & Compton, D. L. (2005). Responding to nonresponders: An experimental field trial of identification and intervention methods. *Exceptional Children, 71*(4), 445–463.

Murray, C. S., Woodruff, A. L., & Vaughn, S. (2010). First-grade student retention within a 3-tier reading framework. *Reading & Writing Quarterly, 26,* 26–50.

Murawski, W. W., & Hughes, C. E. (2009). Response to Intervention, collaboration, and co-teaching: A logical combination for successful systemic change. *Preventing School Failure, 53,* 267–277.

National Center on Response to Intervention. (2010). *Tools charts.* Retrieved from http://rti4success.org/node/699

National Reading Panel. (2000). *Teaching children to read: An evidence-based assessment of the scientific research literature on reading and its implications for reading instruction.* Washington, DC: National Institute of Child Health and Human Development.

Stahl, S., & Nagy, W. (2006). *Teaching word meaning.* Mahwah, NJ: Lawrence Erlbaum.

Vaughn, S., & Chard, D. (2006). Three-tier intervention research studies: Descriptions of two related projects. *Perspectives, 32*(1) 29–34.

Zeno, S. M., Ivens, S. H., Millard, R. T., & Duvvuri, R. (1995). *The educator's word frequency guide.* New York, NY: Touchstone Applied Science Associates.

CHAPTER 6

English
Language Learners and RtI

Elizabeth A. Skinner and Gia Super

English language learners (ELLs) in U.S. schools are those students who speak a language other than English at home. Although accurate, the label ELL provides an overly simplified descriptor of the students in that they are doing much more in school than learning English. In addition to English, ELLs are also learning content area, further developing their skills in their home or native language, and in many cases, learning a new school and social culture. Therefore, a better term for such students may be "emergent bilinguals," as suggested by García and Kleifgen (2010). Throughout this chapter, however, the familiar term ELLs will be used, with an implicit understanding that the teaching and learning of ELLs involves much more than language. In order to demonstrate this, the chapter will first provide readers with background information on the education of ELLs in the United States. Second, successful instructional practices will be outlined, and third, the implementation of Response to Intervention (RtI) with the ELL population will be discussed. The chapter will conclude with a description of RtI implementation at a dual-language school, written by a practicing teacher, which exemplifies not only the complicated nature of educating ELLs but also the thoughtful and careful adaptation of RtI to a specific school population.

Throughout the country there are more than 400 languages other than English spoken by public school children, but the majority of ELLs in U.S. schools speak Spanish as their native language (García & Kleifgen, 2010). Since 1997–1998, the number of ELLs in U.S. schools has grown by 51%

(National Clearinghouse for English Language Acquisition [NCELA], 2011), and all projections indicate that this growth trend will continue, particularly the number of Latino children, which is the fastest growing segment of the U.S. child population (Latino Policy Forum, 2011). Given the current statistics and the projected growth of the ELL population, it is critical that schools and teachers understand the strengths of their emergent bilingual population as well as how to adapt programs and instruction to meet their specific needs. Of late, that instruction has included RtI, which presents possibilities for improving the academic outcomes of ELLs and minimizing their overrepresentation in special education. However, if implemented without taking into consideration the unique linguistic and cultural attributes of ELLs, many feel RtI will not live up to its potential with bilingual students (Brown & Doolittle, 2008; Klingner & Edwards, 2006; Orosco, 2010).

Although the ELL population is diverse, according to García and Kleifgen (2010), there are a few commonalities that are important to understand. These include the fact that most ELLs are Spanish-speaking Latinos, most are poor, and most live in urban areas where schools are often underresourced. Although it may be that the majority of ELLs attend urban schools, it is also true that large numbers of Latinos live in suburban areas and that the population has expanded to geographic regions throughout the United States (Suro & Singer, 2002). Thus, understanding the complexity of the ELL population and how to effectively work with the students in school is no longer a necessity limited to urban teachers, but rather is essential knowledge for all teachers.

First and foremost, a critical understanding for teachers of ELLs is the fact that bilingualism and biculturalism are assets and not deficits. Research demonstrates that proficiency in more than one language allows for greater cognitive flexibility and long-term academic gains, as well as cross-cultural understanding and communication (Chicago Public Schools, 2010; Hakuta, 2011; King & Fogle, 2006). Therefore, schools and teachers do not need to intervene and correct the bilingualism of students; rather, instruction and programmatic implementation should allow students to maintain their home language and culture while adding English to their linguistic repertoire. No bilingual teacher will dispute the fact that ELLs ultimately need to learn English. What is disputed is how best to do that. The following section will offer a brief description of the most widely implemented bilingual education programs in U.S. schools that have varied results in terms of the long-term academic achievement of ELLs.

Program Models

Transitional bilingual education programs (TBE) or early-exit bilingual programs are the most widely implemented program types and, as the name implies, are designed to transition ELLs from a bilingual classroom into a mainstream or English-only classroom within 3–4 years. Most states have guidelines for creating equal access to education for their ELL students. In Illinois, a school district must establish a transitional bilingual education program when there are 20 or more students who speak that language at home (Illinois State Board of Education [ISBE], 2011). Students in a TBE program receive some instruction in their native language and some English as a second language (ESL) support. Generally, the amount of English instruction is increased at each grade level until the student is deemed ready to transition into an English-only classroom. The implementation of TBE may vary widely from school to school, even within the same district. The pressure of standardized testing, which is always in English, has resulted in ELL students being transitioned into mainstream English classrooms well before they are ready to succeed academically in the classroom. In fact, research has shown that realistically it takes at least 4–7 years to reach academic proficiency in a second language or the kind of proficiency that will allow for success in the classroom (Hakuta, 2011). The TBE model is considered subtractive in that the native language, although used for instruction, is not deliberately maintained. In other words, bilingualism is not the ultimate goal but is rather an intermediary stage until the student is moved to the mainstream English-only classroom. In schools where there are fewer numbers of ELLs, TBE may not be an option, and those students are served in what is termed a Transitional Program of Instruction (TPI), which often takes the form of English as a second language (ESL) classes. Often, ESL classes are pull-out in nature and provide concentrated ESL support for 40–50 minutes per day.

Developmental or maintenance bilingual education programs (also known as late-exit bilingual education) allow ELLs a more gradual transition into mainstream English classrooms than the TBE model. In the maintenance model, the home language is maintained, and bilingualism is an ultimate goal. Students may transition into the mainstream English classrooms by the time they reach the upper elementary or middle school grades, with continued opportunity to take literature and other courses in their native language, often called heritage language classes. Thus, developmental bilingual education programs are considered additive in that English is added to the native language of the students.

Dual language (also known as two-way immersion) is a less widely implemented bilingual education program model. Dual-language programs are also considered an additive model of bilingual education because the goal of such programs is for ELLs to learn English while also maintaining and developing academic proficiency in their native language. Although implementation may vary depending upon the linguistic makeup of the students, in dual-language programs there is often a significant population of English-dominant students who are learning the native language of the ELL population. Effective dual-language programs also incorporate the culture of the student population into the curriculum and highlight the benefits of bilingualism and biculturalism for all students. The majority of dual-language programs target Spanish and English speakers, but there are programs that involve other languages. Research shows that dual-language programs (and other additive models) are the most effective in promoting long-term academic achievement for ELLs (August & Shanahan, 2009).

In spite of the programs intended to promote their academic success, as a group, ELLs continue to struggle in U.S. Schools. According to National Assessment of Educational Progress (NAEP) data, ELLs trail English-speaking peers by 39 points in reading scores and 36 points in math on a 500-point scale (Batalova, Fix, & Murray, 2007). This achievement gap leads to unacceptable graduation rates, particularly for Latinos in urban districts. Although a variety of factors contribute to the dismal success rate of ELLs in U.S schools, certainly some of the problem lies in the widely varied and often poor implementation of bilingual education programs. This poor implementation has much to do with the disconnect between research and actual implementation. For example, additive bilingual education programs (such as dual language) demonstrate better long-term academic gains for ELLs, but there are fewer dual-language programs in operation than TBE programs. Additionally, in schools where there is not a clearly defined and implemented bilingual education program, such as districts where the ELL population is relatively new, many teachers have never received training or professional development on working with ELLs. In fact, only 20% of the public school teachers who have an ELL in their class are certified (García & Kleifgen, 2010). Perpetuating this problem is the fact that many colleges of education do not require even one course on teaching culturally and linguistically diverse students for the majority of their graduates.

Effective Instruction for ELLs

Given the general lack of information among many teachers and school personnel as to how to work successfully with ELLs, Response to Intervention (RtI) may provide one opportunity to better address their needs. Regardless of the bilingual education program model implemented and its effectiveness, RtI, because it begins in the general classroom, must include what we do know works for ELLs. Goldenberg (2008) summarized the research on effective instruction for ELLs and provided recommendations that all classroom teachers can take into consideration in order to improve the success of ELLs in school. First it is important to know that "teaching students to read in their first language promotes higher levels of reading achievement in English" (Goldenberg, p. 14). Therefore, if an ELL student is indeed being provided the opportunity to learn, at least some of the initial literacy instruction must be in the native language. Such native language literacy instruction must be research based and in keeping with what works in that language, not simply a translation of English literacy instruction. Understanding bilingual teaching methods and the first- and second-language acquisition process is requisite for classroom teachers if ELLs are to be truly provided equal opportunity to learn and succeed in school.

Second, according to Goldenberg (2008), good instructional practices should be modified for ELLs. Good instruction includes clearly defined objectives and goals, meaningful contexts, rich content, appropriately paced instruction, and active engagement and participation by students. Furthermore, good instruction includes opportunities for practice, frequent and varied assessments, and interaction with fellow students. Such practices, taking into consideration the specific needs of ELLs, allow the general education classroom, whether bilingual or not, to provide optimal learning opportunities for students. In addition to the good instructional practices, ELLs also benefit from consistent classroom routines, graphic organizers, additional time to practice skills, multiple exposure to vocabulary and key terms, vocabulary help, extended interactions with peers and teachers, adjusted rates of speech, and the targeting of both content and language objectives in every lesson (Goldenberg, 2008). Teachers will undoubtedly recognize that the above noted practices are good for all students, not just ELLs.

It is important to further address the notion of engaging instruction in meaningful contexts for ELLs and to think more deeply about the importance of culturally relevant teaching and curriculum. This is true in the general education classroom and in terms of the implementation of RtI with ELL student populations. García and Kleifgen (2010) stated, "social justice and linguistic human rights are the philosophical values that motivate a challenging and creative curriculum for emergent bilinguals" (p. 73); thus, the students' cultural background and prior experience, as well as proficiency in their home language and English, must be considered (Brown & Doolittle, 2008). Culturally relevant teachers take into consideration the social contexts of schooling and rework curriculum and instruction so that it meets the needs of their particular students (Ladson-Billings, 2001). Additionally, culturally competent teachers do not view their culturally and linguistically different students through a deficit lens but rather see the skills and knowledge that every child brings to the classroom. By including the culture and home language of ELLs in the curriculum, the very identity of the student is affirmed (Cummins, 1996). For example, at a public school that implements a dual-language model of bilingual education (see the case study), the social studies curriculum of the school is centered on what the teachers call "The Study of the Americas." The prekindergarten and kindergarten students focus on their individual families' cultural heritage and the local community. The second through fifth graders investigate an indigenous group of the Americas historically relevant to the students and families of the school who represent a diverse Latino population. For example, the second graders study the Taínos (indigenous to Puerto Rico), the third graders, the Incas; the fourth graders, the Mayas; and fifth graders, the Aztecs. The middle school grades study current events in Latin America and how those events impact the indigenous groups studied in grades 2–5. By deliberately and meaningfully connecting the curriculum to the culture and heritage of the students, their identity and home language is affirmed, critical for their success in school.

Implications for RtI

There is a well-documented history of a disproportionate number of ELLs referred to and placed into special education (Artiles, Rueda, Salazar, & Higareda, 2005; Orosco, 2010). Research suggests that this is not the result of actual disabilities but rather of a cultural and linguistic disconnect between teachers and ELL students (Orosco, 2010). RtI has the potential to reverse or at least minimize this trend in that the goal is to successfully intervene before a student is referred and placed in special education. In spite of this potential, questions remain as to how well RtI is implemented at the individual school level for ELL students and if linguistic and cultural considerations are allowed for in the adaptation of the specific interventions. In the following section, issues to be considered for the effective implementation of RtI with ELLs will be discussed.

Tier I: High-Quality Instruction in the General Education Classroom

Tier I consists of high-quality, research-based instruction within the general education classroom. All of the students in the classroom participate in this tier, and it is predicated upon the belief that all students are benefiting from an equal opportunity to learn. In theory, this classwide, initial instructional stage is promising in that it eliminates the instant stigma of being identified as a struggling student who is pulled out of the classroom for special instruction and assessment. However, particularly in the case of ELLs, there is no assurance that the general education classroom is, in fact, providing an equal opportunity to learn. First, given the fact that so few teachers have the background or proper certification to work with ELLs, the curriculum and teaching strategies of the general education classroom may not have been modified in the ways suggested previously to facilitate learning by ELLs who have been transitioned to a mainstream, English-only classroom. Second, even those ELL students in a bilingual education program may not be receiving research-based, effective instruction. Given the wide variation even within schools of the implementation of bilingual education, no matter what the program model, teachers may not be necessarily adhering to the principles of the bilingual program. Further, the fact that the majority of the bilingual education program models are TBE, which is demonstrated to be not as effective for bilingual students as maintenance programs, such as dual language, one can assume that many ELLs are not being provided equal learning opportunities in their classroom. The persistent practice and top-down pressure on teachers to transition ELLs out of bilingual programs and into mainstream, all-English classrooms, in spite of the research that demonstrates that they need more time, is hurting ELLs in their long-term academic prognosis.

In order to be effective for ELLs, Tier I must include evidence-based interventions and instruction by teachers who have developed culturally responsive attributes (Klingner & Edwards, 2006). Such a teacher views the home language and culture of the students as an asset in the classroom and as a starting point in the curriculum, rather than as a deficit. A culturally relevant pedagogy must be accompanied by the knowledge and understanding of the proficiency levels of ELL students in both English and the home language when planning instruction and assessment (Brown & Doolittle, 2008). Brown and Doolittle (2008) include the following as fundamental inclusions for instruction at the Tier I level for ELLs: progress monitoring of ELLs compared to other ELL students, not English-dominant students; culturally responsive instruction; explicit and linguistically appropriate instruction; and instruction in the native language.

In the case study at the end of this chapter, a teacher in a dual-language school discusses and reflects upon her school's effort to reorganize literacy instruction (in both Spanish and English) in order to provide a more optimal learning environment for all students in their classrooms (Tier I). The level of critical analysis undertaken by the administration and teachers of the school, as described by the teacher, exemplifies the approach to RtI necessary for ELL student populations.

Tier II: Intensive and Small-Group Support

Students whose academic achievement occurs at a lower level and more slowly than that of their peers in the general education classroom are provided support in small groups as part of Tier II. Tier II interventions supplement the core curriculum delivered in the classroom and are based on individual student needs (Klingner & Edwards, 2006). Essentially, students in Tier II are receiving a "double dose" of instruction specifically targeted to their needs as identified through the ongoing assessment and monitoring (Brown & Doolittle, 2008). As in Tier I, the interventions in Tier II must be both linguistically and culturally appropriate for ELLs and may include instruction in the home language. Again, the case study that follows describes the careful considerations undertaken by one team of teachers as they moved students from Tier I to Tier II.

Tier III: Increased Intensity of Interventions

Students who require Tier III intervention continue to achieve at a lower level than their peers and at a significantly slower rate (Brown & Doolittle, 2008), even when provided the support of Tier II interventions. At Tier III, a team of specialists works with the child, often individually as opposed to the small-group intervention of Tier II. In the case of ELL students, this team should include a bilingual or ESL specialist and a member who understands and can implement culturally sensitive ongoing assessments (Brown & Doolittle, 2008; Klingner & Edwards, 2006). It is critical to continue to attend to the student's proficiency levels in English as well as the home language and administer assessments accordingly at this level. Careful attention to each student's language-acquisition level through the use of accurate assessment instruments will prevent ELLs from being referred to special education because of language but can also ensure that ELL students who need the support of special education are accurately identified. However, as pointed out in the case study, the teachers may not have complete autonomy at this level, and there may be some district mandates for placement into Tier III and ultimate referral to special education.

Case Study: RtI Implementation in a Dual-Language School and Classroom

Background

I teach second grade at a public elementary school that implements a dual-language model of bilingual education. We serve Spanish-dominant, English-dominant, and bilingual students from diverse backgrounds in a program that aims to cultivate bilingual, biliterate, bicultural, and socially aware students. In the 2009–2010 school year, our faculty took on the daunting task of reevaluating our literacy model and decided to move toward a schoolwide strategy-based concurrent literacy model that we would begin to implement during the 2010–2011 school year. Soon after making that decision, the district informed us that we would be required to create a plan for implementing RtI as well. Although compatible tasks, the schoolwide preparation and then implementation of a new literacy model and RtI caused not only logistical and practical problems to resolve but the dual tasks also forced us to reexamine our theoretical and philosophical approach to bilingual education. What follows is a reflection on my experience collaboratively crafting and implementing an RtI program in the context of our dual-language school. I will describe our work to improve Tier I classroom literacy instruction and the implementation of RtI Tiers II and III, specifically with our ELL students.

Examining Classroom Literacy Instruction

For many years our dual-language school had been implementing an 80/20 model of language distribution and an early literacy program focused on first developing literacy in a child's dominant or native language and then transferring those skills to the developing or second language. In the 80/20 model, 80% of the instructional day was conducted in Spanish and 20% was conducted in English throughout the early childhood years, providing English-dominant students a partial Spanish immersion experience and allowing Spanish-dominant students' access to ESL and to early literacy instruction in their native language. The language distribution percentages gradually changed to 60/40 Spanish/English in fourth and fifth grades, and then 50/50 by sixth grade, preparing students for the predominantly English instruction they would encounter in middle and high school. Although there was no explicit expectation for which 20% of the day was conducted in English, it typically consisted of literacy lessons integrated with social studies or science content. For example, during an 8-week unit on insects, we taught science content in Spanish, and studied insect poetry and fiction during reading time, conducted 3 days per week in Spanish and 2 days per week in English. For reading workshop, students had individual book boxes filled with both Spanish and English books at their reading level, and they were expected to read independently in the language of literacy instruction for that day. Writing was similarly separated by days of the week or in weeklong units in each language. Math was always taught in Spanish, which kept us within our self-prescribed 80/20 division.

The challenge that we had with this model was determining the best use of the 20% of the day conducted in English, given that the needs of our ELLs were quite different from the needs of our English-dominant students. Although our more balanced bilingual students were thriving in the program, there never seemed to be enough time in the day to address the particular English language needs of our true ELL students in order to develop their academic English.

We also grappled with how to best support English-dominant students who were both struggling readers in English and reluctant or even resistant Spanish language learners. Although most English-dominant readers learned to read without difficulty, every year there were a few students in each class who were not receiving enough instructional time in English to support their development and were not engaged or responding positively to the Spanish instruction. A final challenge was maintaining the students' use of the instructional language (Spanish) for discussion and writing during lessons. Many students switched to their dominant language to communicate amongst themselves and resisted writing in their developing language. As teachers, we were concerned that there were deeper problems behind this resistance and that we should address the resistance instructionally. This concern led us to examine and ultimately implement concurrent literacy strategies.

Tier I: Improving Classroom Instruction With Concurrent Literacy

The concurrent literacy model assumes that children are capable of learning to read, write, and speak in both languages concurrently when appropriate support structures are in place. At first, this seemed like a significant shift in our literacy philosophy, which assumed that children would learn in their native language first, but a collective dialogue across grade levels highlighted the fact that many students were already learning Spanish and English concurrently in our program so we began to question our assumptions. We were reluctant to reduce the percentage of the day in Spanish from 80%, fearing that English-dominant students would not learn sufficient Spanish, but because we agreed that model was not working for all students, we were more than ready to try something new. The concurrent literacy model, as now implemented, does provide more balanced instructional time in each language so we are no longer teaching 80% of the day in Spanish. However, the boundaries for language use within those instructional time frames are strict, so instruction is more targeted to either English or Spanish, and student language use is better supported through deliberate planning and instruction.

The school faculty developed three mechanisms to support the implementation of concurrent literacy and improved instruction in the classroom. First, teachers created a schedule, or syllabus, for each unit of study, which outlined the theme, the big ideas, and the objectives for the unit as well as a clear language distribution plan. All units are introduced, studied, and assessed in one language before introducing any related material in the other language. Because of this, students have to be committed to thinking and learning in the language of instruction—they cannot wait to hear about a topic in their language of preference. For the first 4-week block of a semester, literacy is conducted in one language and science/social studies content is conducted in the other language. After 4 weeks, the language of instruction is switched. It is important to note that the previous content is not retaught in English, but rather elaborated and expanded upon.

The second mechanism or feature that enabled the switch to the concurrent literacy model includes a schoolwide strategy-based literacy program in both languages. Like any school, we have teachers who have different strengths, resources, and philosophies and who were trained in various reading methodologies, and we did not have the resources or inclination to retrain all teachers in one particular teaching method. Each teacher bases instruction in a set of common decoding, comprehension, and writing strategies that are consistent from the early childhood grades to middle school and meet standard requirements. Whether using a reading workshop format or the basal reading program that was purchased for the school, all teachers are now working to use their existing and preferred resources and layer strategy-based lessons over their literacy program.

A third structural feature critical in the concurrent literacy instruction is the creation of a "language support time" in the general classroom setting (Tier I) during which students are heterogeneously grouped based on their language needs. This time gives students the opportunity to work on the language and vocabulary important to the content area instruction. Using classroom observations, information from first-grade teachers, and ACCESS test scores, students were placed into one of three groups: bilingual group, developing English group, and developing Spanish group. We then renamed them *grupo sol, grupo luna*, and *grupo tierra* (sun, moon, and Earth groups) to reduce any stigma about being in a particular group.

Students: Samuel, Tomás, and Karina. In spite of the dramatic changes we made in our classroom instruction (Tier I), which included attention to students' individual language assessments and needs, there continued to be students who required further support in Tiers II and III. In order to illustrate our schools' approach to RtI, student cases that represent composite portraits of students will be provided. Although the cases described are not specific students from my classroom this year, they will be discussed because they represent typical students who attend our program and the sort of linguistic and cultural considerations that teachers of ELLs must take into account when planning instruction and intervention.

Samuel is an English language learner and struggling reader and writer in both languages. Tomás, an English language learner, is a fluent reader in Spanish and an emergent reader in English, but his English pronunciation is heavily accented and his English vocabulary is limited. Karina was born to Spanish-speaking parents, and her first language had been Spanish at home, but after years of attending English-speaking daycare and preschool programs, her language of dominance and preference had switched to English, and she generally spoke to her parents in English even when they addressed her in Spanish. She was becoming an emergent reader in both languages almost equally, but her vocabulary was not well developed in either language and she struggled to keep up with academic vocabulary and concepts.

Implementing RtI Tiers II and III

Our principal initially scheduled "all-school extra instruction time" for the last 40 minutes of the school day, Monday, Wednesday, and Friday, in order to accommodate Tier II intervention work. We resuscitated an inter-grade reading buddies program for the students not working with teachers in the small groups. When 3 days became too much for our sixth-grade reading buddies, our grade-level team opted for 2 days per week and set some time aside on Fridays for additional pairs reading or writing work-shop time for the second graders not involved in Tier II interventions. We formed three groups, of no more than seven students, for Tier II inter-ventions: one mathematics, one English literacy, and one Spanish literacy group. In order to form the Tier II literacy groups and identify objectives, we analyzed testing data from the fall DIBELS assessment, which tests reading fluency on texts with no picture cues, as well as a running record of students' fluency and comprehension of leveled readers. We also spoke to the first-grade teachers and observed students in our classrooms to inform our decisions. We decided that our highest priority for Tier II literacy groups would be to support students in their dominant language. If there was space for more students, we would also include students in their devel-oping language, but that was not the top priority. One teacher worked with the English literacy group and focused the first quarter interventions on phonemic awareness activities, sight word vocabulary practice, and teach-ing decoding strategies through guided reading of leveled readers at levels C and D. By the third quarter, that group was reading from guided read-ing level I books, and we were working more on comprehension strategies. That teacher considered switching the goals to focus more on writing, but feared that the group would lose ground or plateau if we did not continue working on reading strategies, so she incorporated some writing responses and short games with word families into the end of the reading sessions but did not abandon reading as the main goal. By the end of the year, that group was working on short chapter books and reading with support in level K and L books.

We placed Tomás in the Tier II English group because, though he was reading fluently in Spanish, his target language, his English DIBELS flu-ency test scores were below 20, and the fall goal was 44. We felt that he would benefit from having access to the phonics and strategy instruction in English because he seemed to pick up concepts quickly in class. We were initially worried about this placement, both because we did not want to deny space to another student who might be struggling in his or her dominant language, and because we were unsure that we could provide the vocabulary support that Tomás needed in such a short session with students who had so many needs. We eventually decided to try it out and worked with Tomás in the English group. He worked diligently in our small group, and by the end of the second quarter, he had exceeded the goals we had set for him in fluency and was beginning to improve in comprehension as well. By the end of the third quarter, Tomás had surpassed the Tier II small group in fluency, with a DIBELS score of 80, and was reading level J books in English. His comprehension was also improving so we exited him from the Tier II interventions. This made space for two students to join us who had started the year solidly but were progressing very slowly. Tomás ended the year reading on grade level in both languages.

We placed Karina in Tier II English Literacy as well, because her English and Spanish reading scores were similar and because she was a reluctant, distracted reader with very little stamina in either language. She clearly preferred reading in English, and we wanted to support her in her more dominant language. By the end of the first quarter, she had settled into better reading habits in the classroom and was able to sit and practice reading from her leveled book box during independent reading time. At the same time, her teachers were getting to know her better as a mathematician, and we became concerned that she was struggling much more in math than she was in reading. So even though she could have been in all three of the Tier II intervention groups, we decided to move her to the math group after the first quarter. She remained in Tier II math for the remainder of the school year and would have qualified for Tier III mathematics if we had a pull-out teacher to work with her. Lacking a Tier III intervention for mathematics, during the last quarter of the school year, her classroom teacher used time from the morning preparation period to work one-on-one with her while other students were at morning recess and breakfast. Karina continued to work with the Tier II group 3 days per week. When she was not receiving Tier II intervention in literacy, I worked with her in a small reading group during Tier I classroom time. She seemed to benefit from the concurrent literacy model that allowed her blocks of time to focus on one language. By the end of the year she had increased her fluency from a fall DIBELS score of 10 to a 71 and was reading level I books in English. Although she was still considered at risk by the district, we were impressed with her growth in literacy and will arrange for interventions to start immediately for her in the fall, if necessary.

We were not given the option of determining which students qualified for Tier III support. Rather, the district mandated that students be identified for Tier III interventions based solely on their DIBELS scores from the end of first grade. This was problematic because teachers had no input into who was initially targeted for Tier III interventions, and the DIBELS is purely a fluency test—there is no comprehension component. We continue to be concerned about extra support being tied too firmly to tests that we believe do not adequately assess the abilities of linguistically and culturally diverse children. Samuel was placed in Tier III through this process and was pulled out of our literacy lessons for daily instruction with a reading teacher. The reading teacher started the year working solely in Spanish, Samuel's dominant language, but by midyear we were concerned that Samuel was missing so much instructional time in both Spanish and English literacy that he was losing out on the English instruction that other students received in the classroom. We adjusted our goals for him, and the reading teacher continued to work with him 4 days per week, but this time following the language of our literacy instruction for that unit—4 weeks in Spanish, followed by 4 weeks in English. We felt that this choice was more in line with the concurrent literacy approach and would help him develop more skills in both languages. He ended the year still a struggling reader, but his English DIBELS scores went from a 5 in September to a 28 in January and a 52 in May (the May goal was a 90). He is not yet a fluent reader, but he has become a reader in English. We have taken steps to pursue a referral for school-based problem-solving services if he continues to struggle with decoding.

Although we would have chosen Samuel for Tier III intervention whether or not the district had chosen him based on the DIBELS scores, we were frustrated by some of the students who were *not* initially chosen based on the district standard for Tier III intervention. By January we were able to gather enough data to argue for some other students to be included in Tier III, but they had already missed half a year of Tier III intervention.

Despite the difficulties we faced in implementing so many changes this past year, we have been impressed by some of the positive outcomes we have observed in our students. We continue to reevaluate the way we are implementing RtI and anticipate making further changes to improve our program. For example, we plan to refine our placement procedures by looking more closely at the data we have across the grade level from the beginning of the school year, rather than placing a few students from each classroom as we did this year. We will focus on more targeted interventions for Tier II RtI that are better linked to the reading strategies that we are studying during our literacy block for that instructional period. We also plan to make better use of the time non-RtI students spend with partners or reading buddies during RtI time by training reading buddies more carefully and establishing better routines for partner work and a quieter classroom environment. Finally, we will spend time grappling with the following questions: What other data can we use to target students for intervention so that we are not so dependent on standardized tests that may not adequately measure the skills of ELL students? How can itinerant school teams streamline and support the process of preassessing and referring Tier III students for special education so the burden of referral is not all on classroom teachers who are not highly trained in that type of assessment? What additional professional development and collaborative planning time do we need to make this program work for our school and make it sustainable?

Conclusion

Many educators are hopeful that RtI will alleviate the disproportionate placement of ELL students into special education. The fact that RtI is implemented on the premise that students can strengthen skills and strategies when provided instruction and opportunity is more promising than simply identifying their weaknesses and deficits. Additionally, the practice of early intervention is compatible with the need of ELLs to be given time to acquire English while learning content in their native language. By providing ELL students with research-driven instruction and appropriate assessments, first within the comfort of their own classroom, we allow them to develop socially and academically in an inclusive environment. The concern is that bilingual and ESL teachers be allowed to appropriately adapt the RtI model to meet the needs of their ELL population, as is demonstrated in the above case study. RtI will not work for the ELL population if it is implemented in a one-size-fits-all manner. Culturally and linguistically diverse students require culturally relevant curriculum and implementation that takes into account their rich and varied backgrounds and linguistic abilities. For bilingual education students, instruction in their native language is critical in their acquisition of English and should be provided as part of the curriculum.

References

Artiles, A. J., Rueda, R., Salazar, J. J., & Higareda, I. (2005). Within group diversity in minority disproportionate representation: English language learners in urban school districts. *Exceptional Children, 71*, 283–300.

August, D., & Shanahan, T. (Eds.) (2009). *Developing literacy in second-language learners: Report of the national literacy panel on language-minority children and youth.* Retrieved from http://www.cal.org/projects/archive/nlpreports/executive_summary.pdf

Batalova, J., Fix, M., & Murray, J. (2007). *Measures of change: The demography and literacy of adolescent English learners: A report to Carnegie corporation of New York.* Washington, DC: Migration Policy Institute.

Brown, J. E., & Doolittle, J. (2008). A cultural, linguistic and ecological framework for Response to Intervention with English language learners. *Teaching Exceptional Children, 55*(4), 66–72.

Chicago Public Schools. (2010). *Language education: Preparing Chicago public school students for a global community.* Chicago, IL: Chicago Public Schools.

Cummins, J. (1996). *Negotiating identities: Education for empowerment in a diverse society.* Ontario, CA: California Association for Bilingual Education.

García, O., & Kleifgen, J.A. (2010). *Educating emergent bilinguals: Policies, programs, and practices for English language learners.* New York, NY: Teachers College Press.

Goldenberg, C. (2008). Teaching English language learners: What the research does—and does not—say. *American Educator, 32*(2), 8–23, 42–44.

Hakuta, K. (2011). Educating language minority students and affirming their equal rights: Research and practical perspectives. *Educational Researcher, 40*(4), 163–174. doi: 10.3102/0013189XII404943

Illinois State Board of Education. (2011). *Part 228 Transitional Bilingual Education.* Retrieved from http://www.isbe.net/bilingual/conf/2010/part_228_rule_revisions_pres.pdf

King, K., & Fogle, L. (2006). *Raising bilingual children: Common parental concerns and current research.* Retrieved from http://www.cal.org/resources/digest/raisebilingchild.html

Klingner, J., & Edwards, P. (2006). Cultural considerations with Response to Intervention models. *Reading Research Quarterly, 41*, 108–117.

Ladson-Billings, G. (2001). *Crossing over to Canaan: The journey of new teachers in diverse classrooms.* San Francisco, CA: Jossey-Bass.

Latino Policy Forum. (2011). *The facts on Latinos and early child-hood education in the U.S. and Illinois.* Retrieved from http://www.latinopolicyforum.org/assets/Early%20Childhood%20Education%20Fact%20 Sheet%20Illinois.pdf

National Clearinghouse for English Language Acquisition. (2011). *The growing numbers of English learner students, 1989/99–2008/09.* Retrieved from http://www.ncela.gwu.edu/files/uploads/9/growingLEP_0809.pdf

Orosco, M. (2010). A sociocultural examination of Response to Intervention with Latino English language learners. *Theory Into Practice, 49,* 265–272.

Suro, R., & Singer, A. (2002). *Latino growth in metropolitan America: Changing patterns, new locations.* Retrieved from http://www.brookings.edu/reports/2002/07demographics_suro.aspx

CHAPTER 7

Culturally
and Linguistically Diverse Students and RtI

Festus E. Obiakor and Michelle J. McCollin

Chioma was an African American urban middle school student. She was one of the few culturally and linguistically diverse (CLD) students in her school. Her parents were successful professionals in Nigeria. However, to make ends meet in the United States, they worked as certified nursing assistants (CNAs). They worked so hard that they had less time to focus on their daughter's schoolwork. As new immigrants to the United States, they had problems adjusting culturally, linguistically, socially, economically, and politically. They barely had time to sleep, let alone focus on Chioma's educational studies. In class, Chioma was ridiculed by her peers for not speaking "good" English. When she spoke to the teacher about it, nothing was done to remediate it! Her classmates complained that she could not get along with them—they also noted that she was mean and had difficulty relating and interacting. As a result, no one wanted to work with her on group projects. Although Chioma did not talk much in class because she felt that neither the teacher nor her peers liked her, she acted out by hitting or fighting her classmates. At home, Chioma's parents expected her to do well in school even though they failed to help her with her school work. Because her performance was below their expectations, she was frequently beaten and abused by her parents. The school administrators had threatened to contact appropriate authorities if the abuse continued. Clearly, Chioma, her parents, her peers, and her teachers were frustrated. Some service providers and teachers in the school had advocated putting her in programs for students with behavior disorders, even without the necessary precautions. Chioma's teachers, principal, and parents had tried to meet several times, but the parents could never make it. After a series of attempts to meet, they all finally met to agree on the best solutions for Chioma. School administrators and related professionals wanted to intervene before her situation got worse. They believed they could help her through the Tier I services of Response to Intervention (RtI). One thing became very clear: To help Chioma deal with her learning and behavioral problems, her parents and the school personnel had to collaborate, consult, and cooperate with each other. Because of the RtI model that was put in place for her, her problems were reduced and she began to function appropriately in school. In addition, the school infused culturally relevant activities (e.g., inviting the parents to speak at several school functions). Though some of her classmates still find it difficult to interact with her, Chioma's positive behaviors increased and her academic performance improved.

Looking at Chioma's case, there are many questions and answers that deserve the attention of general and special educators. Working with students like Chioma is not easy, and simplistic emotional solutions are unproductive for such students. How can educational professionals provide such students with services that could help them to increase appropriate school-related behaviors and decrease inappropriate behaviors without labeling/categorizing them as having behavior disorders or learning disabilities? What culturally responsive/relevant strategies can maximize such students' fullest potential in school without doing so much damage to their self-worth? In this chapter, we advocate the use of RtI as a way to increase school-related appropriate behaviors without labeling students like Chioma. Although there are caveats, when done right, RtI can help maximize the potential of such students in culturally responsive ways.

Though significant progress has been made in the establishment, implementation, and evaluation of scientifically based practices, interventions, strategies, methodologies, and pedagogies for students with exceptionalities, there are still endemic institutionalized issues that seem endless and often quite confounding (Brozo, 2010; Gargiulo, 2006; Vaughn & Fletcher, 2010). More specifically, issues surrounding inappropriate identification, assessment, categorization, and placement practices for CLD students still plague the field, researchers, and school systems (Obiakor, 2001, 2007). One would think that with all of the safeguards in testing/ accountability and interventions, special education services would truly address the needs of all learners. As it appears, it has morphed into a different creature, one not intended by its originators. In addition, it has become laden with issues of misidentification, over- and underrepresentation of CLD students, and legalistic and legislative mandates with no substantial funding or training for students, parents, staff, or the community at large.

Endemic Problems Facing CLD Learners

CLD students like Chioma face many risk factors in their quest for educational equity. Many of them live in poverty within urban centers, and poverty has been shown to sometimes have a harmful effect on academic performance, self-esteem, and behavior (Gargiulo, 2006; Obiakor & Beachum, 2005; Williams & Obiakor, 2009). For example, many urban students classified as having a learning disability are not truly learning disabled—they may be children ravaged by poverty and poor teaching (see Gargiulo, 2006). Teachers and service providers are further confronted with significant challenges of cultural dissonance and bias in their attempts to address educational needs of CLD students, particularly when they have limited English proficiency. One of the major issues for professionals is distinguishing between learning problems that may arise from cultural differences or poor teaching and those that are due to learning disabilities (Obiakor, 2007). Cultural and linguistic differences are sometimes interpreted as disabilities, inevitably leading to inaccurate placements (Meyer & Patton, 2001; Wilkinson, Ortiz, Robertson, & Kushner, 2006).

The political and ethical concerns about the misdiagnosis and disproportionate representation of CLD children in special education caused Congress to commission the National Research Council (NRC, 2002) to conduct a comprehensive study to ascertain and assess educational trends and transitional services to CLD children, the number of them referred and/or receiving special education services, as well as state assessments and graduation data. Findings of the NRC report revealed that CLD students are still, at an astoundingly disproportionate rate, placed in high-incidence special education programs. In addition, it was revealed that the proportion of CLD students in the population of school-age children served under the Individuals with Disabilities Education Improvement Act (IDEA, 2004) has risen dramatically (by 35%) since 2000. Because of the recursive issues about disproportionate representation of CLD learners in special education, Congress now requires that states maintain records according to race and ethnicity for enrollment, educational placement, school exiting status, and discipline.

Determining the factors that influence special education referrals continues to be a source of contention. There is some thinking that teacher referrals of CLD students for special education services may be racially or ethnically biased (Abidin & Robinson, 2002; NRC, 2002). There are other contentions that causal factors may be based on biological factors, resource inequalities, power relationships between school authorities and CLD parents, and other variables (Coutinho & Oswald, 2000). Teacher referrals account for approximately 90% of children tested, of which 74% are identified as eligible to receive special education services (Ysseldyke, 2001). Researchers investigating teacher referrals have revealed that teachers refer children who are problematic to them. These referrals are generally based on affective, contextual, and/or sociopolitical beliefs (see Ysseldyke, 2001). Clearly, the recursive dilemma of CLD student overrepresentation in special education shows factors such as unconscious racial biases of teachers (who are primarily responsible for referral to special education services), cultural differences, lack of highly qualified/culturally responsive teachers, resource inequalities, inappropriate and unrealistic teacher expectations, subjective referral practices, and unjustifiable reliance on intelligence quotient (IQ; Obiakor, 1999, 2001; Obiakor & Beachum, 2005). Despite an array of litigation, legislative initiatives, pedagogical and procedural strategies, federal compliance mandates, and monitoring and enforcement protocols, there has been no significant change in the elevated patterns of teacher referrals and the subsequent placement of CLD students in special education programs (Artiles, Rueda, Salazar, & Higareda, 2005; Artiles, Trent, & Palmer, 2004; Meyer & Patton, 2001).

The RtI Model and CLD Students

The academic outcomes of CLD students with exceptionalities are appalling. Using the learning disabilities category as an example, the National Longitudinal Transition Study-2 (NLTS-2; Newman, 2006) found that approximately 40% receive instruction from teachers who do not address their instructional needs, while less than 12% of classified students receive appropriate accommodations and modifications to access the general education curriculum. As a result, by the time these students enter secondary schools, they perform an average of 3.3 years below grade level in both reading and mathematics. Without a doubt, the extent of these academic deficiencies raises important questions not only about the lack/limited use of appropriate accommodations needed to access the general education curriculum and the lack of guidance provided to general education teachers in meeting students' needs, but also the lack of involvement of the student, school, family, community, and government agencies in the learning process (Fuchs & Fuchs, 2009; Gargiulo, 2006; Hallahan, Kauffman, & Pullen, 2009; Obiakor, 2007; Vaughn, Gersten, & Chard, 2000).

Plausible explanations for the dismal outcomes for CLD populations are the disjointed and disconnected policies, procedures, strategies, and protocols that are in place to address their overall needs. In much of the research on CLD students, there seems to be a void in the connection between the student, the family, the school, the greater community, and the government. The RtI model looks to have all stakeholders collaborate and consult to bring about success for all learners (Fuchs & Fuchs, 2009; Obiakor, 2007; Obiakor, Grant, & Dooley, 2002; Obiakor, Harris-Obiakor, & Smith, 2002; Vaughn, Linan-Thompson, & Hickman, 2003). Clearly, as disability classification criteria and trends in services change, further modifications in special education assessment practices can be expected (NRC, 2002). RtI is a scientifically based and legislatively mandated prereferral strategy used to address issues such as overrepresentation and misdiagnosis. RtI, addressed in the No Child Left Behind Act (2001) and IDEA, seeks to standardize and incorporate the best of scientifically based instructional interventions, screenings for curriculum-based problems, and thorough data-based decision making. Additionally, it seeks to improve accountability for both instruction and referral for special education services (Brown-Chidsey & Steege, 2005; Brozo, 2010; Vaughn & Fuchs, 2003).

The Multiple Tiers of RtI

RtI shows potential as an alternative to the traditional culturally biased testing methods of identifying CLD students for special education services. In an ideal world, RtI has the capacity to both promote effective instructional practices and assist in closing the gap between identification and intervention (Hallahan et al., 2009). RtI could greatly benefit CLD students by (a) identifying them by area of risk rather than by area of deficit, (b) providing early identification and instructional intervention to students, (c) reducing inherent testing bias, and (d) focusing on student academic outcomes (Fuchs & Fuchs, 2005). According to IDEA, RtI invites schools to use a percentage of their special education allocations for intensive general education interventions that utilize research-based instructional strategies implemented by highly qualified personnel. The law portrays RtI as both an instructional strategy for identifying students (replacing the outdated and antiquated IQ discrepancy model), and a strategy for decreasing the number of misidentified students classified as having disabilities (Vaughn et al., 2003).

Generally, RtI represents various models that share several common characteristics: (a) multiple tiers of scientific, research-based interventions; (b) continuous progress monitoring; and (c) systematic progress monitoring intervals to screen students for an evaluation for special education services (Fuchs & Fuchs, 2005; Ham, 2006). The multiple tiers in RtI represent a continuum of high-quality instructional supports ranging from whole class to the most specialized instruction for those demonstrating at-risk behaviors for academic failure (Fuchs & Fuchs, 2007; Vaughn et al., 2003). The tiers of RtI are:

Tier I: High-Quality Instruction for All.
> All students (including CLD students) receive scientifically based instruction provided by a highly qualified teacher (HQT) to ensure that their difficulties are not due to inadequate instruction or poor pedagogy.
> All students (including CLD students) are screened/monitored on a periodic/systematic basis to establish academic and behavioral baselines and to identify learners who may need additional support.
> Students (including CLD students) identified as being "at risk" through multidimensional screenings and/or results on state or districtwide tests receive supplemental instruction during the school day in the general education classroom. At the end of this period, students (including CLD students) not showing adequate progress are moved to Tier II.

Tier II: Targeted Instruction.
> Students (including CLD students) not making adequate progress in the regular classroom in Tier I are provided with intensive smaller group instruction based on performance levels and progress. Intensity varies across group size, frequency and duration of intervention, and level of training of the professionals providing instruction or intervention. Students who continue to show too little progress at this

level of intervention are then considered for more intensive interventions as part of Tier III.

Tier III: Intensive Intervention and Comprehensive Evaluation.

▹ Students (including CLD students) receive individualized, intensive interventions that target the students' skill set deficits/gaps.

▹ Students (including CLD students) who do not respond to intervention (i.e., achieve the determined levels of progress) are then referred for a comprehensive evaluation and considered for eligibility for special education services under IDEA. The data collected during Tiers I, II, and III should be included and used to make the eligibility decision.

On the whole, RtI's foci on prevention, early intervention services (EIS), and practical action are aimed at providing students with high-quality instruction before they experience academic failure. These foci make it more than just an alternative method to identifying students with disabilities; it ensures better academic outcomes for *all* students (Vaughn & Fletcher, 2010). Based on RtI, policy makers, governmental agencies, students, educators, and parents find ways to effectively address the challenges related to providing appropriate accommodations and modifications. Structured and framed as a strategy for the identification and prevention of academic failure, RtI becomes an instructional program that focuses on (a) teacher quality, (b) culturally responsive teaching, (c) instructionally useful assessment, and (d) contextual improvement of pedagogy and methodology (Fuchs & Fuchs, 2009). Within RtI, school-level screenings are more likely to reduce the bias inherent in the current referral and identification processes for CLD students. Screenings would take place earlier in the student's academic career to determine at-risk characteristics. And based on the outcomes of the screenings, students would be engaged in intense supplemental instruction. Reducing biases in CLD student referral and identification is critical to understanding the disproportionate representation of students in special education (NRC, 2002). By using RtI as the basis of a multidimensional screening, monitoring, and supplemental instruction system, schools would be provided with a method by which assessment bias could be significantly reduced or eliminated (Fuchs & Fuchs, 2009). Hence, RtI provides an effective implementation of strategies for CLD students who are sometimes ravaged by poor teaching and limited access to resources.

As indicated, RtI requires highly qualified teachers to provide scientifically research-based instruction to students at varying levels of intensity throughout the curriculum. For the proper and effective implementation of the RtI program, a teacher or service provider must possess a strong sense of self-efficacy, an essential characteristic of successful functioning within any given society (Bandura, 2001). Self-efficacy beliefs mediate the choices people opt for and the line of actions they follow (Bandura, 2001; Schunk, 2000). Within the RtI framework and with CLD students, it is critical to focus on teacher efficacy to avoid making the same mistakes that have plagued education in the past. Self-efficacy beliefs also direct an individual's thinking, deliberation, forethought, behavior, and emotional reactions (Bandura, 2001; Pajares, 2002; Schunk, 2000). Moreover, Bandura (2001) agreed that self-efficacy is responsible for understanding (a) challenges people choose to tackle, (b) how much effort they expend on their endeavor, (c) how long they persevere in the face of adversity, and (d) "whether failures are motivating or demoralizing" (p. 10). Individuals with a high sense of self-efficacy approach seemingly difficult tasks with confidence and composure and are more likely to attain higher levels of achievement. Without the belief that one can succeed on specific tasks, he or she will not make the concerted effort needed to master a task believed to be difficult (Schunk & Gunn, 2001). On the other hand, individuals with low self-efficacy approach difficult or taxing situations as daunting, unmanageable tasks that may result in great apprehension, pressure, and despair (see Bandura, 2001). For an educator responsible for the effective implementation of an RtI program, a high sense of self-efficacy is needed to provide necessary strategies for all learners. And when efficacy is low, it will lead not only to continued misdiagnosis and disproportionate placements in special education services but also to dismal success rates in RtI. As such, "teacher efficacy" may be viewed as both an outcome and a moderating variable relative to implementing innovations such as RtI. As teacher efficacy increases, the perception of responsibility for and capacity to effectuate positive outcomes also increases, thus reinforcing the strength and direction of teacher-student interactions. For instance, in the introductory case, Chioma's teacher might have made some initial mistakes in judging her; however, her unwillingness to label/categorize her before intervention was worthy of note. Clearly, the teacher did not want to get rid of her or assign a destructive label to her—she wanted to work with her parents and other related professionals (for instance, she even tried to save her from abuse). As her efficacy grew, her pedagogical power grew.

Avoiding Traditional Mistakes: A Look at the Future

We acknowledge that there will never be a perfect intervention technique. However, the critical question is, "How culturally responsive is the RtI model?" This is a question that will continue to haunt general and special education programs, including new programs such as RtI. It is great to have an intervention technique that strives to eradicate traditional identification, referral, assessment, categorization, placement, and instructional predicaments of CLD learners like Chioma. It is right to wonder, however, if RtI is a new wine in an old bottle or an old wine in a new bottle. In education, we have confronted many research-proven strategies (e.g., Functional Behavioral Assessment [FBA], behavior intervention plans [BIP], Individualized Education Programs [IEP], Individual Family Support Programs [IFSP], multidisciplinary teams [M-Team], authentic assessment). Where is the beef today? Misidentification, misassessment, miscategorization, misplacement, and misinstruction are still burning issues in general and special education (Obiakor, 2001, 2007, 2008; Obiakor & Beachum, 2005; Williams & Obiakor, 2009).

Without being too skeptical, it is important for general and special educators and service providers to watch out for false RtI prophets and fraudulent multiculturalists who play political games with other people's children. Scientifically proven techniques are excellent in buttressing educational accountability; however, feelings matter too! We need educators and service providers with "hearts" as they meander through the tiers of RtI. No amount of technique can remediate problems befalling CLD learners unless programs are designed to respect and value their humanity (Frankl, 1985; Holmes, 1994; Obiakor, 2001; Obiakor, Mehring, & Schwenn, 1997). Race matters in educational programs such as the RtI model, and it will continue to matter until we take well-organized measurable steps to do something about it. We must shift our socioeducational paradigms and deconstruct our prejudicial thinking on how we value each other as human beings. Although there are many great teachers and service providers, we cannot continue to pretend that we are (a) prepared or willing to teach every child in our classrooms, (b) an equal-opportunity nation, (c) a nonracist society, and (d) not xenophobic in our actions. We need to acknowledge that some White teachers and service providers (in spite of their level of training and knowledge-power about RtI) may not be prepared or willing to work with CLD persons. Sadly, their ultimate goal may just be to get rid of CLD learners in schools and send them to other institutions. Finally, we need to dig deeper in our hearts as we formulate and implement educational policies like RtI. We must truly value individual differences in the way we talk, teach, behave, and learn. In recounting his traumatic experiences in a Nazi camp, Frankl (1985) concluded that

> our answer must consist, not in talk and meditation, but in right action and in right conduct. Life ultimately means taking the responsibility to find the right answer to its problems and to fulfill the tasks which it constantly sets for each individual. (p. 98)

We believe RtI can be beneficial to all learners, including those from CLD backgrounds. In addition, for RtI to do what it is supposed to do for CLD learners, general and special educators must understand that:

1. Race and culture matter in all interventions.
2. Identification of students must be based on needs and not on racial and cultural identities.
3. Language differences should never be misconstrued as a lack of intelligence.
4. Empathy is an important part of good referral or intervention.
5. Differences in human attributes are not deficits.
6. Students are best served when their legal and due process rights are respected.
7. Intraindividual and interindividual differences in learning must be valued by all interventionists.
8. The best intervention technique is the one that values the human being.
9. Prejudicial identification leads to prejudicial referral, which leads to prejudicial intervention.
10. An intervention technique must lead to a continuous process of growth.

Conclusion

In this chapter, we have addressed the endemic problems confronting CLD students and RtI as a scientifically supported intervention strategy to remediate these problems. As an intervention model, RtI integrates efforts of self (i.e., learner), families, schools, communities, and governments in responding to the needs of at-risk populations (e.g., CLD students). Local, state, and federal governments should be utilized for continual funding and for holding institutions accountable to ensure that CLD students such as Chioma receive appropriate educational resources, interventions, and instruction that maximize their potential. Finally, we note that RtI encourages teachers to be self-efficacious and quality oriented to reduce risk factors impacting CLD students. Although there is no perfect model for any one student, we conclude that adding the "heart" to what we do as professionals will help RtI to respond to the multidimensional needs of CLD and other at-risk students.

References

Abidin, R. R., & Robinson, L. L. (2002). Stress, biases, or professionalism: What drives teachers' referral judgments of students with challenging behaviors? *Journal of Emotional and Behavioral Disorders, 10,* 204–212.

Artiles, A. J., Rueda, R., Salazar, J. J., & Higareda, I. (2005). Within group diversity in minority disproportionate representation: English language learners in urban school districts. *Exceptional Children, 71,* 283–300.

Artiles, A. J., Trent, S. C., & Palmer, J. (2004). Culturally diverse students in special education: Legacies and prospects. In J. A. Banks & C. M. Banks (Eds.), *Handbook of research on multicultural education* (2nd ed., pp. 716–735). San Francisco, CA: Jossey-Bass.

Bandura, A. (2001). Social cognitive theory: An agentic perspective. *Annual Review of Psychology, 52,* 1–26.

Brown-Chidsey, R., & Steege, M. W. (2005). *Response to Intervention: Principles and strategies for effective practice.* New York, NY: Guilford Press.

Brozo, W. G. (2010). The role of content literacy in an effective RTI program. *The Reading Teacher, 64,* 147–150.

Coutinho, M. J., & Oswald, D. P. (2000). Disproportionate representation in special education: A synthesis and recommendations. *Journal of Child and Family Studies, 9,* 135–156.

Frankl, V. E. (1985). *Man's search for meaning.* New York, NY: Washington Square Press.

Fuchs, D., & Fuchs, L. S. (2005). Responsiveness-to-Intervention: A blueprint for practitioners, policymakers, and parents. *TEACHING Exceptional Children, 38*(1), 57–61.

Fuchs, D., & Fuchs, L. S. (Eds.). (2007). Responsiveness to Intervention [Special issue]. *TEACHING Exceptional Children, 39,* 14–20.

Fuchs, L. S., & Fuchs, D. (2001). Responsiveness to Intervention: A blueprint for practitioners, policymakers, and parents. *TEACHING Exceptional Children, 38,* 57–61.

Fuchs, L. S., & Fuchs, D. (2009). Creating opportunities for intensive intervention for students with learning disabilities. *TEACHING Exceptional Children, 42*(2), 60–62.

Gargiulo, R. (2006). *Special education in contemporary society: An introduction to exceptionality.* Belmont, CA: Wadsworth.

Hallahan, D. P., Kauffman, J. M., & Pullen, P. C. (2009). *Exceptional learners: Introduction to special education* (11th ed.). Boston, MA: Merrill.

Ham, B. (2006, November). *Understanding the core components of RTI: Taking stock of what's in place & planning for next steps.* Paper presented at the Oregon RTI Summit: Scaling-tip Response-to-Intervention in Schools, Eugene, OR.

Holmes, C. B. (1994). *Like a lasting storm: Helping with real-life problems.* Brandon, VT: Clinical Psychology.

Individuals with Disabilities Education Improvement Act, Pub. Law 108-446 (December 3, 2004).

Meyer, G., & Patton, J. M. (2001). *On the nexus of race, disability, and overrepresentation: What do we know? Where do we go?* Newton, MA: National Institute for Urban School Improvement. (ERIC Document Reproduction Service No. ED 462 487)

National Research Council. (2002). *Minority students in special and gifted education.* Washington, DC: National Academic Press.

Newman, L. (2006). *Facts from national longitudinal transition study-2: General education participation and academic performance of students with learning disabilities.* Menlo Park, CA: SRI International.

No Child Left Behind Act of 2001, 20 U.S.C § 6301 *et seq.* (2002).

Obiakor, F. E. (1999). Teacher expectations of minority exceptional learners: Impact on accuracy of self-concepts. *Exceptional Children, 66,* 39–53.

Obiakor, F. E. (2001). *It even happens in "good" schools: Responding to cultural diversity in today's classrooms.* Thousand Oaks, CA: Corwin Press.

Obiakor, F. E. (2007). Multicultural special education: Effective intervention for today's schools. *Intervention in School and Clinic, 42,* 148–155.

Obiakor, F. E. (2008). *The eight-step approach to multicultural learning and teaching* (3rd ed.). Dubuque, IA: Kendall Hunt.

Obiakor, F. E., & Beachum, F. D. (2005). *Urban education for the 21st century: Research, issues, and perspectives.* Springfield, IL: Charles C. Thomas.

Obiakor, F. E., Grant, P. A., & Dooley, E. A. (2002). *Educating all learners: The comprehensive support model.* Springfield, IL: Charles C. Thomas.

Obiakor, F. E., Harris-Obiakor, P., & Smith, R. (2002). The comprehensive support model for all learners: Conceptualization and meaning. In F. E. Obiakor, P. A. Grant, & E. A. Dooley (Eds.), *Educating all learners: Refocusing the comprehensive support model* (pp. 3–17). Springfield, IL: Charles C. Thomas.

Obiakor, F. E., Mehring, T.A., & Schwenn, J. O. (1997). *Disruption, disaster, and death: Helping students deal with crises.* Reston, VA: Council for Exceptional Children.

Pajares, F. (2002). Gender and perceived self-efficacy in self-regulated learning. *Theory Into Practice, 41,* 116–125.

Schunk, D. H. (2000). *Learning theories: An educational perspective* (3rd ed.). Upper Saddle River, NJ: Prentice Hall.

Schunk, D. H., & Gunn, T. P. (2001). Self-efficacy and skill development: Influence of task strategies and attributions. *Journal of Educational Research, 79,* 238–244.

Vaughn, S., & Fletcher, J. (2010). Thoughts on rethinking Response to Intervention with secondary students. *School Psychology Review, 39,* 296–299.

Vaughn, S., & Fuchs, L. S. (2003). Redefining learning disabilities as inadequate response to instruction: The promise and potential problems. *Learning Disabilities Research & Practice, 18,* 137–146.

Vaughn, S., Gersten, R., & Chard, D. J. (2000). The underlying message in LD intervention research: Findings from research syntheses. *Exceptional Children, 67,* 99–114.

Vaughn, S., Linan-Thompson, S., & Hickman, P. (2003). Response to treatment as a means of identifying students with reading/learning disabilities. *Exceptional Children, 69,* 391–409.

Williams, G. L., & Obiakor, F. E. (2009). *The state of education of urban learners and possible solutions: The Milwaukee experience.* Dubuque, IA: Kendall Hunt.

Wilkinson, C. Y., Ortiz, A. A., Robertson, P. M., & Kushner, M. I. (2006). English language learners with reading-related LD: Linking data from multiple sources to make eligibility determinations. *Journal of Learning Disabilities, 39,* 129–141.

Ysseldyke, J. (2001). Reflections on research: Generalizations from 25 years of research on assessment and instructional decision making. *Exceptional Children, 67,* 295–310.

CHAPTER 8

Assessment
and Instruction in Reading in an RtI Classroom

Linda Wedwick and Sarah Urbanc

Introduction

Samantha is a typical third grader in Mrs. Smith's room at Central Elementary School. She has been at Central since kindergarten. From the outside, it appears that Samantha learned to read on target with her peers. The literacy curriculum utilized in Mrs. Smith's classroom is research based and implemented with fidelity and integrity. Samantha does not seem to be responding favorably to the lessons and is beginning to fall behind with the increased complexities of third-grade reading material.

Mrs. Smith decided to begin gathering data on Samantha in order to pinpoint her areas of strength and weakness. The entire class took part in a fluency benchmark, and Samantha's words read per minute were on grade level. Other informal reading experiences have led Mrs. Smith to believe that Samantha is a fluent reader, yet she is having difficulty comprehending what she has read. As her teacher, Mrs. Smith must consider how Tier I instruction will support Samantha's progress in reading.

Tier I instruction is that which all general education students receive, and there is a fundamental belief that schools must use a research-based curriculum (Marston, 2005). However, researchers are uncovering that students are having problems in reading due to a lack of proper instruction and not necessarily a learning disability (Johnston, 2010) or as the result of the curriculum. Instructional decisions will have the most impact on a student's reading progress.

Teachers like Mrs. Smith will need to support every student's reading progress through a variety of assessment and instructional responses. Therefore, the focus of this chapter will be on best practice Tier I instruction and what to do when reading problems still occur. This will be explained through the use of a case study outlining the reading difficulties of one particular student, Samantha. In the first part of this chapter, we will discuss an instructional framework for reading instruction, followed by a number of tools that can be utilized for data collection in order to provide a comprehensive assessment that can be used to provide information about a student's reading process. More specifically, a focus on comprehension will be evident and an in-process comprehension tool will be shared, including directions for implementation. We will revisit Samantha, our third-grade student, presenting specific data from her assessments, and finally our instructional response. Although we provide a literacy framework, we are working under the assumption that educators have a literacy curriculum they must abide by; therefore, our strategies and methods will be presented in a way that can supplement any program.

Instructional Framework for Reading

The National Reading Panel (NRP, 2000) report led many schools to focus their reading instruction on five components of reading: phonemic awareness, phonics, vocabulary, fluency, and comprehension. Consequently, some interpreted the findings from the NRP report to mean that reading consists of these five skills, and therefore, that instruction should focus on these skills in isolation (Howard, 2009). Reading, however, is more complex, and "instruction is more effective when teachers interweave the [skills] to support the goal of making meaning rather than teach one in isolation" (Howard, 2009, p. 12). If teachers teach these skills in isolation, there will be students who struggle and students who have difficulty remembering what they read. We do not suggest that these components be ignored in our instruction; rather, we believe that meaningful assessments and instruction will incorporate them without a narrow, isolated lens in which to base instruction.

PA
Phonics
Voca
fluenc   Com] 5 components to Reading

146

We understand that educators do not always have the opportunity to choose the curriculum they teach. With that being said, teachers are often looking for ways to supplement the core curriculum in order to ensure that the needs of all learners are being met. In terms of reading instruction, the following instructional framework can be incorporated into any curriculum to support current best practice.

Gradual Release of Responsibility

Shared Readin *RA*

As educators, we know that students do not learn information or skills at the same rate or at the same level of mastery. Rather, the skills that we teach need to be scaffolded to meet the needs of each individual learner. By following a gradual release of responsibility framework, we can allow each learner to be supported, yet learn at a pace that is appropriate to him or her.

When introducing a new concept, educators should start by using a shared-reading technique. Shared reading is when an educator reads aloud to students, modeling strategies or skills being taught, and gradually invites them to take part in the process (Rasinski & Hoffman, 2003). By reading aloud, educators provide students with an example of fluent reading, as well as create an opportunity to think aloud (Dewitz, Jones, & Leahy, 2009). A think aloud is when educators model the use of a comprehension strategy or other literacy skill by voicing their thoughts out loud in order to reveal the thought process for others (Duke & Pearson, 2002). After the first read, educators should reread the text, this time using a think aloud to help bring emphasis to the strategy or skill being highlighted.

Once educators feel students are ready to take the next step in internalizing the skill, educators should incorporate the strategy during guided reading. Guided literacy instruction "is designed to support and empower the development of knowledge they [students] need to move towards independence" (Fisher, Frey, & Lapp, 2009, p. 7). The role of the educator is again one of modeling and explicit instruction (Rasinski & Hoffman, 2003). The area being targeted by educators can be worked on in a small-group setting of five to six students (Fountas & Pinnell, 2001). Because the group is small, educators are in a better position to monitor student comprehension and skill application. During this time, educators should conference with students to gain insight into their level of skill acquisition. Small groups provide a setting in which students can take risks without feeling intimidated.

Prior to completely releasing the responsibility of the strategy or skill directly to the student, teachers should initiate one last think aloud. This time, however, the students should conduct it. This gives educators the opportunity to understand how students are processing the information from the modeled portion of the lesson (Duke & Pearson, 2002). Students who are demonstrating an understanding of a skill are then encouraged to further practice this skill on their own with the remainder of the text. Students who are not showing a command over the skill are then shown further examples of its application until they are able to successfully master the skill on their own.

The final step in the gradual-release model is independent practice. During reading instruction, independent practice should be incorporated, because students need the opportunity to independently practice and apply skills after modeling (Fisher et al., 2009). Students in primary grades should spend at least 20–30 minutes each day independently reading, and intermediate students should take even more time on this task (Cunningham & Allington, 1999). Students should be encouraged to make connections with the text, applying the reading and comprehension strategies discussed during whole-group instruction (Fisher et al., 2009). While reading, students may utilize graphic organizers or interact with the text through a reader response journal; these types of activities have been proven to help students sort their ideas in a way that leads to further understanding (Hancock, 2000).

Comprehension

Because reading is a complex process and making meaning is the goal of any reading event, comprehension must be the basis for our assessment and instruction. All components work together and not in isolation and allow students to make meaning from what they have read (Kieffer & Lesaux, 2007; Pikulski & Chard, 2005). Although comprehension is one of the five components of reading discussed by the National Reading Panel Report, we agree with Howard (2009) and Taberski (2009) that comprehension should be thought of as the umbrella under which phonemic awareness, phonics, fluency, and vocabulary should be taught.

Rather than focus on comprehension after the oral or silent reading is complete, teachers can assess comprehension on two dimensions: comprehension in process and retelling (Goodman, Watson, & Burke, 2005). Comprehension in process is a more suitable alternative to accuracy. The purpose of assessing comprehension in process is to determine the quality of the miscues that readers make. Miscues are those instances when a reader deviates from the printed text. Although some researchers refer to these deviations as errors, we espouse Goodman's (1996) theory that miscues are not random, uncontrolled behavior, but rather cued by the reader's background experiences and knowledge of language. Investigating these instances of deviation and the reader's comprehension in process reveal how a reader is interacting with a text. We will demonstrate data collection with an in-process tool that is combined with a retelling.

Data Collection

According to the International Reading Association and National Council of Teachers of English's Standards for the Assessment of Reading and Writing (2010), the goal of assessment is to improve teaching and learning. Assessment and instruction must be inextricably linked, and our assessments must be comprehensive enough to measure what we want readers to do. For example, if a teacher's assessment for fluency is a one-minute timed reading, the implication is that children will think they are reading when they read fast. Often these children focus only on speed and not on making meaning.

Prior to analyzing a student's reading process, it is important to take a step back and get to know the child as a reader. The first assessment an educator can use is a reading perception tool such as the Burke Reading Inventory (Burke, 1980). The Burke Reading Inventory is used to gather data about a student's perceptions of her own reading abilities and provides insight to the educator as to the strategies students think they use during reading (Goodman et al., 2005). It is known that students' beliefs about their own reading ability (and the reading process in general) affect the ways in which they learn to read (Goodman et al., 2005). By uncovering these beliefs, educators can better plan their next instructional moves.

In addition to utilizing a reading perception assessment, additional tools can also be used to gain a more holistic view of a child's reading process. For example, teachers may use ongoing running records; conduct observations and/or hold conferences; analyze reader response journals, rubrics, and/or graphic organizers; or use reading fluency tests. If possible, an educator may even conduct miscue analysis for more in-depth information. A "miscue analysis examines readers' control and use of the language cuing systems and reading strategies while reading orally" (Goodman et al., 2005, pg. 131). Language cuing systems consist of syntax (the structure of language), semantics (the meaning), and graphophonics, which are the visual features of the print.

149

Although miscue analysis produces a plethora of information, it can be rather timely and requires a high degree of training to be done properly. Therefore, we propose a new tool—one that will reveal a student's level of comprehension without going through a full miscue analysis. The In-Process Comprehension Rubric can be used by any educator during a child's independent reading time and examines his in-process comprehension. When coupled with a retell, this tool gives a wide view of a student's reading ability, without focusing on one isolated component of reading. An example of the In-Process Comprehension Rubric will be provided later in this chapter.

Interventions

Interventions are very fluid in the sense that "no instructional method, approach, technique, strategy, or scheme has ever been found to be 100% effective" (Shanahan, 2008, p. 105). Therefore, it is often left to the personnel designing and implementing the interventions to select the appropriate instructional approach to best aid the students in becoming successful learners. It is important to remember that students who receive extra help should spend that time reading from continuous text and not in isolated skill instruction (Allington, 2009). Oftentimes we see students being pulled from their classrooms in order to receive instruction. We do not recommend this approach for reading because of the content instruction they miss when they are not in the classroom. Also, the amount of time spent with interventions should not be the same for each child. The number of minutes each child needs will depend on his or her grade level and individual needs. However, upper elementary students may need additional time due to the fact that they are usually further behind their peers.

In order to select the most appropriate intervention, meaningful data are necessary. Instructional responses or interventions should not be based on one assessment that determines one aspect of reading. Additionally, assessment data must include a reader's transaction with continuous text.

Case Study

In this section, we will present a framework for assessment. The data collected from Samantha will be used to demonstrate the framework and the accompanying tools for assessment. The main tool we will use is the In-Process Comprehension Rubric. This tool was adapted from Goodman,

Watson, and Burke's (2005) Miscue Analysis and reflects a sociopsycho-linguistic view of reading. In a sociopsycholinguistic view of reading, the reader's construction of meaning is central to assessment and instruction. Additionally, reading is considered a process that integrates skills, context, and background knowledge, rather than isolated skills. Therefore, the rubric encompasses the complexities of comprehension, indicating that comprehension should be the priority in reading assessment, but also takes into account the need for teachers to have an assessment tool that is not too time consuming.

Samantha's Data

How child viewed readin and readers.

The Burke Reading Inventory (BRI) helped Samantha's teacher understand how Samantha viewed reading and readers. On the BRI, Samantha indicated that she likes school and her teacher. She loves to have someone read to her, but does not like to read to others because she says it takes too long. Samantha believes that good readers read fast and do not make mistakes. Samantha would like to be called on more by her teacher during reading time but believes only good readers are called on. She believes that making no mistakes and reading fast looks like fun and may be what she needs to finish a whole book during reading time at school. She also believes that this is the only way that she will get called on to read. When Samantha comes to something she does not know, she usually skips it or tries to sound it out. Occasionally she will seek help from Mrs. Smith, who prompts Samantha to break up the word and sound it out.

*Str
Skip
Soun
ou*

From this data, Mrs. Smith learned that Samantha understands reading to be fast and accurate. This view is likely the result of previous instructional approaches and assessment tools. However, because Samantha's difficulty appears to be comprehension, Mrs. Smith needs to look deeper into Samantha's reading process. Samantha's lack of focus on comprehension and meaning making during reading requires an assessment tool that encompasses more than accuracy and rate. Therefore, Mrs. Smith used the In-Process Reading Comprehension tool. *accuracy + rate to*

Mo

For the case study, Samantha read *Judy Moody Gets Famous!* by Megan MacDonald. The text is Samantha's independent reading time material and is third-grade appropriate. To gather data on Samantha's reading process, Mrs. Smith begins by conducting a reading conference with Samantha and asking her to read orally from the book. As Samantha reads, Mrs. Smith analyzes the oral reading on a sentence level, using tally marks to identify whether the sentences make sense within the context of the story.

(See Appendix A for complete step-by-step directions.) It is important to remember that a sentence can still be marked acceptable and have miscues, as long as the miscues do not alter the overall meaning of the text. Mrs. Smith has Samantha continue reading until she has read enough text to provide a sufficient, meaningful retell. Finally, Mrs. Smith asks Samantha to tell what she remembered about what she read. This retelling should be open-ended at first and followed by some teacher prompts that help the reader extend her responses or recall parts she may have inadvertently left out.

After conducting the retell, Mrs. Smith concludes the reading conference and allows Samantha to continue her independent reading. Mrs. Smith can quickly determine an in-process comprehension percentage, as well as score the remainder of the rubric. From Samanatha's oral reading of *Judy Moody Gets Famous!*, 90 out of the 97 sentences Samantha read retained the text's meaning. This led to an in-process comprehension score of 93%.

The In-Process Comprehension Rubric provides a more in-depth look at the specific comprehension components. Instead of looking at fluency alone, it is important to start breaking down the processes that make up comprehension in order to pinpoint, if necessary, the specific area(s) students need further instruction in.

Data Analysis

Once the information has been collected, the next step is data analysis. We will explain behaviors that developing and proficient readers exude in each category, while focusing on Samantha's outcomes.

Phrasing. Readers who show a high level of comprehension chunk text into syntactically meaningful phrases when they read (Rasinski, 1994). Students who do not properly use phrasing often sound choppy and read text as single isolated words. Also, they may fail to take punctuation into consideration when chunking text. As students move through the developing and transitioning phases, their understanding of how texts and punctuation work increase as they begin to recognize familiar patterns (Flood, Lapp, Squire, & Jensen, 2003). However, students' oral reading will still contain a mixture of run-ons and mid-sentence pauses and will sound partially choppy.

In terms of phrasing, Samantha's oral reading places her in the confident level (see Figure 8.1). She was able to chunk and phrase text in a syntactically appropriate way, paying attention to both phrases and punc-

Date: 10/12/10   Grade: 3rd

Title: Judy Moody Gets Famous

Does the sentence make sense the way the reader left it?

Yes ~~HHT HHT HHT HHT HHT LHT LHT HHT HHT TTTT HHT HHT HHT~~   Total ___90___

No ~~HHT~~ II   Total ___7___

Number of Sentences Read ___97___   **In-Process Comprehension Score** ___93%___

Divide total Yes by total number of sentences for In Process Comprehension Score.

In Process Comprehension Rubric

	Beginning 1	Developing 2	Transitioning 3	Confident 4
Phrasing	Monotonic with little sense of phrase boundaries, frequent word-by-word reading.	Frequent short word phrases, choppy reading; improper stress and intonation that fail to mark ends of sentences.	Mixture of run-ons, mid sentence pauses, and possibly some choppiness; reasonable stress/intonation	Generally well phrased, mostly in clause and sentence units, with adequate attention to expression.
Intonation	Monotonic reading.	Some changes in voice pitch/expression that may not match the text meaning.	Appropriate changes in voice pitch/expression that reflect comprehension of text.	Appropriate changes in voice pitch/expression that reflect comprehension of text and add dramatic emphasis.
Miscues Omissions, Insertions, & Substitutions	Low quality miscues leading to a complete breakdown of comprehension.	Mostly low quality miscues that usually prohibit comprehension.	Uses both high and low quality miscues inconsistently.	Mostly high quality miscues that show confidence in properly editing the text.
Self Monitoring & Correcting	Low quality miscues are not corrected	Inconsistent use of correction when necessary for making sense of the text high quality miscues are corrected	Uses correction, but may not recognize when it is necessary and when it is an overcorrection	Consistently corrects only those miscues that are necessary for making sense of the text
Retell	Fragmented and disjointed even with probing and questioning.	General retell with probing and questioning. Few details and personal interpretation.	Acceptable retell with details and some personal interpretations.	Highly independent retell with details and high levels of personal interpretation.

Figure 8.1. Samantha's In-Process Comprehension Rubric.

tuation. Her fluent reading *should* allow her to shift focus from decoding to comprehension (Pikulski & Chard, 2005).

Miscues. A miscue occurs when the observed response (what the child reads) does not match the expected response (what the author has written; Goodman et al., 2005). They present themselves in the form of omissions (words left out), insertions (words added in), and substitutions (one word or phrase for another). Teachers and students often refer to miscues as "mistakes." However, this can be misleading. The very nature of the word "mistake" signals that the reader unintentionally read something other than the expected response. This is not always the case, especially when analyzing miscues of high versus low quality.

Beginning and developing readers often produce low-quality miscues. Low-quality miscues are those that change the meaning of a text, therefore leading to a breakdown in comprehension (Goodman & Goodman, 2004). An example of a low-quality miscue would be the substitution of *hamster* for the word *house*. As you can see, the reader's prediction would lead to a rather large breakdown in meaning if not corrected.

As readers become more proficient, they are able to create fewer low-quality miscues. However, their number of high-quality miscues may actually increase. High-quality miscues are those that do not inhibit comprehension, and therefore should not be referred to as mistakes (Goodman & Goodman, 2004). For example, saying *home* instead of *house* would not lead to a loss in comprehension. Proficient readers often miscue because they have become confident in editing text, thereby showing a higher level of meaning making.

To score Samantha's miscues on the rubric, Mrs. Smith circles transitioning, because Samantha still produces low-quality miscues that affect her ability to make sense of text. She does show a certain level of comprehension due to her sporadic use of high-quality miscues; however, at this point both uses are inconsistent.

Self-monitoring and correcting. All readers miscue; however, it is what they do following the miscue that provides insight into their comprehension of the text (Goodman & Goodman, 2004). Self-monitoring refers to the consistent use of strategies such as rereading, reflection, and asking questions to ensure meaning is being made from the text one reads (Schwartz, 2005). When a reader is successfully self-monitoring, low-quality miscues will get corrected to reestablish meaning making, and high-quality miscues will be confirmed as meaningful.

Readers at the beginning level of self-monitoring and correcting often focus on each individual word as they read. Subsequently, low-quality miscues are produced. If a reader is not monitoring his understanding, these miscues will often go uncorrected, leading to a breakdown in overall comprehension (Schwartz, 2005).

As readers become more proficient, they begin to focus on meaning making, and therefore begin to monitor their understanding. This in turn leads to the correction of miscues that do not fit the schema the reader has built for the text up to that point, therefore enabling a deeper level of comprehension to occur (Goodman & Goodman, 2004).

Although we are focusing on self-monitoring and correcting, not all miscues need to be corrected (Goodman & Goodman, 2004). Remember that high-quality miscues are not mistakes but rather a reader's way of interacting with the text in a personally meaningful way. Therefore, even though they do not match the expected response (what is in the text), they do not need to be corrected. This can lead to an overcorrection of text, again shifting the reader's focus away from meaning making back to just getting all of the words right. Overcorrection also inhibits fluency. Therefore, confident readers should only correct miscues that are necessary for maintaining meaning.

Samantha's self-monitoring and correcting is in the transitioning range. She is not yet confident with applying comprehension strategies. We feel this is partly due to misunderstanding about the purpose for reading—comprehension. This lack of understanding leads to her inconsistent use of the self-monitoring strategy. Although Samantha corrected some miscues, she also overcorrected by correcting both low- and high-quality miscues, showing an inconsistent focus on comprehension and meaning making.

Intonation. A reader's intonation reflects her ability to predict text structures and adjust her pitch, pause, or stress accordingly (Goodman et al., 2005). When a reader shows a high level of proficiency, she is able to phrase words, produce high-quality miscues, and monitor her understanding. All of these components come together to allow the reader to connect with a text by understanding its deep complexities.

Readers at the beginning stages of intonation use are easy to spot. They often have very little understanding of the way texts are formed syntactically, and therefore are unable to predict the various text structures that may be found within a text (Flood et al., 2003). This inability often leads to a word-by-word reading that sounds monotonic and flat. On the other hand, proficient readers are able to use appropriate changes in pitch and expression to reflect a deeper level of comprehension. They are able to predict a wide variety of simple and complex text structures and punctuation and adjust accordingly in their ability to maintain meaning (Flood et al., 2003).

Samantha's flat intonation in her oral reading was an immediate red flag that indicated a potential comprehension problem. Although she seems to have an understanding that a voice is supposed to "change" as a person reads, she lacked the ability to predict unfamiliar text structures.

155

This prohibited a deeper connection to the plot and characters and an overall comprehension of the text.

Retell. The final step to the In-Process Comprehension procedure is to have the reader retell the text she has just read. A retell allows the reader to explain the text in a way that is meaningful to her. The unaided portion of a retell acts as the window to the mind of the reader, allowing the educator insight into the interpretations the reader made and the level of comprehension that was constructed while reading (Goodman et al., 2005).

A less proficient reader will often provide a retell that displays minor details or insignificant facts. At times, she will be able to provide meaningful details when prompted. This shows an inability to make the distinction as to what holds meaning in a text and furthers comprehension and what does not (Shea, 2006). A proficient reader's retell will provide an acceptable level of details from the story with personal interpretations of the text. She can often do this without the need for prompting, because she has made meaningful connections to the text and understands the concepts such as main idea, characters, setting, and plot (Shea, 2006). Sometimes, a reader's limited retelling of a text is a learned behavior. In other words, if the reader is not accustomed to being asked what she remembers about the text, she may begin by just providing a one- or two-sentence summary. If readers have only been expected to answer literal and limited inferential questions after reading, they may need teacher modeling of retelling.

Samantha's retelling of *Judy Moody Gets Famous!* scored in the developing range. Her retell was sequential, and she only briefly commented on the overall plot and then told what happened at the end of the chapter. She was able to recall some surface information, as well as most of the secondary characters, but was unsure about their relationship to the main character. Samantha understood parts of the basic plot line of the chapter, but was not able to infer any of the higher level meaning from those facts. She had holes in her retelling where she simply shrugged her shoulders and said she could not remember. In some cases, she invented information that was not in the text or pictures and was not a result of her miscues. Some basic inferences about the characters' feelings were extracted through teacher prompting.

Instructional response. Based on Samantha's scores, we can begin to put together a reader profile that identifies areas of strength and weakness. Prior to doing so, it is important to look at the complex systems that interact with each other in order to allow comprehension to occur. The four cuing systems readers use to make meaning are the graphophonic, syntactic, semantic, and pragmatic systems.

GraphoPhonic – Spell
wo

The graphophonic system is responsible for spelling, punctuation, print features, and oral language sounds (Goodman et al., 2005). The syntactic system deals with the relationship between words and sentences within a text (Goodman et al., 2005). The semantic system focuses on the meaning of words and phrases as well as how they influence each other (Goodman et al., 2005). Finally, the pragmatic system influences the semantic system and considers the context in which language occurs (Goodman et al., 2005).

Based on Samantha's scores and retell, she shows an inconsistent use of the cuing systems and a weakness in integrating these systems to produce meaningful high-quality miscues. These results are consistent with the analysis of her miscues and their indication that she gives most of her focus to graphophonic cues at the expense of meaning construction. She is able to pick up surface information as she reads, but does so irregularly. Her focus on graphophonic cues and her weakness in using predicting and confirming strategies are affecting her ability to make meaning of the texts she reads.

However, in terms of strengths, Samantha is confident in phrasing text. This is what allows her to appear to be a fluent reader. She is also confident in her use of the graphophonic system, as many of her miscues looked and sounded similar to the text. Finally, she scored in the transitioning range for miscues and self-monitoring, and these scores indicate that Samantha understands that words hold meaning, but she does not understand that the overall purpose of reading is meaning making throughout the entire text. This is shown by her production of numerous low-quality miscues, as well as the correction of the high-quality miscues.

The developing scores in intonation and retell pinpoint the areas of weakness that most likely led to her breakdown in comprehension. However, since intonation should not be taught in isolation, Samantha will receive instruction on the very purpose of reading and how to make meaning through context clues, as well as be able to predict sentence patterns that are both simplistic and difficult. Also, because she has the necessary decoding skills to "sound out" words, her teacher's instructional responses will further focus on making meaning from the sentence and entire text level, resulting in an increase in comprehension.

Establishing a purpose for reading. Based on Samantha's scores and responses, it appears that she has adopted a model of reading that focuses on accuracy and speed. Therefore, Mrs. Smith decides to first focus on lessons that help Samantha establish a purpose for reading. While engaged in reading, a reader can take an aesthetic or efferent stance (Rosenblatt, 1978).

Why are we reading this?

An aesthetic stance follows Rosenblatt's reader response theory in which each reader brings different purposes and experiences to a text, therefore constructing his own meaning and feeling (Rosenblatt, 2004). Conversely, an efferent stance is when a reader's purpose is to identify or take away a specific piece of information (Rosenblatt, 2004). Readers often adopt this stance when they read nonfiction texts. The reader, rather than the teacher, should establish the purpose for reading. Establishing a purpose prior to reading will help the reader access background knowledge about text expectations and make deeper connections with the text. These connections elicit a more complex level of overall understanding and meaning making.

a purpose?

At first, setting a purpose for reading can be difficult for emerging readers, especially those like Samantha who generally feel the purpose of reading is to say all of the words quickly and correctly. In order to allow students practice in selecting a purpose for reading, one can take a variety of genres of text and work together to set a purpose for reading. In fact, you can use your own basal reading series or read aloud materials. Prior to reading any text, work together to establish a purpose based upon information gathered from a picture walk and genre discussion. When setting the purpose, it is important to keep the end in mind. What do you hope to achieve by reading this text? Is it to gather new information, be entertained, or elicit a specific response? By identifying the purpose for reading, the reader is better able to use previous knowledge to make predictions in texts to continue to build a knowledge base and extend the meaning-making process.

Rereading. Once a purpose for reading has been established, it is important for Samantha to put these new beliefs into practice. This can be done through the rereading of texts. Rereading helps readers improve their phrasing of texts in order to become more fluent. In a reading conference, Mrs. Smith first reads aloud a short passage to Samantha and then has her read the same passage while trying to match the intonation. As the fluent reader, Mrs. Smith follows the repeated reading with a discussion about how the text was read and how intonation shifted. By conducting a think aloud, the less proficient reader is able to gain insight into how to manipulate text in meaningful ways in order to produce and evoke meaning and feeling (Block & Israel, 2004). Samantha will practice multiple readings from an array of texts that will specifically invoke various feelings based on the purpose.

Teachers should remind the reader that texts are usually not going to invoke only one feeling throughout the entire text. Rather readers should be able to identify the cues in the text that alert a reader to the type of predictions to make while reading that inform them as to the proper level of intonation (Block & Israel, 2004).

Retrospective miscue analysis. In order to help Samantha understand the complexities that lie within the four cuing systems and the strategies she currently uses (or does not use) to make meaning, we recommend that Samantha participate in ongoing retrospective miscue analysis sessions (Goodman, 1996). Retrospective miscue analysis (RMA) is a process in which readers reflect on their own reading process by listening to audio recordings of their oral reading. When readers reflect on their miscues, they come to understand that reading is a process of meaning making rather than a disconnected act of accuracy. RMA can be conducted by taping children reading and then playing it back, allowing them to have a conversation about their miscues and strategies they used to resolve the text. Goodman (1996) recommends a series of 40-minute RMA sessions in which the teacher and student discuss five to seven miscues. Depending on the confidence level of the student and her attitude about herself as a reader, teachers can preselect high-quality miscues and gradually introduce readers to low-quality miscues that were not corrected. Initial sessions should help readers recognize that they are making smart miscues and "that they are using strategies that support their meaning construction as they read" (Goodman, 1996, p. 603).

In the reading conference with Samantha, Mrs. Smith discovered that Samantha thinks good readers do not make mistakes when they read. Therefore, Mrs. Smith will need to begin the RMA sessions with Samantha, preselecting several high-quality miscues that Samantha made in order to emphasize the smart decisions she made while reading and how these smart miscues led to meaning construction. Mrs. Smith may then want to focus on the smart miscues that Samantha corrected so that Samantha can learn that correcting a miscue that already maintains meaning of the text is unnecessary. Finally, Mrs. Smith will engage Samantha in a discussion to reveal her thought process during the times that she produced low-quality miscues without correcting. By allowing Samantha to take part in a reflection of her own miscue analysis, she will be better able to understand how meaning making occurs in text, further leading to her development of an emphasis on comprehension and a holistic view of reading.

Retelling. After conducting the above lessons, it is important to look at the output of meaning—the retell. The reader's retelling of a text provides necessary data for assessment, not just for the teacher to assess a student's understanding, but for the student to assess herself. Through a retell, the student can evaluate whether she has truly understood what she has read or if she needs to revisit parts of the text to monitor his understanding (Shea, 2006). A retell should be treated like any other skill one expects students to display, meaning that it requires modeling and explicit instruction. Students may actually recall more than what they say in a retell, because they are not aware of what is actually important in a text. By providing explicit instruction in how to give an effective retell, the teacher will be able to better analyze whether the student did not comprehend the text or if she was just unaware of which information was important.

An effective retell consists of several parts in which students will need modeling, practice, and teacher feedback. Shea (2006) suggests that a retelling include an introduction; summary; and connections, interpretations, reactions, evaluation, and conclusions (CIREC; Shea, 2006). An introduction normally includes basic information regarding the text such as title, author, and genre or topic. The summary of the text will differ depending upon the genre of the text. A narrative text will include information regarding story elements such as characters, setting, and plot. However, expository-type texts will provide information that revolves more around the main idea and purpose set for reading. It is left to the reader to recognize the structure of the expository text such as compare/contrast or persuasion. The final step to an effective retell is CIREC (Shea, 2006):

> ‣ C: Tell how this compares with what you knew before.
> ‣ I: Share your thinking.
> ‣ R: Explain your reactions. How did it make you feel?
> ‣ E: Tell what was exciting or interesting and talk about the writer's style.
> ‣ C: What conclusions have you made so far?

By teaching Samantha the types of information that can indicate importance to a text, she will be able to better provide a retell that includes these data instead of just the exact words she remembers reading. Explicitly teaching the parts of a retelling and providing Samantha with many opportunities to practice will help her to further recognize the need to make meaning while she reads. With teacher feedback, Samantha will be able to shift her focus from just the surface level meaning to that in which she is able to interpret, showing an increased connection and level of meaning making with the text.

Conclusion

Reading is a multifaceted, complex process consisting of more than just the ability to read quickly and accurately. The purpose of reading should be comprehension or making meaning. We also cannot assume that comprehension will automatically follow quick and accurate reading. Therefore, assessment and instruction should focus on what we want readers to do (Howard, 2009; Owocki, 2010). Otherwise, our instruction may only focus on isolated skills without attention to making meaning.

Conducting the above lessons with Samantha (or any reader with similar difficulties) will help to address her overall lack of comprehension. The miscues that Samantha had been making were evidence that she had not been taking comprehension into consideration when reading. This was also evidenced by her inconsistent use of predicting and confirming. As a result of the process she was using, Samantha substituted words that had a high level of graphic and sound similarity at the expense of meaning. Therefore, we recommended intervention activities that immersed her into the complexities of comprehension in the areas of establishing a purpose for reading, rereading, retrospective miscue analysis, and giving meaningful retells.

Using a comprehensive assessment tool, like the In-Process Comprehension Rubric introduced in this chapter (see Appendix 8A), teachers can gather data about readers that provide a broader lens for instructional responses in Tier I settings. Assessment over a period of time with this rubric can show a pattern of increased focus on the purpose for reading—meaning construction.

Appendix 8A
In-Process Comprehension Rubric

Teachers often wonder if students comprehend the texts they are reading. However, educators often feel that without having read the text themselves, they are unable to have meaningful discussions with students with regard to what they are reading. The attached rubric will allow you to just "drop in" on students and spot check their comprehension at any step along the way in order to ensure that they are indeed comprehending what they read. If they are not, this tool will provide insight into the breakdown of the student's reading processes.

Preparation:
1. Make one copy of this sheet and the attached rubric for each student whom you would like to "drop in" on.
2. Place paper on a clipboard and complete the reader, teacher, date, and selection fields for the first student.
3. Read the rubric prior to starting. This will allow for easy markings after the reading.

Directions:
1. Drop in on the student, sit shoulder to shoulder with her, and read the following:
   a. "Please finish the sentence or paragraph you are currently reading, and then stop. I am going to have you read out loud to me. Keep reading until I tell you to stop. I will not interrupt you or help you, so just read how you would normally read. After you are finished, I am going to ask you to tell me about what you just read. Begin whenever you are ready."
2. As the student reads, use the yes or no lines on the next page to keep a tally of the sentences. If the sentence makes sense within the context of the story, mark a yes; if it does not, mark a no. A sentence can score a yes, even if there are miscues, as long as the miscue does not alter the overall meaning of the text.
3. Please note that this is not a timed read; rather, the student should continue reading until she has read an amount that is sufficient for a retell—meaning that she has read something significant that can be discussed.
4. Once you ask her to stop reading, tell her the following:
   a. "I want you to think about everything you have just read. Please tell me in your own words everything you remember."
5. If necessary, you may jot notes in the margin about the details of the retell.
6. Total the yes and no sentences to produce a comprehension score. Then mark the appropriate boxes on the rubric.
7. Pinpoint areas of weakness and provide interventions or enrichment as needed based upon results.

Reader: _____ **Date:** _____ **Grade:** _____

Title: _____

Does the sentence make sense the way the reader left it?

Yes:_____ **Total:**_____

No: _____ **Total:**_____

Number of   **In-Process**

Sentences Read: _____ **Comprehension Score:**_____

Divide total number of yes responses by total number of
sentences read for In-Process Comprehension Score.

Note. Adapted from *Reading Miscue Inventory: Alternative Procedure* (p. 251), by Y. M. Goodman, D. Watson, and C. Burke, 2005, Katonah, NY: Richard C. Owen. Copyright 2005 by Richard C. Owen.

In-Process Comprehension Rubric

	Beginning 1	Developing 2	Transitioning 3	Confident 4
Phrasing	Monotonic with little sense of phrase boundaries, frequent word-by-word reading	Frequent short word phrases, choppy reading, improper stress and intonation that fail to mark ends of sentences	Mixture of run-ons, mid-sentence pauses, and possibly some choppiness, reasonable stress/intonation	Generally well phrased, mostly in clause and sentence units, with adequate attention to expression
Intonation	Monotonic reading	Some changes in voice pitch/expression that may not match the text meaning	Appropriate changes in voice pitch/expression that reflect comprehension of text	Appropriate changes in voice pitch/expression that reflect comprehension of text and add dramatic emphasis
Miscues (Omissions, Insertions, and Substitutions)	Low-quality miscues leading to a complete breakdown of comprehension	Mostly low-quality miscues that usually prohibit comprehension	Uses both high- and low-quality miscues inconsistently	Mostly high-quality miscues that show confidence in properly editing the text
Self-Monitoring and Correcting	Low-quality miscues are not corrected	Inconsistent use of correction when necessary for making sense of the text, high-quality miscues are corrected	Uses correction, but may not recognize when it is necessary and when it is an overcorrection	Consistently corrects only those miscues that are necessary for making sense of the text
Retell	Fragmented and disjointed even with probing and questioning	General retell with probing and questioning, few details and personal interpretation	Acceptable retell with details and some personal interpretations	Highly independent retell with details and high levels of personal interpretation

References

Allington, R. L. (2009). *What really matters in Response to Intervention: Research-based designs.* Boston, MA: Pearson.

Block, C., & Israel, S. E. (2004). The ABCs of performing highly effective think-alouds. *The Reading Teacher, 58,* 154–167.

Burke, C. (1980). The reading interview: 1977. In B. P. Farr & D. J. Strickler (Eds.), *Reading comprehension: Resource guide* (pp. 82–108). Bloomington: Language Education, Indiana University.

Cunningham, P. M., & Allington, R. L. (1999). *Classrooms that work: They can all read and write* (2nd ed.). New York, NY: Longman.

Dewitz, P., Jones, J., & Leahy, S. (2009). Comprehension strategy instruction in core reading programs. *Reading Research Quarterly, 44,* 102–126.

Duke, N. K., & Pearson, P. D. (2002). Effective practices for developing reading comprehension. In A. Farstrup & J. Samuels (Eds.), *What research has to say about reading instruction* (3rd ed., pp. 205–242). Newark, DE: International Reading Association.

Fisher, D., Frey, N., & Lapp, D. (2009). *In a reading state of mind.* Newark, DE: International Reading Association.

Flood, J., Lapp, D., Squire, J. R., & Jensen, J. M. (Eds.). (2003). *Handbook of research on teaching the English language arts* (2nd ed.). Mahwah, NJ: Lawrence Erlbaum.

Fountas, I. C., & Pinnell, G. S. (2001). *Guiding readers and writers grades 3–6: Teaching comprehension, genre, and content literacy.* Portsmouth, NH: Heinemann.

Goodman, Y. M. (1996). Revaluing readers while readers revalue themselves: Retrospective miscue analysis. *The Reading Teacher, 49,* 600–609.

Goodman, Y. M., & Goodman, K. S. (2004). To err is human: Learning about language processes by analyzing miscues. In R. Ruddell & N. Unrau (Eds.), *Theoretical models and process of reading* (5th ed., pp. 620–639). Newark, DE: International Reading Association.

Goodman, Y. M., Watson, D., & Burke, C. (2005). *Reading miscue inventory: Alternative procedures.* Katonah, NY: Richard Irwin.

Hancock, M. R. (2000). A celebration of literature and response: *Children, books, and teachers in K–8 classrooms* (2nd ed.). Upper Saddle River, NJ: Pearson Education.

Howard, M. (2009). *RTI from all sides: What every teacher needs to know.* Portsmouth, NH: Heinemann.

International Reading Association. (2010). *Standards for the assessment of reading and writing.* Newark, DE: Author.

Johnston, P. H. (2010). *RTI in literacy: Responsive and comprehensive.* Newark, DE: International Reading Association.

Kieffer, M. J., & Lesaux, N. K. (2007). Breaking down words to build meaning: Morphology, vocabulary, and reading comprehension in the urban classroom. *The Reading Teacher, 61,* 134–144.

Marston, D. (2005). Tiers of intervention in Responsiveness to Intervention: Prevention outcomes and learning disabilities identification patterns. *Journal of Learning Disabilities, 38,* 539–544.

National Reading Panel. (2000). *Teaching children to read: An evidence-based assessment of the scientific research literature on reading and its implications for reading instruction.* Washington, DC: National Institute of Child Health and Human Development.

Owocki, G. (2010). *The RTI daily planning book: Tools and strategies for collecting and assessing reading data & targeted follow-up instruction.* Portsmouth, NH: Heinemann.

Pikulski, J. J., & Chard, D. J. (2005). Fluency: Bridge between decoding and reading comprehension. *The Reading Teacher, 58,* 510–519.

Rasinski, T. (1994). Developing syntactic sensitivity in reading through phase-cued texts. *Intervention in School and Clinic, 29,* 165–168.

Rasinski, T. V., & Hoffman, J. V. (2003). Oral reading in the school literacy curriculum. *Reading Research Quarterly, 38,* 510–522.

Rosenblatt, L. M. (1978). *The reader, the text, the poem: The transactional theory of the literary work.* Carbondale, IL: Southern Illinois University Press.

Rosenblatt, L. M. (2004). The transactional theory of reading and writing. In R. B. Ruddell & N. J. Unrau (Eds.), *Theoretical models and processes of reading* (pp. 1363-1398). Newark, DE: International Reading Association.

Schwartz, R. M. (2005). Decisions, decisions: Responding to primary students during guided reading. *The Reading Teacher, 58,* 436–443.

Shanahan, T. (2008). Implications of RTI for the reading teacher. In D. Fuchs, L. Fuchs, & S. Vaughn (Eds.), *Response to Intervention: A framework for reading educators* (pp. 105–122). Newark, DE: International Reading Association.

Shea, M. (2006). *Where's the glitch? How to use running records with older readers, grades 5–8.* Portsmouth, NH: Heinemann.

Taberski, S. (2009). *It's all about comprehension.* Portsmouth, NH: Heinemann.

CHAPTER 9

RtI

in Writing: Suggested Screening, Intervention, and Progress Monitoring

Bruce Saddler and Kristie Asaro-Saddler

One of the most important goals in a child's education is to learn to write well. While in school, teachers often use writing as the primary means to document student knowledge and the major instrument to evaluate academic performance (Graham & Harris, 2005). In addition, there is growing emphasis on writing in federal and state-mandated accountability testing and college entrance examinations. When students leave school and enter the workforce, they will find that writing is a key communicative avenue and that good communication skills are essential in many areas of life. For these reasons, teachers must ensure that students learn to write effectively.

However, writing is a difficult skill to learn and can be intimidating to even highly skilled writers. In classrooms, writing can pose challenges for many students and is very daunting to teach. For example, how best to teach writing is debatable, and although there are specific techniques that have been empirically proven to be effective, there is no single technique that will work with all writers. Furthermore, after a writer has been taught to write, how to most effectively score that writing is elusive, because even defining "good" writing is highly subjective. For these reasons, writing has been thought to be the most complex facet of the language arts curriculum

(Mercer & Mercer, 1989), one that represents "the summit of the language hierarchy" (Polloway & Smith, 1982, p. 256).

Not surprisingly, many students struggle with writing. In fact, according to the latest version of the National Assessment for Educational Progress (NAEP; Salahu-Din, Persky, & Miller, 2008), 45% of students with disabilities and 8% of students without disabilities could not write above a basic level of proficiency at eighth grade. This increased to 56% of students with and 15% of students without disabilities in grade 12.

As these numbers indicate, children with writing disabilities present uniquely challenging instructional needs. Typical characteristics of these children indicate that they approach writing tasks far differently than their regularly achieving peers. For example, children with writing disabilities may not engage in effective planning prior to writing (Harris & Graham, 1996a). They may also write very brief stories that are not well organized or cohesive and that may lack important details or elaborations that could make the story more enjoyable or understandable to a reader (Harris, Graham, & Mason, 2006). Sadly, they usually cannot improve the story through revision (Newcomer, Nodine, & Barenbaum, 1988). Furthermore, children with writing disabilities may struggle with handwriting, grammar, punctuation, and spelling. Deficits in these areas may slow their ability to translate their ideas while often making the final product less readable and enjoyable. Because of the struggles they face while writing, many children with writing disabilities may also have more negative images of their writing abilities (Graham & Harris, 1989). Finally, they may be particularly deficient in the use of metacognitive strategies. While a skilled writer can draw upon a repertoire of strategies for planning, writing, and revising text that can be activated as needed, less skilled writers may not be as purposeful or mindful with their writing. Interestingly, many of these same characteristics may also apply to less skilled writers in classrooms who do not have an identified disability.

Therefore, an important goal for our writing instruction needs to be helping less skilled writers and writers with disabilities develop effective strategies for planning, writing, and revising text while increasing their knowledge of the executive procedures necessary for regulating these strategies and the process of writing in general (Harris & Graham, 1996b). It is equally important for us to help our students develop and maintain positive attitudes about writing and their writing capabilities. Although these are compelling goals, many teachers may struggle with how they can be achieved in classrooms containing children on many different levels of writing development.

If we are to improve outcomes for our students, we must apply best educational practices to all students upon entering school while identifying and remediating difficulties right away. This concept is supported by the current educational policy push toward evidence-based disability identification, intervention, and remediation as envisioned in the Individuals with Disabilities Education Improvement Act (IDEA, 2004). That same act encouraged states to utilize an alternative method to identify students with learning disabilities while also providing additional academic supports for struggling students. This method, called Response to Intervention (RtI), has prompted educators to define what adequate instruction means for all learners (O'Fiesh, 2006). In the following case study, a fictitious school is used to illustrate how RtI in writing could be successfully implemented in other schools.

RtI in Schools: A Case Study

The RtI approach was embraced by an elementary school in the Northeast. This school, Garfield Elementary, believed that RtI could help identify struggling learners and remediate deficiencies. One academic area in particular the administrators and teachers at Garfield believed could be improved through an RtI approach was written expression.

The teachers at Garfield believed that their approach to writing instruction included many research-supported interventions. For example, instruction was highly interactive and directed at helping students construct their own understandings of writing and the writing process. While teaching writing, they routinely emphasized that writing is a process, and can best be accomplished with a writing workshop approach. Students worked on meaningful tasks that they wanted to write about, received frequent responses from peers and teachers, and wrote through a series of organized routines including planning, drafting, revising, and publishing. However, even with these supports in place, many students at Garfield still struggled with writing, and the teachers believed that employing RtI could help them identify the students who needed additional support early in their academic careers while also providing a systematic framework for all teachers to intervene with their students.

Collecting Appropriate Data

In typical RtI models, students are universally screened, empirically validated interventions are taught in a three-tiered model of increasing instructional intensity, and progress is systematically monitored (cf. Glover, 2010; Lembke, Garman, Deno, & Stecker, 2010). This general approach is supported by research indicating the efficacy of early identification and intervention (Scanlon, Vellutino, Small, Fanuele, & Sweeney, 2005).

Garfield's RtI model follows this same framework. Garfield's school-wide universal screening, which consists of assessing all students for potential reading problems at the beginning of the year and again in the middle of the year (Compton, Fuchs, Fuchs, & Bryant, 2006), is geared to initially identify students at risk for future difficulties. In Garfield's scheme, kindergartners and first-graders are screened using Dynamic Indicators of Basic Early Literacy Skills (DIBELS) assessments in the fall and spring. The school also uses DIBELS fluency and accuracy assessments for students in the second through fifth grades. Cut scores have been set based on district recommendations, and all students who fall below these cut scores on their assessments are closely monitored. No single score stands alone in determining interventions for students, but rather data from multiple sources (e.g., classroom test scores, fluency screenings, and DIBELS) are used together to determine which students need instruction beyond Tier I and which interventions will be most effective in meeting student needs.

In Tier I, all students are instructed in general education until evidence indicates they are not responding to the instruction as anticipated. In Tier II, teachers provide more intense interventions than are typically provided in general education for students who are identified on the screening instrument or who demonstrate weak progress. However, interventions at this tier are less individualized than special education. For example, students might receive small-group instruction targeted toward specific skill development. In Tier III, more intensive interventions are provided for students who fail to progress in Tier II. These interventions could include specially designed programmatic education delivered by special education teachers and related personnel or by other teachers. This instruction includes individualized and recursive instruction based on careful monitoring and analysis of student performance.

In each of these tiers, systematic progress monitoring of success occurs in increasing frequency in Tiers II and III to assist teachers in identifying needs and designing interventions. Garfield teachers believed that by systematically monitoring progress, diagnostic information is created that helps determine if a student needs a tier change or an adjustment of instruction/curriculum/materials within tiers (Fuchs & Fuchs, 2006).

For writing, Garfield's teachers consider that evaluation for educational decision making requires a comprehensive approach that includes qualitative and quantitative measures of handwriting, spelling, and prose. To this end, their RtI program includes a screening measure administered early in the school year to identify the presence of possible writing difficulties. For this initial screen of writing ability, each teacher in Grades 1–3 provides the students with two pictures of activities children should enjoy writing about. The children are told to choose a picture and then to write a story about that picture. They are given 15 minutes to write their story. The stories are then analyzed quantitatively by counting the number of words and qualitatively by two teachers using a holistic scoring guide to create an overall impression of the selection. See Figure 9.1 for an example of a typical holistic scoring guide. The teachers compare their scores and discuss any paper whose score differed by two or more points. Each teacher practices scoring sample student papers beforehand to help ensure their scoring is as similar to each other's as possible. Students scoring in the bottom 20% in each class are identified as possibly needing more academic support coupled with more systematic progress monitoring. Elizabeth was one of these students.

Elizabeth

Elizabeth had transferred to Garfield at the start of her second-grade year, and the early screening suggested that she struggled with writing. Her story was short and scored very poorly on the holistic scoring guide. The screening results were supported by Elizabeth's performance on several writing projects. Her teacher, Mrs. Donohue, noted that when writing, Elizabeth quickly jotted down a few ideas with no time devoted to planning and little thought toward how the composition sounded. Her stories were short and missing typical elements such as a setting or a believable ending. Finally, she struggled with spelling, punctuation, and capitalization, making her writing very difficult for others to read and enjoy.

Effective teaching methods. Mrs. Donohue had a very effective approach to writing instruction. Mrs. Donohue's typical Tier I instruction was designed to give all students opportunities to develop as writers. Her writing instruction was highly interactive, individualized, and directed at helping students improve transcription skills (writing or word processing), conventions of print, sentence construction, and genre requirements (Graham & Perin, 2007). Her students write across the content via a collaborative process approach where they attempt personally meaningful writing tasks while engaging in a series of organized routines (prewriting/planning, drafting, revising, and publishing). Students receive frequent

---

High Story (7–8)

> A story in the typical sense that has all of the parts (who, what, when, where, why, and emotions)
> Contains extra detail and action
> Many ideas and much imagination
> Well organized
> May have some errors (e.g., capitalization, punctuation, verb tense)
> Flows well, but may still be choppy in a few places

Medium Story (4–6)

> A story in the typical sense, but in part incomplete (missing important parts; for example, the goal is not resolved)
> Has some organization
> Needs more detail and elaboration
> One idea flows to the next, but is not well organized

Low Story (0–3)

> Not a story in the typical sense; no ending, no real beginning, no time described, no action related
> Merely a description of the picture
> No consistent thought flow
> Choppy sentences
> Poor sentence structure
> Lacks imagination

Figure 9.1. Description for holistic story quality anchor points.

---

feedback from peers and teachers. Clear and specific goals are set for assignments, and inquiry activities are implemented to create data that could be used for content. Finally, students are taught how to create written summaries of reading selections and use technology that can support the writing process, such as Microsoft Word spellchecker, speech-to-text software, and Kidspiration and Inspiration, to make graphic organizers to aid in the planning and content generating stages of writing.

Mrs. Donohue decided to employ Tier II interventions and progress monitoring for Elizabeth and several other students in her classroom whose holistic quality scores on the screening instrument were in the bottom 20%. Garfield's Tier II instruction is more explicit, comprehensive, and intense than the instruction provided in Tier I. In general, Tier II instruction would include empirically validated interventions that are part of a plan designed to meet the individual needs of the student. Garfield believes that most students would benefit from this instruction if the teacher presented the interventions with fidelity. To discover if the instruction is beneficial, progress in Tier II is carefully and frequently monitored, no less than biweekly for written expression, using multiple outcome measures to determine to what degree students respond or do not respond. Responders demonstrate progress after tutoring; nonresponders do not respond or respond to a lesser degree. Responders are seen as typical disability-free learners whereas nonresponders require a more intensive, individualized, tertiary intervention (Reschly, 2005; Vaughn & Fuchs, 2006). Garfield's teachers use CBMs to determine responsiveness and target instruction (Hessler & Konrad, 2008). In general, curriculum-based measures are tied directly to the curriculum, can be sensitive to change in student performance, and are quickly administered (Tindal & Hasbrouck, 1991). They can provide specific data for IEP goal development and monitoring and are considered to provide a stronger link between assessment and instruction than standardized tests. CBMs have been recommended for use as an important source of information in informing screening and placement decisions about students (Fewster & MacMillan, 2002).

Garfield teachers use the slope of the student's data from the CBMs to determine response. In this method, students are assessed, a slope of academic improvement is computed, students above a normative cut point referenced to the grade level at the school are deemed responsive, and others are designated nonresponsive. Nonresponders are those who require the most intensive, nonstandard instruction available in the RtI framework or Tier II intervention. For example, in Figure 9.2, Jim, whose data points are above the goal, or aimline, is considered to be a responder to the intervention, while Elizabeth, with data points below the aimline, is a nonresponder.

In Mrs. Donohue's classroom, Tier II writing instruction includes small-group (four to eight students) tutoring sessions with clearly articulated durations (generally 10–15 weeks of 20- to 40-minute sessions), and frequencies (generally 3–4 times per week). These sessions supplement the students' regular writing instruction. During these sessions, she would help students create effective sentences, select topics, plan for using graphic organizers, complete first drafts, and then revise and edit those drafts.

Before Mrs. Donohue began to write paragraphs and longer units of print with her group of students who needed Tier II supports, she taught and practiced sentence construction skills using sentence combining techniques. Sentence combining provides direct, mindful practice in arranging and rearranging basic sentences into more syntactically varied structures (Saddler & Preschern, 2007). For example, if a student characteristically composes simple kernel sentences such as "The tree is tall. The tree is green," he can learn through sentence combining practice to change these

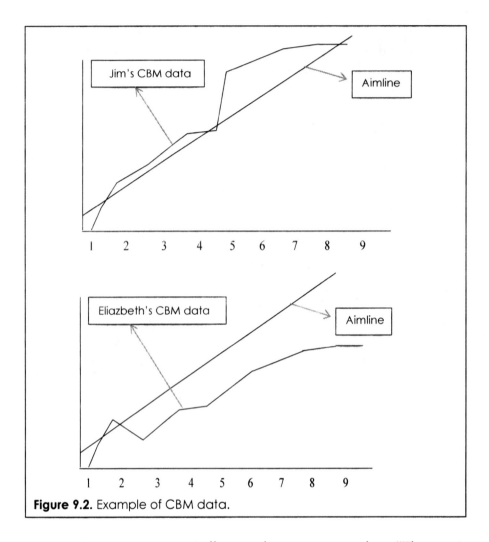

Figure 9.2. Example of CBM data.

sentences into more syntactically complex sentences such as "The tree is tall and green." Sentence run-ons and fragments can also be corrected via sentence combining practice. (For a full treatment of sentence combining, see Saddler & Preschern, 2007). Sentence combining practice can help young writers compose a wider variety of more effective sentences while also improving the overall quality of stories and the amount and quality of revisions (cf. Saddler & Graham, 2005). Mrs. Donohue carefully monitored the children's progress with the sentence combining skills taught by administering a 10-problem curriculum-based measurement (CBM) probe (see Figure 9.3 for an example) each week and graphed each child's results.

After 2 months of direct instruction and practice in sentence combining, students' CBM results improved to a minimum of 8/10 correct responses. These results indicated that the children's skill in crafting a vari-

1.	The cake was delicious. The cake was chocolate.	6.	The bird flew. The bird was white.
2.	The cat chased the ball. The cat was old.	7.	The band played. They played my favorite song.
3.	The winter is boring. The winter is long.	8.	The monkey climbed a tree. The tree was tall.
4.	The girl looked at the boy. She looked sadly.	9.	The hamster was small. The hamster was furry. The hamster was gray.
5.	The man was wearing a hat. The hat was blue.	10.	Chandler turned off the lights. He walked upstairs. He went to bed.

Figure 9.3. Sample sentence combining probe.

ety of sentences had improved to the point where Mrs. Donohue believed she could move into working with longer segments of text. She chose story writing because the class had already been working in this genre and the children were familiar with the basic structure of a story.

Mrs. Donohue believes that one of the best things a teacher can do for their students is to explain the purposes of writing and then model how skilled writers approach the craft. First, she explained to the group that people write to make their thoughts known to others. She then began to model the writing process directly for the children by explaining her thought processes as she picked a topic, set goals, solved problems, and maintained a positive attitude while writing. As she composed a story she would overtly discuss how she was navigating the writing process. She included specific statements about problem definitions (e.g., Why am I writing this? Who is my audience?), goal statements (e.g., I want to include three strong reasons for my argument.), coping statements (e.g., This is hard, but I can do it.), reinforcing statements (e.g., I really like the way that sounds.), and problem resolutions (e.g., Let me try a different word here.). She then read the story aloud to the children and discussed the qualities of the story while also asking questions about the process of writing to reinforce the effective writing behaviors she engaged in (e.g., How did I plan what to say? What kinds of things did I say to myself to help me?).

After modeling the entire process, Mrs. Donohue dedicated time in subsequent sessions to model each step of the writing process for the students, beginning with creating ideas for a story. To do this, she overtly brainstormed ideas and placed them on an organizer. She reinforced the practice of writing in phrases or single words on the organizer, as many of the students wanted to write in complete sentences. She then explained that complete sentences take more time to write, and that writing in short phrases makes it easier to arrange and rearrange ideas.

The next time the group met, Mrs. Donohue modeled translating the notes on the graphic organizer into text by taking logical pieces of information from the notes and fitting them together in a rough draft. She then added additional information while also rearranging information to explore how it best fit together.

After completing an initial draft, Mrs. Donohue worked with the children to make improvements through revisions. She discussed how revising is a problem-solving process involving three steps: problem detection, definition, and correction. She explained and demonstrated that during problem detection a writer may notice an area of text that can be corrected or improved. Then, once detected, the problem must be defined. For example, "This word does not really describe the character as I wanted." She then explained that after defining a problem, the problem must be corrected through revisions that actually make improvements. She discussed several sources to help with textual corrections including a thesaurus for a more expressive or colorful word, restructuring sentences to emphasize a key idea using the sentence combining skills learned earlier, and/or rearranging sentences or paragraphs for a more coherent or consistent flow.

To effectively model revisions, Mrs. Donohue would guide the students in the steps they should take with their own pieces by working through sample stories they had written. She would ask each student to read the current piece he was drafting and then prompt the student's peers to suggest areas for improvement. As classmates suggested revisions and pointed out sources of confusion, the author of the paper learned which concepts or ideas were confusing or which words were vague. In later sessions, Mrs. Donohue structured these revision sessions by using an approach suggested by Wong (2000). In Wong's approach, two students meet with their teacher. The student author provides the teacher and the other student (editor or critic) a copy of her composition to read. While reading, any confusing parts of the text are underlined, and then the editor and the teacher ask the author to provide explanations and elaborations. The teacher assists the editor in formulating questions and the author in improving her text by suggesting effective revisions. When the editor is finished, the teacher may make suggestions for any problematic areas missed. This cycle is then repeated with the students switching roles. The students then make the recommended revisions and return individually for a second conference with the teacher only. To help her students think about specific areas of the texts, Mrs. Donohue also provided checklists and revision guides (see peer editing worksheet in Figure 9.4).

Finally, Mrs. Donohue modeled editing. While editing, she explained that students should identify and correct errors in spelling, grammar, usage, punctuation, or capitalization. She noted that the students had difficulty editing their work because they were often unable to identify the errors in their writing, and when they are able to identify the errors, they did not know how to correct them. She found that one way to help these students increase and improve their editing skills was to provide them with a checklist or a guide such as SCOPE (Bos & Vaughn, 2002; see Figure 9.5) to help them focus on specific areas of editing.

After Mrs. Donohue had completely modeled each step of the writing process, the children began to collaboratively write stories with her. She provided several accommodations for the students including using a voice recorder and computer speech-to-text software to get their thoughts on paper. She also provided word banks containing lists of adjectives, action words, transitions words, and colorful, "million dollar" words, among others.

For all of the students in the Tier II group, Mrs. Donohue carefully monitored their progress on story writing CBMs biweekly. She administered the probes in the same manner in which she administered the probes for screening and rated them using both qualitative and quantitative measures. For a qualitative score, she used a primary trait, or analytic holistic scoring rubric, which allowed her to make decisions about the quality of their writings based on a number of dimensions (Espin, Weissenburger, & Benson, 2004) including ideas, organization, voice, word choice, sentence fluency, and conventions (Spandel, 2008). See Figure 9.6 for a typical analytic scoring rubric. For a quantitative score, she monitored the amount of production by counting the number of words written and the number of words spelled correctly, which she knew to be effective measures of early writing ability (cf. Gansle et al., 2004).

Evidenced-based strategies. Unfortunately, even with Tier II instruction, Elizabeth failed to make adequate progress in writing. Her CBM scores were consistently at approximately 60%, while many others receiving Tier II interventions were achieving scores of 80%–100%. These scores indicated that her response to the instruction Mrs. Donohue provided was not sufficient. Her stories were still short and lacking key elements. Because of Elizabeth's overall lack of progress in Tier II, Mrs. Donohue believed she could benefit from Tier III instruction.

Directions: Use the following guide while you read the rough draft. Put as much detail as you can into each question. The more comments, the better the work will become. Make sure you include any questions you have for the author. Use the back of the sheet if you need more space to write.
- What made the story interesting?
- What were the characters like?
- How was the setting unique?
- Was the ending what you expected?
- What did you like best about the story?
- What was the most exciting part of the story?
- What part of the story do you want to know more about?
- Was the story organized and easy to follow?
- Did the author use a variety of different sentences?
- What vivid vocabulary did the author use?

Peer Editor Comments:_____

_____

_____

_____

Figure 9.4. Peer editor worksheet.

- **S**pelling: Is the spelling correct?
- **C**apitalization: Are the first words of sentences, proper names, and proper nouns capitalized?
- **O**rder of words: Is the syntax correct?
- **P**unctuation: Are there appropriate marks for punctuation where necessary?
- **E**xpress complete thought: Do your sentences contain a noun and a verb, or are they only phrases?

Figure 9.5. SCOPE checklist.

At Garfield, Tier III is characterized by small instructional groupings of one to four students and is implemented for a longer time period than Tier II. Instruction is more explicit and intense and highly individualized to meet specific student needs. School personnel with extensive training in working with students with severe learning difficulties are often responsible for Tier III instruction. At Garfield, special education teachers in either a resource room or the general education classroom delivered this instruction, and individual long-term learning goals with materials that coincided with the level of the child were employed. The instructional methods were more intensive versions (generally meaning longer sessions and smaller groups)

Overall Rubric for Holistic Quality

	5 (Highest)	3	1 (Lowest)
Ideas and Content	Paper is clear and focused; includes details; holds readers' attention	May be somewhat clear and focused but not as interesting; has some details but main ideas not always clear	The paper lacks a main idea and has few details
Organization	Paper makes sense and reader can easily follow along; has good transitions	Reader can follow along but not as easily; transitions may be used less frequently or may be weak	Organization is disjointed; no clear direction and no transitions
Voice	Writer "speaks" to the reader in an interesting way; shows the writer's style	The paper may have some personality, but not as fully involved in the topic	Writer seems indifferent or uninvolved; makes no connection with the reader
Word Choice	The writer uses powerful yet natural vocabulary	Language conveys the message but is ordinary	Vocabulary is limited and does not convey main idea clearly
Sentence Structure	Paper has a good rhythm, with a variety of sentence structures effectively used	Paper may sound "mechanical" and lack variety in sentence structure	Paper is difficult to follow; sentences are choppy, incomplete, or run-ons
Conventions	Proper mechanics are used; few or no errors present	Errors may be present, but the reader can still get the main idea	Numerous errors are present that take away from the reader's ability to understand the paper

Figure 9.6. Sample analytic scoring rubric. Adapted from *Creating Writers Through 6-Trait Writing Assessment and Instruction* (5th ed.), by V. Spandel, 2008, Columbus, OH: Allyn & Bacon. Copyright 2008 Allyn & Bacon.

of the tutoring program used in Tier I and Tier II and included modifications based on the continuous and frequent (usually weekly) monitoring of student performance such as individualized goals and materials, repetitions of a skill, an increase in praise-to-corrective feedback, and criterion versus time-based instruction to allow students the opportunity to acquire a skill or strategy at their own pace (Fuchs & Fuchs, 2009; Harlacher, Walker, &

Sanford, 2010). We must remember that Tier III instruction is in addition to instruction in Tiers I and II.

The special education teacher working with Elizabeth was Mrs. Griffin. After careful consultation with Mrs. Donohue, she believed that Elizabeth could benefit from the use of metacognitive writing strategy instruction, as she lacked awareness of the cognitive aspects of writing, and did not engage in self-regulatory processes while writing. In general, strategy instruction involves explicitly and systematically teaching steps that guide writing processes while also providing structure that helps organize writing behavior. This instruction helps students think strategically about managing the writing process (cf. Graham & Harris, 1989) and is especially valuable for students with learning problems (Harris, 1982).

Mrs. Griffin utilizes a well-validated method to teach strategies called the self-regulated strategy instruction model (SRSD; Graham & Harris, 1989). SRSD was developed with the premise that skilled writers use self-regulation procedures, including goal setting, planning, self-monitoring, self-assessment, self-instruction, and self-reinforcement, to guide the way they think and feel during writing (Harris & Graham, 1996a). Mrs. Griffin knew that SRSD is used to teach a variety of writing skills including planning, semantic webbing, goal setting, monitoring production, peer response to revising, and revision. Furthermore, SRSD has been used to teach story writing and persuasion to students with various disabilities including learning, emotional, attention deficit, and autism spectrum disorders beginning in the early elementary grades and proceeding through middle school. (See Asaro-Saddler & Saddler, 2010; Baker, Chard, Ketterlin-Geller, Apichatabutra, & Doabler, 2009; and Rogers & Graham, 2008, for a summary of the research base. See Harris et al., 2006, and Harris, Graham, Mason, & Friedlander, 2008, for detailed lesson plans and instructional materials.)

Implementation steps. First Mrs. Griffin met with Elizabeth and asked her to write a story based on a picture. The story was analyzed for length, number of basic story elements (e.g., who, what, when), and overall quality. Mrs. Griffin graphed the results of the analysis and established a slope of academic improvement.

Mrs. Griffin noted that Elizabeth did not plan prior to writing; therefore, she selected a planning strategy she believed could help Elizabeth. The strategy Mrs. Griffin chose to teach Elizabeth included a mnemonic device, POW, which helped organize the planning and writing process. POW reminds writers to **P**ick My Ideas (i.e., decide what to write about), **O**rganize My Notes (i.e., develop an advanced writing plan), and **W**rite and Say More (i.e., expand the plan while writing). A second mnemonic—WWW, What = 2, How = 2—reminded students to create notes for basic story elements. Each letter of this mnemonic keyed the students to write notes for each of the following questions: **W**ho are the main characters? **W**hen does the story take place? **W**here does the story take place? **What** do the main characters want to do? **What** happens when the main characters try to do it? **How** does the story end? **How** do the main characters feel? The strategy was taught through several instructional stages including: (a) developing background knowledge, (b) discussion of the strategy, (c) modeling of the strategy/self-instruction, (d) memorization of the strategy, (e) support/collaborative practice, and (f) independently practicing the strategy.

Developing background knowledge. During this stage, the quality of the story Elizabeth had written for Mrs. Griffin was discussed along with what strategies she used while writing that story and how those strategies helped. Mrs. Griffin then discussed the potential benefits of the proposed strategy and asked Elizabeth to commit to working with her to learn and use the strategy.

Discussion of the strategy. They then spent time discussing the strategy itself, its purposes, how and when to use it, and how it could be used in other classes and for other types of writing. One of Elizabeth's previous pieces of writing was used to illustrate what parts of the story she already included and what she could add to make her story better. Mrs. Griffin also helped Elizabeth create and write down writing goals and self-instructions to help reach those goals. In addition, Mrs. Griffin showed Elizabeth how to self-monitor and self-reinforce her performance using a chart to document the number of words written and the number of key story elements included.

Modeling of the strategy and self-instructions. Mrs. Griffin then modeled the use of the strategy for Elizabeth. During this modeling she talked out loud using self-instructions. To Mrs. Griffin, this step represented "taking the top of her head off" and letting Elizabeth see and hear what she was thinking. She included self-instructions for problem definition (What do I need to do here?), planning (What do I see in this picture?), strategy use (What is the next step of the strategy?), self-evaluation (How does this sound to me?), coping and error correction (That isn't quite what I wanted to say), and self-reinforcement statements (Way to go!).

Memorization of the strategy. During each instructional session, Mrs. Griffin would prompt Elizabeth to practice memorizing the strategy steps. She provided Elizabeth with a visual illustration detailing each of the steps, which they reviewed during each lesson. In addition, Elizabeth was prompted to take the illustration home to practice memorization with her family. Mrs. Griffin understood that if Elizabeth could not remember the steps, she likely could not use the strategy effectively in Mrs. Donohue's class.

Supportive practice. Mrs. Griffin continued to provide guidance while practicing the strategy until Elizabeth was comfortable enough to run the strategy on her own. Elizabeth continued to monitor her own performance by graphing the words in her stories and the number of story elements on a chart.

Independent performance. By this stage, Mrs. Griffin expected Elizabeth to be using the strategy fairly independently, with little prompting. She also expected to see evidence of strategy use in Elizabeth's writing—meaning that because this strategy involved creating a plan for writing a story, she wanted to see Elizabeth create a written plan before beginning to write a story. Mrs. Griffin checked Elizabeth's progress toward independence by administering weekly writing probes that were analyzed for the number of story elements, length, and overall quality.

However, Mrs. Griffin planned booster sessions for maintenance of the strategy and writing assignments that required Elizabeth to generalize the strategy. In addition, she discussed how Mrs. Donohue should encourage Elizabeth to use the strategy when writing stories in her classroom and made plans with Mrs. Donohue to continue the progress monitoring Elizabeth was accustomed to using to help ensure continued strategy use.

Working through these stages of instruction took several months for Elizabeth, which is not atypical. Changing writing behaviors takes time and cannot be addressed with quick fixes. However, as a result of the SRSD strategy, Elizabeth's planning ability improved tremendously. She produced written plans that helped her to better incorporate the story elements (such as who, when, why, what, and how). In addition, her stories were longer and more enjoyable to read.

Clearly, Elizabeth was making progress as a writer; however, Mrs. Griffin decided to keep Elizabeth in Tier III to help her generalize the strategy to new writing tasks and to support the other writing demands she faced in Mrs. Donohue's classroom such as other writing genres (e.g., persuasion, expository) and unique writing tasks (e.g., letter writing, dialogues).

Conclusion

Although writing is challenging to teach and to learn, it is a critical skill for students to master. Effective writing instruction will help less skilled writers and writers with disabilities develop effective strategies for planning, writing, and revising text while increasing their knowledge of the executive procedures necessary for regulating these strategies and the process of writing in general (Harris & Graham, 1996b). Instruction will also aid students' development and maintenance of positive attitudes about writing and their writing capabilities.

To improve students' writing ability, we must identify writing disabilities early enough to remediate, aggressively apply appropriate research-based interventions such as sentence combining and SRSD, and systematically monitor student progress using both qualitative and quantitative curriculum-based writing assessments such as those suggested in this chapter. All of these tasks are encapsulated within an RtI framework. In typical RtI models, students are universally screened, empirically validated interventions are taught in a three-tiered model of increasing instructional intensity, and progress is systematically monitored. As demonstrated in this chapter, an RtI framework to organize identification and instruction in writing certainly makes sense. However, schools will need to consider the types of writing interventions that will best enhance student outcomes, the length of instruction, and how best to monitor progress as they establish their writing programs.

References

Asaro-Saddler, K., & Saddler, B. (2010). The effects of planning and self-regulation training on the writing performance of young writers with autism spectrum disorders. *Exceptional Children, 77,* 107–124.

Baker, S., Chard, D., Ketterlin-Geller, L., Apichatabutra, C., & Doabler, C. (2009). Teaching writing to at-risk students: The quality of evidence for self-regulated strategy development. *Exceptional Children, 75,* 303–318.

Bos, C., & Vaughn, S. (2002). *Strategies for teaching students with learning and behavior problems.* Boston, MA: Allyn & Bacon.

Compton, D. L., Fuchs, D., Fuchs, L. S., & Bryant, J. D. (2006). Selecting at-risk readers in first grade for early intervention: A two-year longitudinal study of decision rules and procedures. *Journal of Educational Psychology, 98*(2), 394–409.

Espin, C. A., Weissenburger, J. W., & Benson, B. J. (2004). Assessing the writing performance of students in special education. *Exceptionality, 12*(1), 55–67.

Fewster, S., & MacMillan, P. (2002). School-based evidence for the validity of curriculum-based measurement of reading and writing. *Remedial & Special Education, 23,* 149–157.

Fuchs, D., & Fuchs, L. (2009). Responsiveness to Intervention: Multilevel assessment and instruction as early intervention and disability identification. *Reading Teacher, 63,* 250–252.

Fuchs, D., & Fuchs, L. S. (2006). Introduction to Response to Intervention: What, why, and how valid is it? *Reading Research Quarterly, 41,* 93–99.

Gansle, K., Noell, G., VanDerHeyden, A., Slider, N., Hoffpauir, L., & Whitmarch, E. (2004). An examination of the criterion validity and sensitivity to brief intervention of alternate curriculum-based measures of writing skill. *Psychology in the Schools, 41,* 291–300.

Glover, T. A. (2010). Key RTI service delivery components: Considerations for research-informed practice. In T. A. Glover & S. Vaughn (Eds.), *The promise of Response to Intervention: Evaluating current science and practice* (pp. 7–22). New York, NY: Guilford Press.

Graham, S., & Harris, K. R. (1989). Improving learning disabled students' skills at composing essays: Self-instructional strategy training. *Exceptional Children, 56,* 201–214.

Graham, S., & Harris, K. R. (2005). *Writing better.* Baltimore, MD: Brookes.

Graham, S., & Perin, D. (2007). A meta-analysis of writing instruction for adolescent students. *Journal of Educational Psychology, 99,* 445–476.

Harlacher, J. E., Walker, N. J., & Sanford, A. K. (2010). The "I" in RTI: Research-based factors for intensifying instruction. *Teaching Exceptional Children, 42*(6), 30–38.

Harris, K., & Graham, S. (1996a). Memo to constructivists: Skills count, too. *Educational Leadership, 53,* 26–29.

Harris, K., & Graham, S. (1996b). *Making the writing process work: Strategies for composition and self-regulation* (2nd ed.). Cambridge, MA: Brookline Books.

Harris, K. R. (1982). Cognitive-behavior modification: Application with exceptional students. *Focus on Exceptional Children, 15*(2), 1–16.

Harris, K. R., Graham. S., & Mason, L. (2006). Improving the writing knowledge and motivation of struggling young writers: Effects of self-regulated strategy development with and without peer support. *American Educational Research Journal, 43,* 295–340.

Harris. K., Graham, S., Mason, L., & Friedlander. B. (2008). *Powerful writing strategies for all students.* Baltimore, MD: Brookes.

Hessler, T., & Konrad, M. (2008). Using curriculum based measure to drive IEPs and instruction in written expression. *Teaching Exceptional Children, 41,* 28–37.

Individuals with Disabilities Education Improvement Act, Pub. Law 108-446 (December 3, 2004).

Lembke, E., Garman, C., Deno, S., & Stecker, R. (2010). One elementary school's implementation of Response to Intervention (RTI). *Reading & Writing Quarterly, 26,* 361–373.

Mercer, C. D., & Mercer, A. R. (1989). *Teaching students with learning problems.* Columbus, OH: Merrill.

Newcomer, P., Nodine, B., & Barenbaum, E. (1988). Teaching writing to exceptional children: Reaction and recommendations. *Exceptional Children, 20,* 559–564.

O'Fiesh, N. (2006). Response to Intervention and the identification of specific learning disabilities: Why we need comprehensive evaluations as part of the process. *Psychology in the Schools, 43,* 883–888.

Polloway, E. A., & Smith, J. E. (1982). *Teaching language skills to exceptional learners.* Denver, CO: Love Publishing.

Reschly, D. J. (2005). LD identification: Primary intervention, secondary intervention, then what? *Journal of Learning Disabilities, 38,* 510–515.

Rogers, L., & Graham, S. (2008). A meta-analysis of single subject design writing intervention research. *Journal of Educational Psychology, 100,* 879–906.

Saddler, B., & Graham, S. (2005). The effects of peer-assisted sentence combining instruction on the writing of more and less skilled young writers. *Journal of Educational Psychology, 97*(1), 43–54.

Saddler, B., & Preschern, J. (2007). Improving sentence writing ability through sentence-combining practice. *Teaching Exceptional Children, 39*(3), 6–11.

Salahu-Din, D., Persky, H., & Miller, J. (2008). *The nation's report card: Writing 2007* (NCES 2008–468). Washington, DC: National Center for Education Statistics, Institute of Education Sciences, U.S. Department of Education.

Scanlon, D., Vellutino, D., Small, S., Fanuele, D., & Sweeney, J. (2005). Severe reading difficulties. Can they be prevented? A comparison of prevention and intervention approaches. *Exceptionality, 13,* 209–227.

Spandel, V. (2008). *Creating writers through 6-trait writing assessment and instruction* (5th ed.). Columbus, OH: Allyn & Bacon.

Tindal, G., & Hasbrouck, J. (1991). Analyzing student writing to develop instructional strategies. *Learning Disabilities Research & Practice, 6,* 237–245.

Vaughn, S., & Fuchs, L. S. (2006). A response to "Competing views: A dialogue on Response to Intervention." *Assessment for Effective Intervention, 32*(1), 58–61. doi: 10.1177/15345084060320010801

Wong, B. Y. L. (2000). Writing strategies instruction for expository essays for adolescents with and without learning disabilities. *Topics in Language Disorders, 20,* 29–44.

Using
RtI in the Mathematics Classroom

Diane Pedrotty Bryant and Brian R. Bryant

In today's classrooms, it is important that mathematics instruction focus on developing and supporting students' "conceptual understanding, computational fluency, and problem solving skills" as they engage in daily mathematical activities (National Mathematics Advisory Panel [NMAP], 2008). By doing so, educators are building mathematics competence and promoting successful performance across the grades, which is critical for preparing students for postsecondary education and competitive career opportunities. To promote conceptual understanding of the mathematics being taught and problem-solving abilities, core or Tier I mathematics classroom instruction should involve students investigating and learning about problem-solving strategies. Oftentimes, students should be interacting with their peers in small groups to discuss and explain their mathematical reasoning about mathematics activities (Baxter, Woodward, & Olson, 2001; National Council of Teachers of Mathematics [NCTM], 2000). In this environment, for example, teachers facilitate discussions and prompt students' thinking by asking probing or clarifying questions and helping students make connections to mathematical ideas they know, which can help solve new problems. Students need to be able to communicate effectively using mathematically precise language and multiple representations to build their knowledge about mathematical ideas through classroom interactions.

Core mathematics instruction should be responsive to the needs of *all* students, including students with mathematics difficulties and disabilities, students who are gifted and talented, and students from culturally and linguistically diverse backgrounds. Yet, we know that there is a group of students who struggle with Tier I core mathematics instruction. In addition to receiving differentiated core instruction, these struggling students may also require additional supplemental intervention, which can be conducted as part of Tier II or Tier III instruction, to improve their mathematics performance. Thus, educators are challenged each day to teach mathematical ideas as part of a multitiered approach to instruction in ways that are beneficial for all students to prepare them for more advanced mathematics course work.

This chapter describes how teachers can address the instructional needs of their students who have difficulties learning mathematical concepts and skills through a multitiered approach to instruction. We begin by describing curricula recommendations from policy makers, which should be present in all tiers of mathematics instruction. We next describe examples of teaching practices, which should also be part of any tier of instruction, that are important to help students focus on the mathematics of the lessons. We then turn our attention to discuss those students who receive mathematics core instruction but also require additional intervention to improve mathematics performance within a Response to Intervention (RtI) model. In doing so, we describe ways to collect data, provide information about effective teaching methods, and give specific examples of evidence-based strategies.

Core Mathematics Curriculum

The provision of high-quality research-based core instruction is a key ingredient of the RtI model (Mellard, 2004). Fortunately, within recent years, research-based publications have emerged that have significantly impacted the knowledge base of what should constitute mathematics curriculum content and pedagogical practices (NCTM, 2000, 2006; National Research Council [NRC], 2009), spurred by less than proficient performance on national (i.e., National Assessment of Educational Progress [NAEP], 2009) and international mathematics assessments (Gonzales et al., 2009), especially as compared to the performance of other countries (e.g., Japan, Korea, Belgium). Moreover, there is a significant emphasis on preparing students for algebra by emphasizing algebraic readiness instruction beginning in PreK and extending through eighth grade.

Algebra is considered by many as the gatekeeper for more advanced mathematics coursework and is an integral part of current college readiness efforts. As such, the NMAP (2008) indicated that in order to prepare students for algebra, schools need to (a) streamline the grades PreK–8 mathematics curriculum by emphasizing a set of topics most critical in these grades; (b) embrace the evidence about how children learn and focus on the role of "conceptual understanding, procedural fluency, and automatic recall of facts" (p. xiv) in mathematics instruction; and (c) focus on evidence-based instructional practices that include features from instructional approaches (i.e., student centered and teacher directed) that produce success in mathematical learning. In particular, a more focused grade-level curriculum is necessary to help educators better understand just how to provide a more focused curriculum. Recommendations from the NMAP's report along with NCTM's (2006) publication, *Curriculum Focal Points for Pre-Kindergarten Through Grade 8 Mathematics: A Quest for Coherence* (located at http://www.nctm.org), and the *Common Core State Standards for Mathematics* (National Governors Association Center for Best Practices & Council of Chief State School Officers, 2010; located at http://www.corestandards.org) clearly delineate how districts, curriculum developers, and mathematics specialists can analyze their grade-level mathematics content and the progressions of concepts and skills across grades.

Thus, there is a great deal of support for district leaders to examine their curriculum that constitutes core instruction for all students. Equally important are practices that teachers should embrace to instill important grade-level mathematical ideas and prerequisite knowledge for students who are lacking critical concepts and skills.

Teaching Practices That Support Mathematics Performance

A focused curriculum is important; equally important is how the curriculum is taught in an RtI multilevel approach to meeting the needs of all students. There are key teaching behaviors that can promote strong mathematical instruction. For example, a teacher should engage students in meaningful mathematical discussions, using "math talk" or the language of mathematics representations that help students develop the conceptual understanding as well as procedural knowledge of the mathematics they are studying. Students should be prompted to share their thinking aloud about their mathematical understanding and their problem-solving approaches (Gersten, Beckmann et al., 2009).

Teachers should use mathematically precise definitions of terms that are developmentally appropriate and expect students to use correct math language as well (Milgram, 2007; Wu, 2006). Students must use and talk about models of mathematics they build to represent mathematical ideas as they work in various grouping structures (e.g., small heterogeneous and same-ability groups, with peer partners, in whole group with the teacher). For instance, when using an array to model "3 groups of 4," students should take about how they set up the array to show the problem and how they manipulated the model to show the commutative property of "4 groups of 3." In yet another area, teachers should translate between verbal and symbolic statements and representations (Wu, 2005). In the following example, the verbal statement is translated to the symbolic:

Verbal: The cost, including tax, of renting a car is $83 per day plus $0.43 for each mile driven. Which equation can be used to determine c, the total cost of a rental car that has been driven m miles?
Symbolic: $C = 0.43m + 83$

Finally, teachers should make connections among mathematical ideas using previously taught ideas to help students learn more difficult concepts. For example, students can build an area model to show 4 x 3; the area model can also be used to help students understand 4 x 1/3 or 1/3 of 4. By starting with an area model of 4 x 3, the teacher can then help students use a grid (area model) to show units of 4 x 1/3. Other connections should be made to real-life contexts by applying mathematical ideas and procedures to solving problems meaningful to students. For instance, word problems can include situations such as buying video games, clothes to wear to school, or trendy collectibles; cooking; or playing sports. These real-life contexts help students connect the action of solving word problems to their background knowledge.

We have discussed components of evidence-based core instruction as recommended by policy makers and teaching practices that should be included as part of a multitiered approach to instruction for all students. However, students who do not benefit from a solid core program will likely require additional supplemental, Tier II, or more intensive intervention, Tier III, to provide the support they will need to learn the mathematical concepts and skills that are taught in core instruction. We now turn our attention to a discussion of how the RtI process can occur in school districts to support solid core instruction, which includes differentiating instruction to meet the needs of students throughout the school year as topics change. Differentiating instruction can be accomplished through various ways for all learners to take into consideration instructional needs, linguistic diversity, and factors associated with disabilities. We begin by presenting a case study as a means of explaining how the RtI model can work when teachers provide differentiated instruction as part of core instruction. For those students who do not benefit from core instruction as the only means for learning mathematics, we discuss procedures for identifying students who require additional support, such as that in Tier II or Tier III, and evidence-based teaching practices to help improve students' mathematics performance.

A Case Study of Differentiation and the Need for Supplemental Mathematics Intervention

This case study illustrates an example of core mathematics instruction for reviewing and teaching equivalent fractions. As you read the case study, notice how the teacher adjusts instruction to accommodate the learning needs of Jason. Remember that other students may require similar adjustments because of similar learning difficulties.

Case Study

Mrs. Salazar is reviewing the concept of equivalent fractions with her fourth-grade class. She opens the lesson by reviewing key background knowledge for vocabulary terms (e.g., equivalence) and concepts (e.g., fractions that are equal to or less than a whole, equal partitioning, unit fractions). She then tells students the purpose of the lesson, which is to identify equivalent fractions by using models to represent them.

To begin, Mrs. Salazar introduces the concept of equivalent fractions by having students fold paper strips (i.e., fraction strips) into parts two times. She draws fraction bars on the whiteboard to illustrate the fraction strips and asks students what they notice about the parts (e.g., they are equal parts, 1/2 is equal to 2/4, the size of the pieces gets smaller with each partition of the whole). She asks them to predict the next fraction if they were to fold the paper another time. Mrs. Salazar then uses number lines to show how fractions, such as 1/2 = 2/4 = 4/8, are equivalent. She continues to ask students what they notice about the numerator and denominator with each partition. She also asks how multiplication is used to create equivalent fractions. She then has students work in small, mixed-ability groups to find various equivalent fractions.

Mrs. Salazar provides students with graph paper to create fraction bars for their assigned fractions and paper to show their equivalent fractions using number lines. As she circulates among the small groups, she listens to group discussions as students work with the fraction bar models. She notices that one of her students, Jason, who struggles with mathematics, seems confused with the activity. She listens as he talks about how to partition the fraction bar to create equivalent fractions and show the equivalent fractions using number lines. Mrs. Salazar determines that adaptations are needed based on Jason's explanations. She models how to find equivalent fractions and decides that Jason might better conceptualize fractional parts by using the fraction strips once again. She notes in her assessment notebook the need for Jason to return to the concrete model, the paper strip, for representing equivalent fractions and for additional modeling of how to use the strip to find equivalent fractions.

Mrs. Salazar calls the small groups back together for a whole-class discussion. She calls on several students to present their answers, using the document camera and whiteboard, by explaining how they created equivalent fractions using fraction bars and number lines for their assigned fractions. She asks questions about how the students approached the task and the steps they took to complete the assignment. She asks the class probing questions such as what they noticed about the size of the pieces with each partition, what portions are the same on the fraction bar (e.g., 1/2 = 4/8), and how they used multiplication to demonstrate that their fractions were equivalent.

She concludes the lesson by providing a daily check or quiz on the lesson's objectives that students complete independently. Mrs. Salazar checks all papers with particular attention to those students who need extra help with the concept and may continue to need differentiated instruction (e.g., changing the materials, providing more specific instruction) in future lessons. She notes in her assessment record sheet that Jason scored only 40% correct; thus, he did not achieve the mastery score of 90% accuracy for the day's lesson despite the differentiated support. Moreover, in terms of Jason's performance over time, he continued to lag significantly behind his peers on regular assessments, and he scored only slightly above the cut score on the fall screening for mathematics difficulties.

Case study analysis. Jason is a fourth-grade student who struggles with understanding equivalent fractions. Mrs. Salazar also knew through a timed facts test that he has difficulties with the ability to quickly recall multiplication and division facts, which is a necessary skill for more advanced work such as identifying equivalent fractions (NCTM, 2009). During small-group work, Mrs. Salazar used an observation technique to gather information about Jason as he worked with his peers on an equivalent fractions activity. Mrs. Salazar realized that Jason required differentiated or adapted instruction to benefit from group work. Although adaptations were provided, Jason was not sufficiently responding to instruction, and thus was not keeping up with his peers. In reviewing her assessment notebook, Mrs. Salazar concluded that Jason's overall mathematics performance was well below that of the rest of the class.

Mrs. Salazar also consulted with Jason's third-grade teacher about his mathematics performance across the previous year, particularly with concepts and skills related to fractions. In the area of multiplication and division facts, Jason needed extra practice using pictorial representations, such as arrays and area models, to demonstrate his understanding of the meaning of multiplication and with partitioning and equal sharing to represent division. According to the teacher, he struggled with learning and remembering strategies for basic multiplication facts and the related division facts. Difficulty with learning and retrieving arithmetic facts quickly is a typical problem among students who struggle with mathematics. According to Geary (2004), challenges with arithmetic facts are persistent with and characteristic of a developmental difference that may be some form of a memory or cognitive deficit.

In the area of fractions, his teacher explained that Jason had problems using number line representations to compare fractions and benefitted from using concrete models such as fraction strips. The teacher emphasized that Jason needed extra practice and instructional adaptations for the lesson being taught, yet he continued to lag behind his peers on mathematics performance measures such as the district's curriculum-based assessments, which were conducted at 6-week intervals. According to Hecht, Vagi, and Torgesen (2007), solving problems with fractions is a persistent difficulty exhibited by students with mathematics difficulties and represents a major barrier for learning higher-order math topics in later school years. Moreover, fundamental understandings of fractions and decimals must be mastered to prepare students for more challenging work (e.g., computation that includes fractions, proportional reasoning, algebra; Brown & Quinn, 2007; NMAP, 2008). Unfortunately, studies have shown that students with mathematics difficulties demonstrate a weak understanding of fraction equivalency (Mazzocco & Devlin, 2008).

Collecting appropriate data. In our case study, as part of core instruction, Mrs. Salazar observed her students' performance while engaged in a small-group activity on creating equivalent fractions. Teachers gather assessment information every time they watch students engage in their assignments. In assessment terminology, this is called observation, and it involves not only watching students do something, but also them thinking about what they are doing, why they are doing specific things, and what the doing means for the students and those around them. Teachers' observations occur over time and are ongoing, which makes them a valuable tool to record academic concerns, successes, and the need for adaptations or differentiation (Venn, 2004).

Mrs. Salazar could have also used a clinical interview technique to more specifically determine Jason's understanding of creating equivalent fractions. The clinical interview technique can be used to identify, as much as possible, the strategies students use to solve mathematics problems (McLoughlin & Lewis, 2005). The clinical interview approach would include asking Jason to think aloud as he completes the task of creating fractions bars for fractions equivalent to 1/2, in this case. Mrs. Salazar would ask Jason to explain how he would go about creating one fraction that is equivalent to 1/2. By observing his approach to the task and listening to him think aloud, Mrs. Salazar could ask more probing questions that tap prerequisite knowledge about the task and prompt Jason to solve the task. For example, she could ask: (a) "If we start with a whole, how do we partition the whole into halves?" (b) "What do we know about the size of each partition in relation to the other parts?" (c) "How can you partition 1/2 to show an equivalent fraction?" (d) "What happens to the size of the pieces as you partition the fraction bar?" and (e) "How do we know that 2/4 is equal to 1/2?"

Observations and clinical interviews are effective ways to learn more about student understanding of mathematical concepts, skills, and tasks. Additionally, as part of RtI, universal screening to identify students who are manifesting significant difficulties in math compared to their peers and progress monitoring with supplemental intervention tutoring and small group work are needed.

Universal screening to determine students who qualify for supplemental Tier II or Tier III intervention. In Mrs. Salazar's school district, as part of its RtI model, universal screening of mathematical concepts and applications is conducted with all students in the fall, and further benchmark assessments of similar concepts and applications are conducted in the winter and spring. Examples of universal screening and progress monitoring measures can be found at the National Center on Response to Intervention website (http://www.rti4success.org/progressMonitoringTools).

Using data to support decisions is a key component of RtI. In the fall, results from the universal screening of mathematics difficulties showed that Jason scored slightly above the school district's cut score (25th percentile) for qualifying for supplemental intervention, Tier II in the district's RtI model. Although he did not qualify for supplemental intervention, his performance was monitored carefully because his score was only slightly above the cut score for Tier II intervention. The winter benchmark testing results showed Jason now performing below the 25th percentile cut score, and thus qualifying for Tier II intervention, which in Mrs. Salazar's school is conducted by a math interventionist.

Progress monitoring of supplemental Tier II or Tier III intervention. Educators must have access to progress-monitoring techniques that can be easily and reliably used to identify students in need of intervention and to determine their response to intensive instruction (Bryant, Smith, & Bryant, 2008). Progress-monitoring data not only help the Tier II math interventionist identify whether students are working toward their goal, but also inform the instruction that follows. For example, progress monitoring data can inform grouping structures for Tier II intervention. Small groups of students who demonstrate persistent difficulties in an area can be grouped in same-ability groups of three to six students. This grouping structure enables teachers to systematically target specific individual needs by providing multiple opportunities for students to actively engage in much-needed practice and correcting errors that might go undetected in whole-group or small-group mixed-ability work.

Daily Checks are one aspect of progress monitoring to determine whether the student met the daily objective of the lesson (Bryant & Bryant, 2010; Cuillos, SoRelle, Kim, Seo, & Bryant, 2011). By examining Jason's performance on Daily Checks that were representative of the day's instructional activity (i.e., identifying, showing, and writing equivalent fractions), the Tier II math interventionist can determine whether Jason demonstrated an understanding of what was taught. If Jason fared well, the next lesson can be delivered as written. However, if Jason did not meet the objective, the math interventionist should review the previous day's lesson during the next day's warm-up. Because much of mathematics is cumulative, that is, builds upon previously learned information, conducting the next lesson without taking into account Jason's lack of previous understanding diminishes the chances that Jason will understand the new lesson, which builds upon the lesson of the previous day. Thus, data from the Daily Check inform instruction for the next day; that is, some information needs to be retaught or reviewed.

Most progress-monitoring programs also use measures that are administered periodically (often biweekly) to see how the students are progressing toward their annual goal (Bryant & Bryant, 2010; Cuillos et al., 2011). In our work, we call those measures Aim Checks. The math interventionist created a graph for Jason, on which she placed the number of items correct on the y-axis and the Aim Check administrations along the x-axis (see Figure 10.1). Jason's initial universal screening score was recorded with a dot, and an additional dot was placed representing the end of year benchmark score. Finally, the math interventionist drew a line connecting the two points. This aim line shows the progress that Jason must make during intervention to meet the end of year goal and, thus exit Tier II intervention.

Every 2 weeks the math interventionist administers the progress monitoring measure and records Jason's scores. In Figure 10.1, we show Jason's performance on three Aim Checks, showing satisfactory progress along the aim line. As long as he is continuing to progress adequately toward the benchmark, that is, scoring closer to where the aim line shows he should be scoring, intervention continues as is. However, if Jason were to plateau over a couple of weeks and not approach the aim line, the intervention would be changed. For example, the math interventionist might use different materials for representing mathematical concepts, or instructional objectives might be task analyzed to provide smaller chunks in content for students to learn in the day's lesson.

Daily Checks and Aim Checks provide the math interventionist with useful data that can be used to demonstrate Jason's knowledge of concepts and skills learned daily, and also to provide evidence that Jason is progressing satisfactorily toward his goal. When progress monitoring demonstrates that Jason is not sufficiently benefiting from the intervention, the math interventionist can alter the intervention to help Jason learn the skills that are being taught.

Effective Teaching Methods for Tier II and Tier III Intervention

In this section, we describe the use of explicit and systematic instruction, which can be used to teach mathematical concepts and skills. Next,

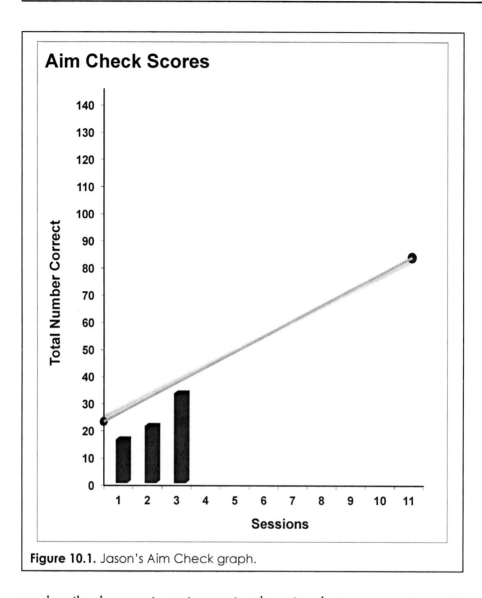

Figure 10.1. Jason's Aim Check graph.

we describe the steps in an instructional routine that uses concrete, semi-concrete (e.g., pictures, tallies), and abstract (e.g., symbols) representations to teach many mathematical concepts. Finally, we discuss the use of visual representations that should be included in mathematics instruction as a means for helping to build conceptual understanding for abstract mathematical ideas. These procedures and the use of visual representations are illustrated in the Evidence-Based Strategies and Implementation Steps section.

Explicit and Systematic Instruction

The use of explicit and systematic instruction is well documented for teaching mathematical concepts and skills including computation and word problems (Baker, Gersten, & Lee, 2002; Butler, Miller, Crehan, Babbitt, & Pierce, 2003; Gersten, Chard et al. 2009; Swanson, Hoskyn, & Lee, 1999) and research studies have shown strong evidence for the use of these procedures (Gersten, Beckmann et al., 2009; Swanson, Hoskyn, & Lee, 1999). Both lessons in the next section employ the critical features of explicit and systematic instruction, which involve (Stein, Kinder, Silbert, & Carnine, 2006):

> providing cumulative review of previous concepts,
> modeling or demonstrating how to solve problems,
> thinking aloud the procedures for solving problems or using cognitive strategies,
> engaging students in guided practice with sufficient opportunities to practice new skills and concepts,
> providing error correction procedures to correct mistakes and mathematical misunderstandings, and
> providing independent practice (e.g., quizzes, homework) that do not require direct teacher supervision or guidance.

As part of systematic, explicit instruction for teaching a new concept, skill, or strategy, teachers initially provide structure and assistance (i.e., scaffolding instruction) as students practice under their guidance. As students become more adept with the instruction, the teacher fades assistance (e.g., cues, prompts, manipulatives, stating the steps of a strategy), allowing the student to take more responsibility for the learning.

Concrete–Semi-Concrete–Abstract (CSA) Teaching Sequence

CSA is another instructional routine that has been applied in studies to teach basic facts (Miller & Mercer, 1993) and fractions (Butler et al., 2003) to students with mathematics difficulties. The instructional routine includes the following steps, which are taught to criterion (e.g., 90% accuracy):

> Step 1: Concrete Representation
  o Use manipulatives to represent number concepts or skills (e.g., Base 10 models or bean sticks to represent place value).

- > Step 2: Semiconcrete Representation
  - o Use tally marks or pictures to illustrate the concept or skill.
- > Step 3: Abstract Representation
  - o Provide problems that include numbers similar to those presented in Step 1 and Step 2.

Visual Representations

Visual representations are concrete models, such as Base 10 models and counters, and pictorial depictions, such as drawings, number lines, tallies, and ten frames, that are intended to promote conceptual understanding of mathematical ideas. Gersten, Beckmann et al. (2009) explained that the relationships between visual representations and abstract symbols (e.g., numbers, < and > signs) could strengthen students' understanding of mathematical concepts. For example, when teaching fractions, the use of the number line is highly recommended as a "central representational tool" to help build students' conceptual understanding (Siegler et al., 2010, p.1). Moreover, Gersten, Chard et al. (2009) found positive, moderate effects for the use of visual representations in mathematics instruction and positive effects on mathematics performance when the use of visual representations was paired with explicit and systematic instruction. Thus, mathematics instruction should include teaching students how to visually represent mathematical ideas and to translate these representations into abstract symbols.

Evidence-Based Strategies and Implementation Steps

In this section, we present examples of evidence-based strategies and implementation steps that interventionists can use to teach multiplication and division facts and equivalent fractions. To teach multiplication and division facts to middle school students with learning difficulties, Harris, Miller, and Mercer (1995) used the CRA (similar to CSA) sequence. They began with concrete objects to build conceptual understanding, including paper plates to represent groups and plastic counting discs to show the objects in each group. From there they used visual representations by drawing pictures of boxes with dots or tallies to show the multiplication problems. After six lessons at the concrete and representational levels, the students moved to the abstract and symbolic level. A mnemonic strategy was taught to help students remember how to solve the problems.

The DRAW strategy is a mnemonic intended to help students recall the steps of a problem solution. The strategy includes a mnemonic in which each letter of the word signals a procedure for students to follow (e.g., D = Discover the sign). The mnemonic features of the DRAW strategy are described in detail below.

Explicit and systematic practices were used as part of the CRA sequence along with concrete objects and pictures; repetition was used with rule instruction. A total of 21 lessons over 8 weeks were conducted with all of the students. As part of each lesson, students independently completed a Learning Sheet with 10 problems; the lesson was retaught to students who did not achieve a score of at least 80% accuracy. Additional student progress-monitoring data included completion of a Multiplication Minute sheet under timed conditions throughout the study.

Implementation Steps for the DRAW Strategy

The teacher (a) explained the purpose of the lesson; (b) modeled, using "think aloud," how to use the mnemonic to solve a problem; and (c) taught students the mnemonic (i.e., "say the mnemonic, name the letters, and tell what action to do for each letter"). The following steps were used to teach students the strategy.

> **D** = Discover the sign (The student looks at the sign to figure out the operation.)
> **R** = Read the problem (The student says the problem aloud.)
> **A** = Answer or draw and check (The student thinks of the answer or draws tallies to solve the problem.)
> **W** = Write the answer. (The student writes the answer in the answer space.)

Once students set up the problem, they use DRAW to solve the computation. The goal is that students learn the mnemonic steps and apply them independently to successfully solve both multiplication and word problems. The results of this study showed that all students with learning difficulties improved their performance ranging in improvement from 50–85 percentage points.

To teach equivalent fractions, we provide an example of a lesson (see Appendix 10A) including the use of area models and paper strips (i.e., visual representation).

The first page of the lesson includes information for the teacher including the lesson number, the lesson objectives, and instructional materials. Page 2 includes references to the Cumulative Review, the Preview, and ways to Engage Prior/Informal Knowledge. The DM letters refer to Display Masters. Beginning on page 3, instructions for how to demonstrate the content to the students are provided. On page 6, activities are provided to help students practice the concepts for the lesson, and on page 7, the independent practice is featured. Finally, the lesson concludes with a closure. The lesson also includes Teacher Notes to provide sideline information for teachers about the lessons and a Watch For to alert teachers to possible misconceptions that should be corrected.

Conclusion

In this chapter, we provided information about how RtI is implemented within the context of teaching mathematics to students who demonstrate persistent difficulties with certain aspects of the core curriculum and instruction. We framed our discussion around a case study of Jason, who despite efforts to address his needs as part of core instruction continued to manifest difficulties that affected his mathematics performance. We chose fractions instruction as a difficult topic for Jason because understanding fractions is a critical readiness topic for algebra (NMAP, 2008).

Collecting appropriate data using universal screening measures to identify struggling students and progress monitoring measures to frequently assess the effects of Tier II or Tier III intervention are important aspects of RtI. Examples of ways to collect data were provided as a means for monitoring progress and making instructional decisions. Three effective teaching methods were presented including explicit and systematic instruction, the CSA instructional routine, and the use of visual representations. Finally, evidence-based strategies and implementation steps focused on an example for teaching equivalent fractions and multiplication and division facts. Specific steps and instructional procedures were featured in both examples.

Mathematics instruction is a major component of any RtI model in school districts. Educators must identify ways to ensure that all students—struggling, typical, and gifted students—benefit from mathematics instruction. A multilevel approach provides more differentiated intervention to those students who are most in need of instructional support to achieve success in mathematics.

Chapter 10, Appendix A

EQUIVALENT FRACTIONS

Lesson 7: Model Equivalent Fractions with Area Models

Lesson Objectives

- Students will identify equivalent fractions represented as area models.

- Students will model and visually represent equivalent fractions by folding paper strips.

- Students will create an equivalent fraction, given a fraction represented as an area model.

Instructional Materials

Material	Quantity	Description
How Am I Doing? graph	1 per student	
Crayons, markers, or colored pencils	1 per student	
Display Masters	1 each	• Demonstrate: Key Ideas: Model Equivalent Fractions with Area Models • Engage Prior/Informal Knowledge: Area Model of a Fraction
Master	1 each	• Demonstrate: Paper Strips 1
Handouts	1 per student	• Cumulative Review • Paper Strips 2 • Practice • Independent Practice
Answer Keys	1 each	• Cumulative Review • Practice • Independent Practice

1 of 8

Lesson 7: Model Equivalent Fractions
with Area Models

EQUIVALENT FRACTIONS

Cumulative Review

Have students answer the questions on the Cumulative Review handout. Go over the answers. Correct misconceptions. Have students use a colored pencil to make corrections as needed. Collect student papers to determine who needs additional instruction.

Preview

This lesson will build on students' conceptual knowledge of fractions. Students will model and visually represent equivalent fractions by folding paper strips. Students will use the knowledge taught in this lesson when identifying and computing equivalent fractions.

TEACHER NOTE
Students can use the same strips in subsequent lessons, so you may want to store them for later use.

Display and introduce through a brief explanation the key ideas for this lesson:

- Fractions are equivalent if they represent the same amount of area.

- Equivalent fractions represent the same value

Use the Key Ideas: Model Equivalent Fractions with Area Models **DM** display master as needed.

Engage Prior/Informal Knowledge

To open the lesson, present questions to activate students' background knowledge related to the content to be taught in this lesson. Display the fraction $\frac{7}{3}$ as an area model. Use

©2011 The University of Texas System/The University of Texas at Austin

203

the Area Model of a Fraction **DM** display master as needed. Be sure students understand that each strip shown represents 1 whole. Ask students questions such as:

- What fraction is shown? ($\frac{7}{3}$)

- For the fraction shown, is it less than, equal to, or greater than 1? (greater than 1)

If students cannot answer these questions, stop and explicitly teach the material.

Demonstrate

1. Model equivalent fractions using paper strips.

Use paper strips cut from the Paper Strips 1 master.

Think aloud as you perform each step. First, demonstrate each step, and then help students do the same step.

Show students the paper strip.

> **Say:** *What fraction does this strip represent? (1 or 1 whole)*

If students do not say 1, guide them to understand that the paper strip is one whole.

> **Say:** *I want to represent the fraction $\frac{1}{2}$.*

> **Say:** *I am folding my paper strip in half. Now fold yours in half.*

> **Say:** *I am going to mark the crease by drawing a line. Fold and mark the crease on your paper strip.*

Lesson 7: Model Equivalent Fractions
with Area Models

EQUIVALENT FRACTIONS

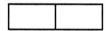

Say: *I am going to shade one section of my strip. You shade yours.*

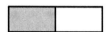

Say: *Since we have shaded one part out of 2 equal parts, we can say the shaded part represents $\frac{1}{2}$.*

Say: *The shaded portion of the paper strip is $\frac{1}{2}$. I am labeling the shaded part as $\frac{1}{2}$.*

Be sure students are comfortable with the idea that the shaded portion of the strip represents $\frac{1}{2}$ before you go on.

Say: *We are going to fold our strips in half again.*

Refold the strip in half and then, fold in half again.

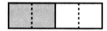

Say: *Mark the new creases with a line.*

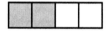

Say: *We have not changed the size of the shaded part of our strip, but we can give it a new name. What name do you think we could use?*

TEACHER NOTE
Remind students that fractions can be used to describe the area shaded because the parts have equal areas.

4 of 8

©2011 The University of Texas System/The University of Texas at Austin

205

Help the students understand that the shaded part could now be represented by the fraction $\frac{2}{4}$.

> **Say**: *Did we change the size of the shaded portion?*
> *(No.)*

Help students understand that the number of parts is different, but the size (area) of the shaded portion of the paper strip does not change.

> **Say**: *Since, the size of the shaded part of the paper does not change: $\frac{1}{2}$ and $\frac{2}{4}$ are equal; $\frac{1}{2}$ and $\frac{2}{4}$ can be called equivalent fractions.*

Label the shaded part of the strip with $\frac{2}{4}$.

2. Model equivalent fractions by illustrating equivalent fractions.

Help students draw what they have done on paper.

Have students draw a separate picture for each fraction made.

3. Model 3 equivalent fractions using paper strips and drawings.

Repeat the process to create $\frac{4}{8}$, but fold the strip in half horizontally.

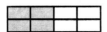

> **Say**: *What fractions can represent the shaded part now?*

TEACHER NOTE
Have students who have trouble drawing free hand use the Paper Strips 2 handout or grid paper to draw and shade what they have just done.

TEACHER NOTE
Students may be able to more easily visualize equivalent fractions if the picture for $\frac{2}{4}$ is drawn directly beneath the picture for $\frac{1}{2}$.

Help students understand that the number of parts is different, but the area of the shaded portion of the paper strip does not change.

Say: *The area of the shaded part does not change so $\frac{1}{2}$, $\frac{2}{4}$, and $\frac{4}{8}$ are equivalent fractions; they all represent the same area.*

Label the strip with the fraction $\frac{4}{8}$.

Help students create a picture of $\frac{4}{8}$.

Say: *When we folded our strip to make $\frac{1}{2}$ into $\frac{2}{4}$, what happened to the number of parts? What about when we folded to make $\frac{4}{8}$?*

Guide students to notice that the total number of equal parts is doubled, but the area of each part is smaller.

Repeat the process to model equivalent fractions for a fraction greater than 1, such as $\frac{3}{2}$.

TEACHER NOTE
If you have students who would benefit from additional examples of equivalent fractions, such as $\frac{1}{3}$, $\frac{2}{6}$, $\frac{4}{12}$, repeat the process as needed.

Practice

For each practice activity, provide detailed feedback to students, highlighting what was done correctly and what needs improvement. Provide opportunities for students to correct their errors. Collect student work to review and monitor student progress.

Activity 1: Help students draw pictures of equivalent fractions, starting with fractions such as $\frac{3}{4}$, $\frac{7}{2}$, and $\frac{4}{2}$. Select a few students to verbalize their reasoning. Listen for the development of any misconceptions within the reasoning. Be alert for students who still need to physically fold paper.

As students are working ask questions such as:

- What fraction of the strip is shaded?

- When you folded it, what fraction of the strip was shaded?

- When you folded it again, what fraction of the strip was shaded?

- What is a fraction equivalent to...?

- What is another fraction equivalent to...?

Activity 2: Have students work in pairs or small groups to complete the activity on the Practice handout. Have students verbalize their reasoning for each step in the process to their partners. Listen for the development of any misconceptions within the reasoning.

WATCH FOR

Some students may believe that fractions are equivalent only when they look identical or have the same number of selected parts. Tell students that because the same amount of area is represented, the fractions may look different but they have the same value.

Independent Practice

1. Have students work independently to complete the activity on the Independent Practice handout.

2. Go over the answers (students self-check and correct, using a colored pencil).

3. Have students record the number correct in the box and complete their How Am I Doing? graph.

4. Collect the papers to review and monitor student progress.

©2011 The University of Texas System/The University of Texas at Austin

Lesson 7: Model Equivalent Fractions
with Area Models

EQUIVALENT FRACTIONS

Closure

Review the key ideas. Have students provide examples from the lesson. Ask
questions such as:

- How would you describe to someone else what we did to create equivalent
  fractions?

- How can you tell if two fractions are equivalent when comparing their area
  model representations?

Clear up any misconceptions. Students who believe equivalent fractions must
look the same or have the same number of selected parts need additional
instruction.

References

Baker, S., Gersten, R., & Lee, D. (2002). A synthesis of empirical research on teaching mathematics to low-achieving students. *The Elementary School Journal, 103,* 51–73.

Baxter, J., Woodward, J., & Olson, D. (2001). Effects of reform-based mathematics instruction in five third grade classrooms. *Elementary School Journal, 101,* 529–548.

Brown, G., & Quinn, R. J. (2007). Investigating the relationship between fraction proficiency and success in algebra. *Australian Mathematics Teacher, 63*(4), 8–15.

Bryant, D. P., & Bryant, B. R. (2010, October). *Early mathematics assessment and intervention.* Paper presented at the Division for Learning Disabilities Conference, Baltimore, MD.

Bryant, D. P., Smith, D. D., & Bryant, B. R. (2008). *Teaching students with special needs in inclusive classrooms.* Boston, MA: Allyn & Bacon.

Butler, F. M., Miller, S. P., Crehan, K., Babbitt, B., & Pierce, T. (2003). Fraction instruction for students with mathematics disabilities: Comparing two teaching sequences. *Learning Disabilities Research & Practice, 18*(2), 99–111. doi:10.1111/1540-5826.00066

Cuillos, S., SoRelle, D., Kim, S. A., Seo, Y. J., & Bryant, B. R. (2011). Monitoring student response to mathematics intervention: Using data to inform tier 3 intervention. *Intervention in School and Clinic.* Retrieved from http://isc.Sagepub.com/content/early/recent doi: 10.1177/1053451211414188

Geary, D. C. (2004). Mathematics and learning disabilities. *Journal of Learning Disabilities, 37,* 4–15.

Gersten, R., Beckmann, S., Clarke, B., Foegen, A., Marsh, L., Star, J. R., & Witzel, B. (2009). *Assisting students struggling with mathematics: Response to Intervention (RtI) for elementary and middle schools* (NCEE 2009-4060). Washington, DC: National Center for Education Evaluation and Regional Assistance, Institute of Education Sciences, U.S. Department of Education. Retrieved from http://ies.ed.gov/ncee/wwc/publications/practiceguides

Gersten, R., Chard, D., Jayanthi, M., Baker, S., Morphy, P., & Flojo, J. (2009). Mathematics instruction for students with learning disabilities: A meta-analysis of instructional components. *Review of Educational Research, 79,* 1202–1242.

Gonzales, P., Williams, T., Jocelyn, L., Roey, S., Kastberg, D., & Brenwald, S. (2009). *Highlights from the TIMSS 2007: Mathematics and science achievement of U.S. fourth- and eighth-grade students in an international context.* Washington, DC: National Center for Education Statistics.

Harris, C. A., Miller, S. P., & Mercer, C. D. (1995). Teaching initial multiplication skills to students with disabilities in general education classrooms. *Learning Disabilities Research & Practice, 10,* 180–195.

Hecht, S. A., Vagi, K. J., & Torgesen, J. K. (2007). Fraction skills and proportional reasoning. In D. B. Berch & M. M. M. Mazzocco (Eds.), *Why is math so hard for some children?* (pp. 121–132). Baltimore, MD: Brookes.

Mazzocco, M. M. M., & Devlin, K. T. (2008). Parts and holes: Gaps in rational number sense in children with vs. without mathematical learning disability. *Developmental Science, 11,* 681–691.

McLoughlin, J. A., & Lewis, R. B. (2005). *Assessing students with special needs* (6th ed.). Upper Saddle River, NJ: Pearson.

Mellard, D. (2004). *Understanding Responsiveness to Intervention in learning disabilities determination.* Retrieved from http:www.nrcld.org/publications/papers/mellard.pdf

Milgram, R. J. (2007). What are some of the potential problems of the various "New Math" techniques being taught in some American schools? *Teachers College Record.* Retrieved from http://www.tcrecord.org/content.asp?contentid=14560

Miller, S. P., & Mercer, C. D. (1993). Using data to learn about concrete-semiconcrete-abstract instruction for students with math disabilities. *Learning Disabilities Research & Practice, 8,* 89–96.

National Assessment of Education Progress. (2009). *The nation's report card.* Washington, DC: Author.

National Council of Teachers of Mathematics. (2000). *Principles and standards for school mathematics.* Reston, VA: Author.

National Council of Teachers of Mathematics. (2006). *Curriculum focal points for prekindergarten through grade 8 mathematics: A quest for coherence.* Reston, VA: Author.

National Council of Teachers of Mathematics. (2009). *Focus in grade 3.* Reston, VA: Author.

National Governors Association Center for Best Practices, & Council of Chief State School Officers. (2010). *Common core state standards.* Common Core State Initiative. Retrieved from http://www.core standards.org

National Mathematics Advisory Panel. (2008). *Foundations for success: The final report of the National Mathematics Advisory Panel.* Washington, DC: U.S. Department of Education.

National Research Council. (2009). *Mathematic learning in early childhood: Paths toward excellence and equity.* Washington, DC: Author.

Siegler, R., Carpenter, T., Fennell, F., Geary, D., Lewis, J., Okamoto, Y., . . . & Wray, J. (2010). *Developing effective fractions instruction for kindergarten through 8th grade: A practice guide* (NCEE #2010-4039). Washington, DC: National Center for Education Evaluation and Regional Assistance, Institute of Education Sciences, U.S. Department of Education. Retrieved from http://whatworks.ed.gov/publications/practiceguides

Stein, M., Kinder, D., Silbert, J., & Carnine, D. W. (2006). *Designing effective mathematics instruction: A direct instruction approach* (4th ed.). Upper Saddle, NJ: Prentice Hall.

Swanson, H. L., Hoskyn, M., & Lee, C. (1999). *Interventions for students with learning disabilities: A meta-analysis of treatment outcomes.* New York, NY: Guilford Press.

Venn, J. J. (2004). *Assessing students with special needs.* Upper Saddle River, NJ: Pearson.

Woodward, J. (2006). Developing automaticity in multiplication facts: Integrating strategy instruction with timed practice drills. *Learning Disability Quarterly, 29,* 269–289.

Wu, H. (2005). *Must content dictate pedagogy in mathematics education?* Berkeley: University of California.

Wu, H. (2006). *Professional development: The hard work of learning mathematics.* Berkeley: University of California.

CHAPTER 11

Using
RtI in the Science Classroom

Kullaya Kosuwan, Jeffrey P. Bakken, and Barbara M. Fulk

Case Study

Ted was always the first student to enter the seventh-grade science class. In fact, he generally entered the science classroom shortly after the passing period began, several minutes before the final bell. His difficulties remembering his combination, combined with poor motor skills when trying to manage the lock, resulted in his carrying all of his books in his backpack, which greatly enhanced his timeliness to class. Ted also preferred chatting with his science teacher, Mrs. Torres, to any peer interactions, which further motivated him to hurry to science class.

Ted loved the demonstrations as well as the lab activities in science. He carefully listened and tried to meaningfully contribute during demonstrations and discussions. He and his father spent lots of time together tending their flower and vegetable gardens, which made the plant science chapters particularly interesting to Ted. He could not read much of the science text, although he could often make good sense of diagrams and tables. As the school year progressed, however, Ted's reading, spelling, and writing difficulties resulted in failing grades on tests and written projects. Mrs. Torres appreciated Ted's interest and motivation for science. Nonetheless, she became increasingly concerned about ways to accommodate Ted and other low-achieving readers in her classes so they could demonstrate sufficient progress on science tests mandated by No Child Left Behind.

As an active participant on the seventh-grade faculty team, Mrs. Torres was quite interested in extending the school's Response to Intervention (RtI) model to students in her science classes. Ted was a perfect candidate for a three-tiered intervention plan in science.

Science Instruction

Making sure that all students have access to quality science curriculum and instruction has never been more important than it is today. Children have a natural curiosity about the world, and science education provides a significant opportunity for them to have authentic learning experiences and develop insights into the world around them. Science education helps students develop problem-solving skills and understanding of cause-and-effect relationships as well as making them more well-rounded individuals. In addition, institutions of higher education are now requiring more science coursework for potential students.

The National Science Teachers Association, which created the National Science Education Standards with the National Research Council in 1996, emphasized that the standards are written for and apply to *all* students regardless of age, gender, cultural or ethnic background, or disabilities. In addition, the Individuals with Disabilities Education Improvement Act (2004) includes the expectation that students with physical, mental, sensory, and emotional disabilities will have access to the general education curriculum and be included in the general instructional arena. Nationally the No Child Left Behind Act (2001) has placed science in the forefront by requiring that beginning in 2007–2008 all students, including those with disabilities, be administered tests in science achievement at least once in grades 3–5, 6–9, and 10–12.

Significant research has been conducted to investigate the effect of a variety of approaches and techniques in teaching and learning science. Scruggs and Mastropieri (2007) reviewed 20 years of literature and research on science education for students with disabilities. Their effort and the efforts of other researchers lend critical information to those who make curricular and instructional decisions about how best to teach students with disabilities. Different curriculum and instructional approaches are likely to have different results and implications for students with disabilities depending on their particular strengths and needs. In addition, students who do not have identified disabilities may also benefit from the understanding of and application of these approaches.

RtI in Science

In general, a three-tiered approach to Response to Intervention includes the following: Tier I, which includes high-quality research-supported instruction delivered to all students with acceptable progress for the majority (i.e., 80%) of students; Tier II, which consists of Tier I instruction plus additional small-group instruction (needed for a smaller—15%—percentage of students) and additional adaptations provided in the science classroom; and Tier III, which generally includes one-to-one instruction (i.e., 5% of the students). Students would move from Tier I to the other tiers as needed, based on their success in each layer of the intervention. If students did not achieve success in Tier III, they would be referred for possible special education eligibility and testing.

What does success in science look like? High achievers in science have strong background knowledge and above-average vocabulary skills. They skillfully comprehend written text as well as other research materials that further enhance their science learning. They readily apply principles and problem solve during hands-on science activities. They have good writing as well as communication skills that they use not only for note-taking, but also to clearly explain their science learning verbally, as well as on written tests or via other written projects.

However, many students are similar to Ted, in that they enter the science classroom having difficulties in one or more of these skill areas. They may have inadequate background knowledge or limited word knowledge that results in difficulties when learning the science vocabulary. Many students read well below the grade level of the science text and struggle with written expression on tests and projects. Ted had difficulties in all of these areas. In addition, his handwriting was illegible and his spelling was terrible.

Approaches to science instruction. The literature identifies two major approaches to teaching science: traditional and inquiry. Each approach has its unique benefits and applications. Traditional approaches include content-based, factual learning where instruction is delivered via lecture and demonstrations, and the use of textbooks provides opportunities for students to learn vocabulary and general facts. Students who have difficulty with literacy may benefit from instructional adaptations under the traditional approach to teaching science. These adaptations include: (a) providing text-processing strategies where text analysis is explicitly taught (Bakken, Mastropieri, & Scruggs, 1997; Gaddy, Bakken, & Fulk, 2008), (b) using mnemonic devices and direct instruction (Scruggs & Mastropieri, 2007);

and (c) employing cooperative group learning (Scruggs & Mastropieri, 2007). These approaches may provide sufficient support and scaffolding to promote independent learning from science text. When the goal for the student is primarily to learn vocabulary and facts, it appears that for some students, the optimal approach is the traditional one, with these specific adaptations and scaffolding.

An inquiry-based approach, sometimes called a constructivist or hands-on approach, provides unique opportunities for students to engage with and develop thinking and understanding about science concepts (Mastropieri, Scruggs, Boon, & Carter, 2001). The constructivist approach has been defined as the five E's: engage, explore, elaborate, explain, and evaluate (Bybee, 2002). Some researchers have found that students taught using hands-on, experimental methods achieved more and reported more engagement and enjoyment than when they were taught by more direct instructional methods (Scruggs & Mastropieri, 2007). When instruction in science includes activities that are appropriately sequenced and when students are given support and assistance developing their inquiry throughout a science unit, comprehension of key concepts and memory for vocabulary and facts are increased (Mastropieri et al., 2006). Some researchers have found that hands-on models of teaching that use concrete experiences to assist students in developing knowledge appear to result in more depth and comprehension than an approach that emphasizes recall of facts (McCarthy, 2005).

It should be acknowledged that techniques that feature the teacher as facilitator, as in the constructivist approach, alter the learning environment, requiring the student to be more engaged and self-directed than typically is true of a traditional approach where the teacher directs the instruction. It might be expected that students with disabilities would struggle with this level of independence. Some researchers have found, however, that when the emphasis in a classroom is on discovery learning, students who have difficulty with reading text and other literacy skills may actually thrive and demonstrate the conceptual learning that is desired (McCarthy, 2005). Many aspects about the learning situation need to be considered as the teacher plans for diverse learners (including those with disabilities). One promising approach to designing teaching and learning activities to address a variety of student needs and learning styles is Universal Design for Learning.

Data collection in science classrooms. In addition to providing research-based instruction, another component of the RtI model is the need to frequently monitor the progress of all students, but especially those students who were identified as struggling learners based on universal screening results. Students' progress should be assessed at least one time each week for a minimum of 8 weeks (and up to 12 weeks), and the data collected will serve to identify students who are not meeting given benchmarks despite receiving high-quality instruction through the core reading program. Data collected will help teachers make more accurate instructional decisions (Johnson, Mellard, Fuchs, & McKnight, 2006).

To monitor progress, the use of curriculum-based measurements (CBMs) is recommended. CBMs are an effective assessment approach that is directly linked to instruction and is an effective tool that directly and consistently monitors student progress (Cohen & Spenciner, 2011). They are criterion-referenced measures where students are assessed on the curriculum being taught. The skills assessed are selected from all of the skills that should be learned by the end of the year and provide recommended performance levels multiple times throughout the school year (Deno, 2003). CBMs are conducted on a regular basis (e.g., once a week), and all skills in the instructional curriculum are assessed by each test or probe across the year. The probes include items that cover skills the students are expected to master by the end of the school year.

This means that science teachers will need to develop assessment measures to monitor the progress of their students over time. This could consist of quizzes, homework, activities, or exams. The crucial element in the assessment of performance is that teachers need to collect data frequently and often.

Effective Interventions and Evidence-Based Practices

Because students with different abilities and levels are included more in general educational settings, it is necessary for general education teachers to improve their strategies in order to meet the different learning needs of all students. Response to Intervention (RtI), a promising approach, has been introduced into inclusive classrooms for the purpose of identifying students in need and to prevent students who may have low academic performance in schools from failing (Fuchs & Deshler, 2007).

In implementing RtI for prevention purposes, teachers must be knowledgeable and skillful in providing subject content to all students in an effective manner. Therefore, a good teacher should demonstrate effective instructional practices. The effective strategies for teaching science to students with special needs in general education settings are one of the major topics to be elaborated when implementing RtI in schools. It will be more helpful if teachers or practitioners can choose acceptable research-based interventions to teach students. A number of evidence-based practices and effective instructional strategies to use with diverse students in the classroom are described in the following sections. Hunley and McNamara (2010) suggested that "characteristics of effective intervention include: (a) opportunities to respond to tasks requiring the behaviors targeted for improvement, (b) immediate post-work feedback with error correction, (c) positive post-work contingencies, (d) pacing and instructional strategies, and (e) progress monitoring" (p. 113).

Inquiry-Based Instruction

Inquiry-based instruction is a teaching method considered an effective intervention, particularly for science classrooms, as it combines a student's curiosity with the scientific method that promotes critical thinking skills. This approach consists of 5 Es: engagement, exploration, explanation, elaboration, and evaluation (Bybee, 2006). However, teaching students to be inquiry-based learners does not mean just going to the class and asking what they want to learn today. In fact, the teacher needs to set goals and plans prior to the class, in order to encourage students to actively take part in their own learning.

Preparing for effective learning, the teacher needs to consider several factors related to the class and topics such as the students' age, topical focus, skills students need to learn, and available resources. In this process, the teacher should allow students to make as many decisions as possible. Then, the teacher should find out the students' interests using brainstorming techniques. It may be a good idea to ask the whole class to work on one topic or assign groups of students to work on particular aspects of the topic. Implementing an inquiry-based instruction, Dr. Cornelia Brunner (2011) from the Center for Children and Technology suggested the process of teaching as follows:

1. **Pose a real question.** In this step, the teacher encourages students to develop their real questions by using guided questions such as "What do I want to know about this topic?" "What do I need to know?" and "How do I know it?"
2. **Find resources.** All available resources should be introduced to students in order to support their investigation. Questions like "What kinds of resources do I need?" "Where can I find them?" and "What

information do I need?" should be taught to students to facilitate their own learning.

3. **Interpret information.** At this step, students are encouraged to focus on the information they obtained with their hypotheses. Questions that should be used include "How is this relevant to my question?" "Which parts support my answer?" and "How does it relate to what I knew?"

4. **Report findings.** Students may discover their answer and want to share their findings with other groups. The teacher should explain to students that the results that reject their hypotheses should be considered as challenges.

When students engage in inquiry-based learning, they will (a) ask questions, (b) investigate what is happening, (c) use evidences to explain and predict the result, (d) link evidences to knowledge, and (e) share information from the findings (Bybee, 2006). Because of its flexibility, this method can be used with students with different developmental capabilities so that they can learn together. See Figure 11.1 for an example of inquiry-based instruction.

Direct Instruction

Direct instruction, a traditional type of instruction, is a teacher-led instructional approach that focuses on rigorously developed and well-planned lessons that break down students' learning. Direct instruction requires the teacher to provide information with continuous modeling and active interaction with students. The lesson is fast paced, and followed by guided and independent practice until students demonstrate mastery of the content. Direct instruction is more appropriate for providing new learning skills for the students (Whitten, Esteves, & Woodrow, 2009). Typically, direct instruction involves several steps: (a) stating the objectives and the importance of the lesson in an introduction that explains how the objectives are important to real life, (b) reviewing skills or knowledge that has been taught and connected to the new information, (c) presenting the new information in a sequence, (d) providing multiple examples, (e) checking for students' understanding by asking questions or using group activities, (f) providing adequate guided practice such as opportunities for the whole class or groups to practice what they have just learned while the teacher gives immediate feedback and error correction, and (g) providing

Steps of Learning

Before students engage in inquiry activities, Samarapungavan, Mantzicopoulos, Patrick, and French (2009) suggested that the teacher must introduce students to the main ideas of the topic, a procedural framework of their investigations, and the textbooks related to the content to provide students background knowledge.

- ➤ **Step 1: Asking Questions:** The students began their investigations by creating questions and making predictions while observing and recording what happened in their science books. For example, after observing two plants being placed in different places outside the classroom, students asked "Why do the plants grow differently?"
- ➤ **Step 2: Investigation:** Students had background information that all plants need water to grow. They also noticed that these two plants received enough water. They should do research from textbooks until they found, for example, that light is another factor for plants to grow. However, the students observed that the plants received the same amount of light each day.
- ➤ **Step 3: Using Evidence to Explain and Predict the Results:** After the 5-day observation, the students use the data collected each day to conclude that light did not play a key role in the different growth of both plants because they received the same amount of light every day. Then, the students may predict that the temperature may be the main cause of this difference. They may decide to check the temperature of each plant during the same time each day for a week to find that Plant A has a higher temperature than Plant B.
- ➤ **Step 4: Linking Evidence to Knowledge:** The students learned that water, light, and temperature can affect the plants' growth. They also learned that a difference of even one factor can result in different growth among plants.
- ➤ **Step 5: Sharing Information From the Findings:** After the students found the result of the experiment, they shared the project with the class, explaining the experiment procedure and reporting the outcomes and conclusion. During this process, the teacher introduced ways to effectively communicate with peers using a PowerPoint presentation, poster, or charts.

Inquiry-based instruction has been used effectively in science. For example, Cobern and colleagues (2010) investigated the effectiveness of two approaches, inquiry-based instruction and direct instruction, to teach science to eighth graders from different school districts in urban, suburban, and rural areas over a 2-week period. Although the outcomes of the findings showed no significant difference between students' gains from both methods, the inquiry-based instruction has advantages over direct instruction in that it provided the necessary science process to develop all students' thinking skills.

Figure 11.1. Example of inquiry-based instruction.

and monitoring independent practices in class and at home. See Figure 11.2 for an example of direct instruction.

Although a number of studies on direct instruction reported its effectiveness in teaching language and social studies, it can also be used in science classrooms. However, Whitten et al. (2009) commented that the direct instruction approach should be used on a limited basis, because several other strategies (e.g., grouping or interactive classroom activities) can offer more benefits that respond to students' educational needs.

Problem-Based Learning (PBL)

PBL is a student-centered approach that provides opportunities for students to learn in the context of realistic and complex problems. While learning in groups, the students identify what they already know, what they need to know, and what they want to know in order to resolve the problem. Rather than that of a knowledge provider, the teacher's role is to motivate and scaffold students' learning (Goodnough & Nolan, 2008). Key features of problem-based learning include: (a) students' learning is encouraged through challenging, high-level, and open-ended problems; (b) students typically work in groups; and (c) the teacher is a facilitator who poses problems and provides support.

PBL is considered one of several research-based intervention strategies for teaching science as well as other academic areas such as math and social studies. According to Barrows (2000), the problem posed for students should be realistic and open ended and contain several feasible solutions in order to stimulate their learning as well as their problem-solving skills. At the beginning, the teacher may introduce less complex problems and gradually fade out support. As students are mastering this learning strategy, the teacher can increase difficulty and complexity of the problems and make them more realistic. Thus, this instructional practice helps students to become more self-directed. Whitten et al. (2009) suggested that PBL involves the following steps: (a) present the problem or scenario to students; (b) allow the students to work in small groups of 3–5 students; (c) teach them to discuss the problem, talking about what they knew and what their learning needs are; (d) ask the students to investigate the problem, test their hypothesis, and come up with a solution; (e) distribute worked-out examples of the problems as models for the students; (f) challenge their ideas, if necessary, with questions and time to process their thinking and formulate ideas; and (g) focus on the scientific process rather than the solution. Gordon, Rogers, Comfort, Gavula, and McGee (2001) investi-

Topic: Birds

Materials:
1. Five paper bags
2. Five toy birds
3. Styrofoam peanuts

Steps of Teaching

Anticipatory:
1. The teacher passes out five paper bags, each bag filled with a toy bird, and Styrofoam peanuts to the students. Each student gets to hold each bag once.
2. The teacher asks the students to investigate what they received without looking in the bags.
3. Then, the teacher asks the students what they expect to find in the paper bags.

Presentation:
   After showing the toy birds from paper bags, the teacher provides information related to characteristics, food, and location of each particular bird. For example, the teacher presents the first bird (e.g., a cardinal), and describes its characteristics, location, and food, repeating this for all five birds.

Check for Understanding:
1. Ask the students to make the first bird's call.
2. Ask them to describe each kind of bird food.
3. Ask them to say the location of all birds presented today.

Guided Practice:
1. Write a few questions on the board, ask students one at a time to do each question, and provide guidance and feedback.
2. Give each of them a worksheet to work on.
3. Walk around to support students as needed.

Independent Practice:
1. Give the students the second worksheet to practice at home.
2. Give them an assignment to find out additional important information related to the birds learned today.

Closure:
   The teacher and the students make a conclusion from what they learned together.

Figure 11.2. Example of direct instruction in science.

gated PBL with middle school students and found that the use of PBL with the middle school curriculum with minority students resulted in improved behaviors and science achievement.

Hands-On Science Activities

Hands-on activities have long been recognized as a critical strategy in teaching science. Students usually work in groups to manipulate a variety of objects. This strategy provides the students with opportunities to ask questions and collect data, as well as interact with their peers. Numerous studies showed positive effects of hands-on activities in teaching science for students (e.g., Bay, Staver, Bryan, & Hale, 1992; McCarthy, 2005; Scruggs, Mastropieri, Bakken, & Brigham, 1993). In a 2-year qualitative study in a special education science classroom, it was reported that students enjoyed the science activities and benefitted significantly from the activities with real-world materials (Scruggs & Mastropieri, 1994). Moreover, Scruggs et al. (1993) compared the effects of hands-on activities and textbook-based instruction in eighth-grade special education science classes of students with learning disabilities and behavioral disorders. They found that the students taught with hands-on activities using the science materials significantly outperformed those who used the textbook-based method. In her review of the literature, Satterthwait (2010) found that three factors have made a major contribution to the effectiveness of this strategy. These include peer interaction through cooperative learning, object-mediated learning, and embodied experience. See Figure 11.3 for an example of a hands-on science activity.

There have been a number of reports and studies claiming the effectiveness of hands-on activities. For example, Mastropieri et al. (2006) reported that collaborative hands-on activities statistically facilitated learning of middle school science content for all students including those with disabilities in inclusive classrooms. In McCarthy's (2005) study, a traditional textbook approach and a hands-on thematic approach were compared in teaching 18 middle school students with serious emotional disturbances who were instructed on the topic of matter. McCarthy found that students in the hands-on activity group performed significantly better than those in the textbook program. Similarly, Gurganus, Janas, and Schmitt (1995) investigated the importance of using science materials and textbooks in order to provide students with more impactful learning experiences in science. The findings revealed that students with disabilities given hands-on

Materials Needed
1. Large, wide-mouth glass container
2. Hot water
3. Ice cubes
4. Small plate to cover the container
5. Index card

Steps
1. The teacher pours 2 inches of very hot water into the glass container.
2. Then, the teacher lets a student cover the container with a plate and allows the water to sit for a few minutes.
3. The teacher asks another student to place ice cubes on the plate.
4. All students observe what happens after that.

Students will notice the droplets under the plate and how they drop to the container. This is because the moisture in the warm air rises and meets the cold temperature of the plate. It then condenses to form water droplets. The same thing happens in the atmosphere as warm and moist air rises and meets colder temperatures in the atmosphere. It condenses, forms droplets, and falls to the Earth as rain (Web Weather for Kids, 2011).

Figure 11.3. Example of hands-on science activity: To make it rain.

thematic instruction in science showed significantly better performance than those in the textbook-driven instruction group.

Differentiated Instruction

Differentiated instruction is an appropriate approach to teach students in inclusive education settings, as it requires teachers to adjust their pace, style, and level of instruction in responding to the needs of each student (Appelbaum, 2009). Differentiated instruction is a process that needs professional development and time before it can be implemented in the real classroom. Generally, teachers can differentiate their instruction in three areas: content, process, and product (Tomlinson, 2001). Science content can be differentiated in multiple ways, including using different levels of textbooks and presenting ideas through various means. Teachers can differentiate the process of science learning by using flexible grouping, implementing tier activities, providing hands-on materials, and allowing varying timeframes to complete the task. Examples of differentiating products include providing several options for learning assessments and allowing more choices for students to focus their interests on a product.

Grouping. Grouping should be flexible to meet students' learning style and pace. Students typically work independently in some parts of the day and in groups other parts of the day. In grouping students, a teacher needs to know what the lesson objectives are so that she can prepare how to assign students to each group. Each student should be assigned to a homogeneous group in some activities and placed in a heterogeneous group in other activities, according to the purpose of the lesson. The teacher can use homogeneous groups for particular instructional purposes such as drill and practice. Students will have fun working with peers in preparing answers for the test. For a heterogeneous group, a well-prepared teacher can offer several fun and interesting activities to the class including open-ended discussions on science topics and activities that require critical thinking and analysis, forming the concepts, and finding solutions for science problems (Appelbaum, 2009).

Tiered assignments. Although the use of differentiated instruction has been proven to be effective in providing instruction to diverse students, a number of teachers may hesitate to implement it for several reasons including (a) lack of administrative support, (b) possible result of lower standardized test scores, (c) problems with classroom management, (d) reluctance to change their teaching style, (e) lack of time to plan, and (f) fear of parents' disagreement (Latz, Speirs Neumeister, Adams, & Pierce, 2009). According to Cooper (1998) and Knopper and Fertig (2005), implementing differentiated instruction may take time in the beginning, but it can become more effective and save a teacher's time when students become self-directed learners through anchoring activities that allow students to spend their free time more appropriately and effectively after they complete their assignments in class.

Mnemonic Strategies

Many students, especially those with learning disabilities, frequently have difficulty with long-term memory. These students need study skills on how to remember materials that they have just learned. Mnemonic strategies have been widely used as one of the most powerful methods in teaching students with special needs to promote their memory of new information in inclusive classrooms (Mastropieri, Scruggs, & Levin, 1985; Scruggs & Mastropieri, 1990). The use of these strategies has been proven to be successful for students with different levels of abilities including students with giftedness and typical development as well as those with disabilities. Teachers must not only explain why information is important to students, but also teach them how to recall the content. Therefore, numerous studies (e.g., Mastropieri, Emerick, & Scruggs, 1988; Scruggs & Mastropieri,

1992) have introduced the use of mnemonic instruction to teach a number of subject areas including science. For example, Fulk, Mastropieri, and Scruggs (1992) investigated the use of mnemonic strategies by training students with learning disabilities to generate their own mnemonics in science and social studies. They also found that those students outperformed students who used a rehearsal-based study.

Graphic Organizers, Concept, Idea, and Story Maps

A number of students, including students with learning disabilities, may have difficulty in comprehending expository text. A teacher needs instructional strategies to support this, especially terminology and definitions in science concepts. Graphic organizers, an evidence-based practice, are recommended for teaching students how to map their thinking. A graphic organizer is a visual graphic display that describes a relationship between terms and ideas within a learning task (Strangman, Hall, & Meyer, 2011). It has taken place in many forms such as graphic organizers, concept maps, idea maps, and story maps.

Strangman and colleagues (2011) also showed different forms of graphic organizers that can be used for specific purposes. For example, when students want to organize the concept of learning in a hierarchical set of information that reflects subordinate elements, it is recommended to use a network tree (shown in Figure 11.4). However, when the information is scattered, it is recommended to use a spider map to organize the idea (see Figure 11.5). Another form of graphic organizer is a fishbone map (see Figure 11.6), used to represent complex cause-effect relationships.

Research-based studies suggest that the use of graphic organizers promotes skills including developing and organizing ideas, understanding relationships, and categorizing concepts, as well as enhancing retention and recall of information. However, in successfully implementing the use of graphic organizers, the teacher needs to provide explicit instruction for their use with a demonstration on how to use them (Gardill & Jitendra, 1999; Willerman & Mac Harg, 1991).

It is necessary to note that the effective interventions presented above can be used for enhancing students' science learning at all tiers (i.e., Tiers I, II, and III). However, teachers need to carefully adapt and modify them according to students' educational needs and their contexts.

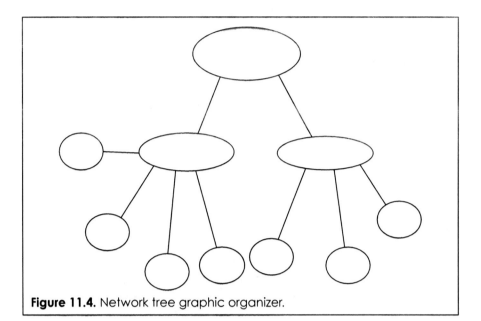

Figure 11.4. Network tree graphic organizer.

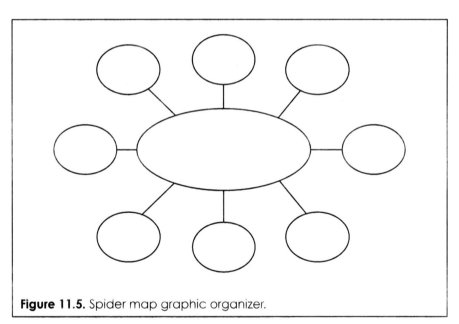

Figure 11.5. Spider map graphic organizer.

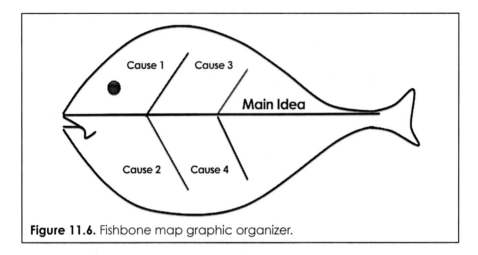

Figure 11.6. Fishbone map graphic organizer.

Evidence-Based Practices and Accommodations in Tiers I, II, and III

To provide accommodations to support students in the science classroom, a variety of strategies can be used such as the following:

1. **Use anchor activities.** Anchor activities are well-planned activities provided for some students who have completed their assignments early that allow them to add to, review, or expand the content being taught. These activities also provide a teacher time to work with other students who have different needs and levels of abilities. Appelbaum (2009) suggested the following examples of anchoring activities:
   a. practicing assignments
   b. reviewing materials
   c. learning science using manipulatives
   d. reading a book
   e. writing in a journal
   f. using graphic organizers (p. 77)

2. **Tier lessons and assignments.** In providing instructions to students, the teacher can tier lessons and/or assignments according to their complexity to meet students' abilities. This strategy enables all students to focus on their assignments at their own pace of learning. However, well-planned instruction with a variety of materials and texts are needed.

3. **Use more concrete materials.** This strategy provides students with more visual cues to better understand the content.

4. **Make students check in**. This one-on-one strategy used before and/ or after class informs teachers if the student is ready to learn and/or has learned the content taught today. For example, the teacher asks a student about what he has learned today or whether he understood the content (Colorado Science, 2011).

5. **Have the student redo a portion of a paper.** Some students may not be able to complete the assignment correctly. To give them more opportunities to work on their assignment, the teacher allows those students to redo the parts of the paper on which they made mistakes. This will provide students with an opportunity to think more carefully and practice again (Colorado Science, 2011).

6. **Scaffold instruction**. The teacher provides several kinds of support at a student's level. This strategy may include but is not limited to detailed explanations, modeling, coaching, reminding, or offering more time and opportunities for students to learn. These support students in mastering the skills being taught and achieving set goals. For example, a few students do not understand how to measure one's heart rate, so the teacher demonstrates to each individual student and asks each of them to practice it (McEwan-Adkins, 2010).

7. **Provide wait time**. Some students may need more time than others to process thinking. Teachers should allow at least 3–5 seconds for the students to recall what is learned and to find out the answer. However, the wait time can last more than 5 seconds, if the teacher feels the student needs more time. This technique allows all students the opportunity to answer questions and to participate in class activities.

8. **Pair students with more advanced skill learners**. Generally, there are students with different skill levels in each classroom. This strategy not only provides multiple opportunities for students to practice, but also gives the teacher more time to plan and to manage students' behaviors.

9. **Use visual representations**. Visual representation is considered a powerful strategy to enhance students' learning, especially those who have difficulty in auditory information processing. Examples of visual representation include pictures, charts, video clips, and graphic organizers, as well as kinesthetic activities. It is noted that incorporating visual representation with verbal description provides students more modalities of learning (Whitten et al., 2009).

10. **Incorporate technology**. Using technology and presentation media can enhance students' learning in science by linking sound, pictures,

animation, and video to lessons in an interactive fashion (Perrault, 2010; Salend, 2005). This includes graphic organizers, video, CD-ROMs, the Internet, television, and other technologies that not only provide students with opportunities to interactively learn the content, but also motivate their curiosity.

Case Study

Think back to the beginning of this chapter, when Ted was always the first student to enter the seventh-grade science class. Ted also preferred chatting with his science teacher, Mrs. Torres, to any peer interactions. Ted loved the demonstrations as well as the lab activities in science. He carefully listened and tried to meaningfully contribute during demonstrations and discussions, but he could not read much of the science text, although he could often make good sense of diagrams and tables. As the school year progressed, however, Ted's reading, spelling, and writing difficulties resulted in failing grades on tests and written projects.

As Mrs. Torres implements the CBMs in class, she records all of her students' progress. She begins to monitor students who are consistently struggling on the weekly CBMs—in both reading and writing (including spelling). After 8 weeks, Mrs. Torres refers three of her students for Tier II services based on their performance. At Mrs. Torres' school, general education teachers with support from a trained paraprofessional provide the Tier II services for science.

For her Tier II services, Mrs. Torres focuses on both students' struggles with the reading comprehension associated with science as well as improving students' literacy in the content areas. Working in a small group, the students are provided specific strategies to approach reading and writing in the content areas as well as thinking skills. For example, Mrs. Torres and her paraprofessional focus on teaching the students to be strategic readers, using strategies such as previewing the text; making predictions and confirming them; making connections from the current text to previous texts, rereading the passage; retelling and summarizing; and discussing the text. Mrs. Torres teaches the students how to take notes and to organize the reading as well as all of the information presented for a particular topic or unit. Mrs. Torres also allows students to have time to work together to discuss the information and then check in with herself or the trained parpaprofessional.

After 20 weeks of Tier II service and continual progress monitoring with the CBMs, two of the three students are determined to have responded to the more intensive instruction; Ted is referred to Tier III services. In addition to the evidenced-based, high-quality science instruction he receives in Mrs. Torres' class, Ted receives supplemental support instruction in the special education classroom by a trained special education teacher. In particular, the special education teacher makes recommendations for appropriate accommodations to be made in the general education classroom for daily class activities as well as for assessments that would benefit Ted in science class. Further, the special education teacher provides more intensive strategic instruction, such as teaching the students to employ a two-column note-taking strategy. After 12 weeks, data suggest that Ted is catching on and becoming more independent with note-taking and better understanding content. At this time, Ted goes back to the general classroom with hopes that these strategies will be what he needs to be successful.

Mrs. Torres continues to collect data on Ted as well as his classmates. Even though she is the content teacher/specialist for science in her school, she needs to monitor all of her students on the skills necessary to be successful in her class.

Conclusion

It is important to make sure that all students have access to science content, curriculum, and experiences. Regardless of age, gender, cultural or ethnic background, or disabilities, this should be emphasized. Teachers should be aware of RtI and how it can impact students in their science classes. Collecting data and constant evaluation through assessment is necessary in order to know and understand how students are doing, what they are learning, and how to plan for future lessons. It is also important for science teachers to understand the demands placed on students and effective interventions and evidence-based practices that have been proven to be effective with different types of students. This chapter presented many different approaches, strategies, and techniques that should aid the science teacher to be better prepared and more efficient in the classroom. Teaching science is a challenge in and of itself, but having learners with different knowledge and abilities can be even more challenging. It is hoped that this chapter will provide some valuable insight and information to help teachers work with all kinds of students in their classrooms.

References

Appelbaum, M. (2009). *The one stop guide to implementing RTI: Academic and behavioral interventions, K–12.* Thousand Oaks, CA: Corwin Press.

Bakken, J. P., Mastropieri, M. A., & Scruggs, T. E. (1997). Reading comprehension of expository science material and students with learning disabilities: A comparison of strategies. *The Journal of Special Education, 31,* 300–324.

Barrows, H. S. (2000). *Problem-based learning applied to medical education.* Springfield, IL: Southern Illinois University Press.

Bay, M., Staver, J. R., Bryan, T., & Hale, J. B. (1992). Science instruction for the mildly handicapped: Direct instruction versus discovery teaching. *Journal of Research in Science Teaching, 29,* 555–570.

Brunner, C. (2011). *How to: Inquiry.* Retrieved from http://www.youthlearn.org/learning/planning/lesson-planning/how-inquiry/how-inquiry

Bybee, R. (Ed.). (2002). *Learning science and the science of learning.* Arlington, VA: National Science Teacher Association Press.

Bybee, R. W. (2006). Enhancing science teaching and student learning: A BSCS perspective. In *Research Conference 2006* (pp. 12–20). Colorado Springs, CO: BSCS.

Cobern, W. W., Schuster, D., Adams, B., Applegate, B., Skjold, B., Undreiu, A., Loving, C. C., & Gobert, J. D. (2010). Experimental comparison of inquiry and direct instruction in science. *Research in Science & Technological Education, 28*(1), 81–96.

Cohen, L. G., & Spenciner, L. J. (2011). *Assessment of children and youth with special needs* (4th ed.). Boston, MA: Pearson.

Colorado Science. (2011). *Evidence-based science education: RtI in science.* Retrieved from http://webcache.googleusercontent.com/search?q=cache:RrvjQlO_d2AJ:sciencecolorado.blogspot.com/2010/10/rti-in-science.html+selfcorrect+rti+science+check-in&cd=1&hl=en&ct=clnk&gl=us&client=safari&source=www.google.com

Cooper, C. (1998). For the good of humankind: Matching the budding talent with a curriculum of conscience. *Gifted Child Quarterly, 42,* 238–244.

Deno, S. L. (2003). Developments in curriculum-based measurement. *Remedial and Special Education, 37,* 184–192.

Fuchs, D., & Deshler, D. D. (2007). What we need to know about Responsiveness to Intervention (and shouldn't be afraid to ask). *Learning Disabilities Research & Practice, 22,* 129–136.

Fulk, B. J. M., Mastropieri, M. A., & Scruggs, T. E. (1992). Mnemonic generalization training with learning disabled adolescents. *Learning Disabilities Research & Practice, 7,* 2–10.

Gaddy, S. A., Bakken, J. P., & Fulk, B. M. (2008). The effects of teaching text-structure strategies to postsecondary students with learning disabilities to improve their reading comprehension on expository science text passages. *Journal of Postsecondary Education and Disability, 20,* 100–121.

Gardill, M. C., & Jitendra, A. K. (1999). Advanced story map instruction: Effects on the reading comprehension of students with learning disabilities. *The Journal of Special Education, 33,* 2–17.

Goodnough, K., & Nolan, B. (2008). Engaging elementary teachers' pedagogical content knowledge: Adopting problem-based learning in the context of science teaching and learning. *Canadian Journal of Science, Mathematics, and Technology Education, 8,* 197–216.

Gordon, P. R., Rogers, A. M., Comfort, M., Gavula, N., & McGee, B. P. (2001). A taste of problem-based learning increases achievement of urban minority middle-school students. *Educational Horizons, 79,* 171–175.

Gurganus, S., Janas, M., & Schmitt, L. (1995). Science instruction: What special education teachers need to know and what roles they need to play. *Teaching Exceptional Children, 27,* 7–9.

Hunley, S., & McNamara, K. (2010). *Tier 3 of the RtI model: Problem solving through a case study approach.* Thousand Oaks, CA: Corwin Press.

Individuals with Disabilities Education Improvement Act, Pub. Law 108-446 (December 3, 2004).

Johnson, E., Mellard, D. F., Fuchs, D., & McKnight, M. A. (2006). *Responsiveness to Intervention (RTI): How to do it.* Lawrence, KS: National Research Center on Learning Disabilities.

Knopper, D., & Fertig, C. (2005). Differentiation for gifted children: It's all about trust. *The Illinois Association for Gifted Children Journal, 6*(1), 6–8.

Latz, A. O., Speirs Neumeister, K. L., Adams, C. M., & Pierce, R. L. (2009). Peer coaching to improve classroom differentiation: Perspectives from Project CLUE. *Roeper Review, 31,* 27–39.

Mastropieri, M. A., Emerick, K., & Scruggs, T. E. (1988). Mnemonic instruction of science concepts. *Behavioral Disorders, 14,* 48–56.

Mastroprieri, M. A., Scruggs, T. E., Boon, R., & Carter, K. B. (2001). Correlates of inquiry in science: Constructing concepts of density and buoyancy. *Remedial and Special Education, 22,* 123–137.

Mastropieri, M. A., Scruggs, T. E., & Levin, J. R. (1985). Maximizing what exceptional students can learn: A review of research on the keyword method and related mnemonic techniques. *Remedial and Special Education, 6,* 39–45.

Mastropieri, M. A., Scruggs, T. E., Norland, J. J., Berkeley, S., McDuffie, K., Tornquist, E. H., & Connors, N. (2006). Differentiated curriculum enhancement in inclusive middle school science: Effects on classroom and high-stakes tests. *Journal of Special Education, 40,* 130–137.

McCarthy, C. B. (2005). Effects of thematic-based, hands-on science teaching versus a textbook approach for students with disabilities. *Journal of Research in Science Teaching, 42,* 245–263.

McEwan-Adkins, E. K., (2010). *40 reading intervention strategies for K–6 students: Research-based support for RtI.* Bloomington, IN: Solution Tree Press.

National Research Council. (1996). *National science education standards.* Washington, DC: The National Academy Press.

No Child Left Behind Act of 2001, 20 U.S.C § 6301 et seq. (2002).

Perrault, A. M. (2010). Making science learning available and accessible to all learners: Leveraging digital library resources. *Knowledge Quest, 39*(3), 12–15.

Salend, S. J. (2005). Using technology to teach about individual differences related to disability. *Teaching Exceptional Children, 38*(2), 32–38.

Samarapungavan, A., Mantzicopoulos, P., Patrick, H., & French, B. (2009). The development and validation of the science learning assessment (SLA): A measure of kindergarten science learning. *Journal of Advanced Academics, 20,* 502–535.

Satterthwait, D. (2010). Why are "hands-on" science activities so effective for student learning? *Teaching Science, 56*(2), 7–10.

Scruggs, T. E., & Mastropieri, M. A. (1990). Mnemonic instruction for learning disabled students: What it is and what it does. *Learning Disability Quarterly, 13,* 271–281.

Scruggs, T. E., & Mastropieri, M. A. (1992). Classroom applications of mnemonic instruction: Acquisition, maintenance, and generalization. *Exceptional Children, 58,* 219–229.

Scruggs, T. E., & Mastropieri, M. A. (1994). The construction of scientific knowledge by students with mild disabilities. *Journal of Special Education, 28,* 307–321.

Scruggs, T. E., & Mastropieri, M. A. (2007). Science learning in special education: The case for constructed versus instructed learning. *Exceptionality, 15*(2), 57–74.

Scruggs, T. E., Mastropieri, M. A., Bakken, J. P., & Brigham, F. J. (1993). Reading vs. doing: The relative effectiveness of textbook-based and inquiry-oriented approaches to science education. *Journal of Special Education, 27,* 1–15.

Strangman, N., Hall, T., & Meyer, A. (2011). *Graphic organizers and implications for universal design for learning: Curriculum enhancement report.* Retrieved from http://aim.cast.org/sites/aim.cast.org/files/GO_UDLNov2.pdf

Tomlinson, C. A. (2001). *The differentiated classroom: Responding to the needs of all learners* (2nd ed.). Arlington, VA: Association for Supervision and Curriculum Development.

Web Weather for Kids. (2011). *To make it rain.* Retrieved from http://eo.ucar.edu/webweather/tornact5.html

Whitten, E., Esteves, K. J., & Woodrow, A. (2009). *RTI success: Proven tools and strategies for schools and classrooms.* Minneapolis, MN: Free Spirit Publishing.

Willerman, M., & Mac Harg, R. A. (1991). The concept map as an advance organizer. *Journal of Research in Science Teaching, 28,* 705–711.

CHAPTER 12

Using
RtI in the Social Studies Classroom

Emily C. Bouck and Sarah Jones

What is social studies? Social studies is perhaps the most challenging of the core content areas in education to understand holistically (No Child Left Behind Act [NCLB], 2001). The term *social studies* represents a class students can take (e.g., sixth-grade social studies), an area of education teachers can be prepared to teach, and a conglomeration of disciplines (i.e., history, geography, civics and government, political science, economics, psychology, philosophy, archaeology, anthropology, sociology, law, religion; National Council for the Social Studies [NCSS], 2008). Although the disciplines of social studies are more distinct at the secondary level (e.g., ninth-grade American History, 10th-grade economics), at the elementary and sometimes the middle school level instruction in social studies can be more interdisciplinary.

Best practice in social studies instruction is unofficially governed by the NCSS—the professional organization associated with social studies. Similar to other professional associations in education, the NCSS (2008) developed curriculum standards for social studies. The social studies curriculum standards from the NCSS are designed to go across the K–12 spectrum and focus on themes by which to organize social studies instruction: culture; time, continuity, and change; people, places, and environments; individual development and identity; individuals, groups, and institutions; power, authority, and governance; production, distribution, and consumption; science, technology, and society; global connections; and civic ideals and practices. We invite the reader to refer to the NCSS website (http://

www.socialstudies.org) for more in-depth information about the social studies standards.

Social studies is a core content area (NCLB, 2001). However, NCLB does not require states to test students in grades 3–8 and once again in high school on social studies content, and hence schools have been replacing social studies instructional time with mathematics or literacy instruction, which are used to determine if schools are making Adequate Yearly Progress (AYP; McCall, Janssen, & Riederer, 2008; NCLB, 2001). Hence, students experience less exposure to social studies than other content areas, with research suggesting less than 90 minutes a week (Lintner & Schweder, 2008; VanFossen, 2005).

Although all students are experiencing a decrease of time devoted to social studies instruction, often students with disabilities experience even less opportunity to learn this content area (Lintner & Schweder, 2008). Historically, social studies has not been a high priority for students with disabilities, especially students with high-incidence disabilities (Patton, Polloway, & Cronin, 1987). This was particularly exacerbated at the secondary level, in which the researchers found almost half of special education teachers surveyed were not teaching social studies (Patton et al., 1987). Although a predisposition toward inclusion has increased over the past few decades, the decreased focus on social studies instruction in general education results in a continued diminished opportunity for access.

Academic Tasks

Given the multidisciplinary nature of social studies, the academic tasks associated with social studies are also varied, and can range from more traditional instruction (i.e., lecture, use of textbooks, individual seatwork) to inquiry-based learning (Harniss, Dickson, Kinder, & Hollenbeck, 2001; Memory, Yoder, Bolinger, & Warren, 2004; Scruggs, Mastropieri, & Okolo, 2008). In fact, the academic tasks associated with truly teaching, learning, and understanding social studies can read like a laundry list: reading texts as well as primary and secondary sources; abstract concepts (e.g., What is democracy?); multiple perspectives (e.g., Is Andrew Jackson a man of the people or a dictator?); critical thinking skills (e.g., Was the Revolutionary war between the colonists and the British justified?); understanding relationships (e.g., cause-and-effect, problem-solution); forming and evaluating arguments; and evaluating sources (Beyer, 2008a; Cuban, 2003; NCSS, 2008; Scruggs et al., 2008). In other words, participating in a social studies class involves lower level (e.g., remembering) and higher

passive vs inquiry

order (e.g., evaluating and creating) thinking skills. Although the majority of history instruction has historically involved passive learning (i.e., lecture, reading from a textbook, individual seatwork; Harniss et al., 2001; Scruggs et al., 2008), instruction in social studies classrooms can be more student-centered. Simulations engage students in critical thinking skills (Steele, 2008), and inquiry allows students to solve problems faced by real social scientists (e.g., historians and economists; Schell & Fisher, 2007).

Scruggs and colleagues (2008) conceptualized social studies instruction as existing on four levels, which involve lower and higher order thinking skills. The first level is factual learning, or in other words, declarative knowledge (e.g., the seventh President of the United States was Andrew Jackson, the definition of the word *anarchy*). The next level involves conceptual learning, which includes concepts (e.g., democracy, market systems). The third level is called procedural learning (i.e., knowing how to do a task), which involves both lower level tasks like "computing how many members of the United States House of Representatives should be allotted to a particular state" (Scruggs et al., 2008, p. 10) as well as the procedures for higher level thinking skills such as completing inquiry. The last level (type of learning) is investigative learning, which integrates the three previous types of learning. Investigative learning uses problem solving to address real-life scenarios and inquiry or exploration of ideas. Ultimately, it is the fourth level educators should strive to reach with their students, although many note the challenges students face both with the lower level skills (i.e., reading and writing in this content domain), as well as with higher level skills (i.e., understanding concepts and multiple perspectives (Baker, Gersten, & Graham, 2003; De La Paz & Graham, 1997; Scruggs et al., 2008; Ward-Lonergan, Liles, & Anderson, 1999).

Beyond knowing what academic tasks typically exist, it is important to understand what it takes for students to be successful. Given the nature of social studies instruction involving reading and writing, language and literacy are key areas for student success (Harniss et al., 2001; Scruggs et al., 2008). Students must be able not only to decode text but also to comprehend text, whether that text is a textbook, a trade book, or a primary or secondary source (Ward-Lonergan et al., 1999). Truly understanding social studies involves students synthesizing and interpreting text, not just providing a regurgitation or recall of what they read (Paxton, 1997). Beyond reading, social studies instruction involves students expressing their understanding through seatwork (i.e., worksheets) or higher order written expression opportunities (i.e., position essays; Baker et al., 2003; De La Paz & Graham, 1997). Written expression poses challenges to students from

S.S Requires a lot

[handwritten margin note: word Planning/ORGANIZING]

planning and organizing to actually composing the work. Other academic tasks exist in the teaching and learning of social studies—from auditorily attending to and comprehending lectures and recalling information for tests to active interpretation, problem solving, reasoning, and understanding both the multiple perspectives inherent in the content as well as that social studies is filtered by the perspectives of those who write about it (Baker et al., 2003; De La Paz & Graham, 1997; Scruggs et al., 2008; Ward-Lonergan et al., 1999).

Response to Intervention (RtI)

Despite the prevalence of Response to Intervention (RtI) in today's schools, an important yet underexamined area is how one applies RtI to social studies. To address this question, it is important to understand that RtI may have two roles in education: (a) RtI as a model to identify students with LD (Barnes & Harlacher, 2008) or (b) RtI as "an innovative approach to service delivery" (Legere & Conca, 2010, p. 33). RtI as an alternative means of identification is fairly familiar to most educators. If not, the authors invite the reader to refer to earlier chapters in this book as well as Marston (2005) and Stecker, Fuchs, & Fuchs (2008). However, RtI as "an innovative approach to service delivery" receives less attention. This model of RtI "seeks to prevent *academic* problems from occurring and to intervene when these problems persist" (Legere & Conca, 2010, p. 33). Because social studies is not an area in which students are identified with learning disabilities (as in literacy and mathematics), it is the prevention and intervention of academic problems that aligns most appropriately with social studies. The application of RtI to social studies may result in students getting additional assistance in this often-neglected content area (Lintner & Schweder, 2008) or bolstering the importance of this necessary and critical content area.

[handwritten margin note: SOCIAL STUD]

Implementation Steps

Significant research, attention, and resources exist to support teachers in implementing RtI in literacy and mathematics (e.g., Fuchs, Fuchs, Hintze, & Lembke, 2007; Vaughn et al., 2010; also see earlier chapters in this text on RtI with reading and mathematics) and even with applying RtI to behavior (Fairbanks, Sugai, Guardino, & Lathrop, 2007; Gresham, 2005). However, little attention has focused on RtI in the social studies classroom (Bailey, Shaw, & Hollifield, 2006; Lintner & Schweder, 2008).

[handwritten margin note: LITTLE RESEARCH SS]

That is not to say, however, that RtI cannot or should not be applied to social studies. Instead, teachers must be more creative and apply what is known in other areas, such as literacy, to the use of RtI in a social studies class.

Most models of RtI involve three tiers (Fuchs & Fuchs, 2006). The first tier involves high-quality, research-based instruction and progress monitoring (Stecker, Fuchs, & Fuchs, 2008). The second tier involves intensive supports within the general education environment. Tier II interventions are designed to target students' specific areas of need related to instruction and provide specific, small-group support for strengthening those areas (Canter, Klotz, & Cowan, 2008). In other words, Tier I instruction is designed to benefit *all* learners; Tier II is designed to bolster those for whom Tier I instruction is insufficient (Stecker, Fuchs et al., 2008). In studies of Tier II intervention in other subject matter (e.g., O'Connor, Fulmer, & Harty, 2003; Tilly, 2003; Vaughn, 2003), Tier II interventions supplement Tier I instruction and last anywhere from 15 minutes three times per week to 30 minutes daily and from 8 weeks to several years (Stecker, Fuchs et al., 2008).

The third tier results in placement in special education or additional evaluation for special education services (Fuchs, Mock, Morgan, & Young, 2003). Tier III interventions, usually based on an Individualized Education Program (IEP), are targeted to the individual student's strengths and needs and are designed to support students' long-term success (Stecker, Fuchs et al., 2008). Although who provides instruction in Tier I and Tier III seems more clear-cut, it is less evident who is always providing the instruction for Tier II interventions (Fuchs & Deshler, 2007). Important in the RtI model is the fluidity of the tiers and the ability for students to move in and out as needed, as evidenced by progress monitoring (Stecker, Fuchs et al., 2008). Additionally, the RtI model includes an implicit expectation that the majority of students will respond to intervention in Tiers I and II; Torgesen (2000) estimated that 2%–6% of the general school population would be eligible for Tier III, or in other words, would be nonresponders to Tier II interventions.

Across disciplines, RtI involves progress monitoring, or in other words collecting, interpreting, and using appropriate data to make decisions about student progress, services, and placement (Stecker, Lembke, & Foegen, 2008). To be most effective, Stecker, Lembke et al. (2008) recommended that progress monitoring "a) be sensitive to student change, b) be educationally meaningful, and c) [not] monopolize instructional time" (p. 49). Curriculum-based measurements (CBMs) accomplish these goals, as CBMs are systematic, brief, and relatively easy for teachers to administer and interpret, and reflect what students should be learning across the curriculum (Stecker, Lembke et al.). CBMs are typically done weekly or biweekly and have a strong evidence base for their use with reading, written expression, spelling, and mathematics (McMaster & Espin, 2007; Stecker, Lembke et al., 2005). However, less research and attention focuses on the use of CBMs in content area instruction such as social studies.

Tier I

Effective teaching methods and evidence-based strategies. Historically and currently, social studies receives less attention in practice and research (Bailey et al., 2006; Lintner, 2006; Lintner & Schweder, 2008). Hence, it is not surprising that less evidence-based strategies or discussions of effective teaching methods of this content area exist. Although RtI and current educational policy (i.e., NCLB, 2001) advocate for evidence-based or scientifically based practices, Marston (2005) noted "in areas where an adequate research base does not exist, data should be gathered on the success of promising practices" (p. 542).

Social studies instruction at Tier I should focus on big ideas—that is, the major themes or conceptual categories (e.g., freedom) found throughout the discipline (Crawford, Carnine, Harniss, Hollenbeck, & Miller, 2011; Schell & Fisher, 2007). Teaching for big ideas means focusing on the standards (i.e., NCSS, 2008) as well as teachers' own objectives through thought-provoking and engaging ideas and questions applicable to students' lives as well as other areas of study (Schell & Fisher, 2007; Wiggins & McTighe, 1998). Teaching with a lens toward big ideas focuses on understanding and making sense of facts, procedures, and concepts as they relate to larger contextualized issues (Wiggins & McTighe, 1998). One way to teach for big ideas is through investigative learning, which combines factual, conceptual, and procedural learning with problem solving in order to address real-life problems (Scruggs et al., 2008).

Applying the big idea principle and investigative learning can occur through the problem-solution-effect approach and multiple perspectives (Crawford et al., 2011). Within this approach, teachers facilitate student discussion and understanding of, for example, the Revolutionary War through addressing the problem(s), solutions(s), and the effect(s) of the war or exploring its multiple perspectives—including the colonists (both revolutionists/patriots/Whigs/rebels as well as Tories/loyalists) in addition to the British. Another way to approach the big idea principle is to use the

242

backward mapping strategy advocated by Wiggins and McTighe (1998). Backward mapping begins with the desired results (e.g., What knowledge do you want students to acquire? What skills are most important? What are the big ideas that transcend the classroom?). From there, the teacher determines the learning possibilities, considering approaches (i.e., simulations, inquires, debates), resources, level of abstraction, and potential for engagement. Next, the teacher focuses on the assessment pieces and how he will measure the learning and what exactly will be measured (i.e., facts, skills, understanding). Finally, the teacher looks at the implementation of a lesson and determines what should be taught on a particular day and how to do that most effectively, as well as the connection of the content to past and future concepts (Wiggins & McTighe, 1998).

Effective teaching and evidence-based teaching strategies for social studies can involve more than just the big idea principle. Effective teaching in social studies also involves use of strategic instruction, making connections—including activating or priming background knowledge—and explicit use of inquiry-based learning and other student-centered approaches (e.g., simulations, cooperative learning; Checkley, 2008; Crawford et al., 2011; McCall et al., 2008; Memory et al., 2004; Schell & Fisher, 2007).

Of course, no instructional strategy can replace generating student interest in social studies (Schell & Fisher, 2007). Despite interest in social studies related ideas and concepts outside of school (e.g., enjoyment of historical-based movies [*Pearl Harbor*], historical-based books, and television shows such as *National Geographic*), interest and motivation do not always transcend into a classroom (Key, Bradley, & Bradley, 2010). In part, the lack of interest and motivation may be attributed to the traditional ways of teaching social studies (i.e., lecture, textbook, individual seatwork, rote memorization), and hence we provide suggestions for alternative approaches to social studies instruction. However, teachers can also undertake tactics to encourage student interest such as the use of hooks like beginning instruction through the presentation of a story; use of primary sources including text and artifacts, political cartoons, and other images (i.e., photography); interviews with members of the community; and KWL charts —a graphic organizer with three columns (what do I **K**now, what do I **W**ant to know, what did I **L**earn; Schell & Fisher, 2007).

Collecting appropriate data. Despite a strong history in other areas, less research and attention focuses on the use of CBMs in content-area instruction such as social studies. Espin, Busch, Shin, and Kruschwitz (2001) discussed two approaches to the application of CBM to content-area instruction: (a) identifying critical skills for the content area (e.g., social studies) or (b) identifying general indicators. Espin and colleagues (Espin et al., 2001; Espin & Deno, 1993, 1995; Espin & Foegen, 1996; Espin, Shin, & Busch, 2005) focused on vocabulary matching (i.e., vocabulary terms, definitions) as CBMs to measure student progress in social studies. For example a teacher could, similar to what was done in the studies by Espin et al. (2001, 2005), create a list of vocabulary words throughout the year or semester's curriculum. These words can come from the textbook or other resources the teacher uses for teaching. The teacher develops a series of probes for the school year by dividing the list of vocabulary terms and their accompanying definitions into the number of needed probes (i.e., weekly or biweekly). The probes each consist of the same number of terms and definitions (e.g., Espin et al., 2001, 2005, used 20 terms and 2 distract-ers—the distracters were terms that did not have their matching definitions provided) randomly selected for placement on the probes (i.e., the order of terms are not aligned with the progression of the curriculum). For RtI progress, students who fail to make progress on the CBMs are considered for additional supports available in Tier II. To note, Espin and colleagues (2001, 2005) included two types of matching questions on their problems, which they termed factual and applied. Factual was matching the term to the definition, while applied involved applying the term to a contextual situation.

Maze fluency is another type of CBM that can be used to assess student progress with informational text (Stecker, Lembke et al., 2008). Although less support exists for maze fluency related to social studies, it has been used as a CBM with upper elementary and secondary students (Espin & Foegen, 1996).

Beyond any research base on CBMs and social studies, monitoring students' progress in this domain may benefit from a more conceptual stance. For example, teachers could determine the higher order thinking content or big ideas they will be teaching across the year and develop questions that elicit student thinking. Multiple-choice or short-answer questions are more aligned with the CBM model, but teachers can think outside of the box and involve more essay-type questions to evoke student problem solving and critical thinking. Similar to the vocabulary matching, teachers would generate the list of yearlong higher order thinking content or big ideas, form questions and assessments, and then randomly assign the assessment throughout the school year (e.g., monitoring weekly or every other week).

When implementing progress monitoring in Tier I, assessments can occur weekly or every other week; however, more frequent assessment can assist in instructional decision making, and as noted in the discussion of later tiers, the frequency should be increased when working with struggling students or students with disabilities (Stecker, Lembke et al., 2008). Determining students' progress, or lack thereof, in social studies is not limited to collecting the data, such as through the use of CBMs, but also involves graphing the data and then tracking or comparing the graphed data over time to determine whether students are progressing at the rate necessary for academic success (Stecker, Lembke et al., 2008).

Tier II

Effective teaching methods and evidence-based strategies. For the purposes of social studies, we discuss recommendations for two separate tracks of Tier II intervention —recommendations for students who struggle with the abstract cognitive processes necessary for social studies (i.e., drawing conclusions, verifying a source's credibility), and recommendations for students who struggle with content-area literacy.

One group of students who may require interventions in social studies are those who struggle with abstract thinking skills (Beyer, 2008a). As discussed earlier, success in social studies requires more than rote memorization of names and dates; social studies requires complex cognitive maneuvers ranging from categorizing and sequencing to sourcing documents and corroborating historical evidence (Leinhardt & Young, 1996). One strategy for helping students with abstract thinking skills is metacognitive reflection (Beyer, 2008a). In metacognitive reflection, a teacher leads a group of students in a thinking activity (e.g., comparing and contrasting Italy under Mussolini with Germany under Hitler). Then, the teacher guides students in a reflection exercise to identify exactly what happened in their minds as they completed the task. The goal is for students to apply these thinking skills to different situations in the future.

However, for those students who do not intuitively use higher level thinking processes, direct instruction may be necessary (Beyer, 2008b). For example, an eighth-grade teacher asks students to read the Declaration of Independence and use it to explain the founders' opinions on government. To do this, students need to know what it means to draw a conclusion, know the steps to drawing conclusions, and recognize they are being asked to draw a conclusion in this instance and should use the steps they know. To teach the associated thinking skills, the teacher begins by modeling the skill, explaining and demonstrating what the skill is, discussing when and why it is useful, and giving the steps for using it (Beyer, 2008a). Thus, a teacher who wanted to give direct instruction in drawing conclusions

245

with the Declaration of Independence example first provides high-quality instruction on the Declaration of Independence and explains how documents like the Declaration of Independence can be better understood when we know how to draw conclusions. The teacher then details the process of drawing a conclusion based on the Declaration, thinking aloud and labeling each step for the students.

Several tools exist for helping teachers and students with Tier II interventions for thinking skills. For example, Martin and Wineburg (2008) developed an online program that uses expert think alouds to show students effective ways to think about history. Beyer (2008a) also recommended checklists, lists of questions, and graphic organizers to help students keep track of the processes involved in specific thinking skills. Teachers can also develop videos that model specific thinking skills, so that students receiving Tier II interventions can benefit from watching the modeling multiple times (Beyer, 2008a).

Beyond struggling with the abstract cognitive processes associated with social studies, other students may struggle with the reading related to social studies instruction. If students struggle with comprehension with social studies materials, Tier II interventions may involve strategies such as previewing, chunking, or changing the text (Hedin & Conderman, 2010). Previewing strategies may include looking at section titles, objectives, or text structure in order to recognize important points. Later, students will be more able to remember and apply that information. Chunking strategies may include stopping after a section or paragraph and asking, "Do I understand what I just read?" and "Do I need to read any part of that again?" If students find they do not understand a chunk of text, they can use rereading as a strategy. Strategies in changing the text may include replacing pronouns with their antecedents or putting keywords at the beginning of sentences in order to boost literal understanding (Hedin & Conderman, 2010).

Finally, teachers can teach reading comprehension strategies with reciprocal teaching. In reciprocal teaching, small groups of students read a section of text, develop a few questions about the text, and answer their questions together. Next, the students ask themselves if anything did not make sense, and if so, they reread the text to clear up their confusion. Third, the group works together to summarize the text they just read. Finally, the group predicts what might come next in the reading. Over time, students get used to asking themselves questions while reading to monitor their own comprehension (Slater & Horstman, 2002).

Collecting appropriate data. Collecting data for students in Tier II is similar to data collection for students in Tier I. The progress monitoring of students can still rely on CBMs, and teachers can continue to use the same CBMs used in Tier I to determine if students are making progress (e.g., vocabulary matching, maze fluency, social studies content focused on higher order thinking). Students should be assessed in similar frequency as during Tier I such as weekly or biweekly. Those who make progress following Tier II interventions can be returned to Tier I, whereas those who still fail to respond are considered for Tier III. Some researchers have speculated that 25%–50% of students receiving Tier II services will fail to respond or be eligible for Tier III services (Marston, 2005; Vaughn, 2003). Vaughn (2003) stipulated that students who fail to make progress after 20 weeks of Tier II interventions could be considered nonresponders.

Tier III   *INQUIRY / PROJ LEARNING*

Effective teaching methods and evidence-based strategies. As with social studies instruction in general, research regarding effective strategies to teach (i.e., pull-out class) or support (i.e., resource room) students with disabilities in social studies is limited. However, emerging evidence-based instructional strategies do exist regarding social studies instruction for students with disabilities. These include inquiry-based or project-based learning (Okolo & Ferretti, 1996a, 1996b), strategy instruction (De La Paz, 2005; Williams et al., 2007), and use of technology (Boon, Fore, Blankenship, & Chalk, 2007).

Okolo and colleagues (Ferretti, MacArthur, & Okolo, 2001; Okolo & Ferretti, 1996a, 1996b) discovered students who explored social studies through problem-based learning with technology (e.g., developing multimedia presentations) experienced improved motivation, self-efficacy, knowledge, and the ability to discuss key ideas in social studies. To implement, teachers select a controversial issue or an issue with multiple perspectives (e.g., immigration, westward expansion) and create groups to explore the different perspectives. Students utilize a variety of resources to understand their perspective on the topic (e.g., trade books, textbooks, videos, movies, interviews, primary and secondary sources) and develop a technology-based presentation to share with the class. The class then learns about all of the different perspectives, although each group engages deeply with one lens.

Aside from student-centered approaches, strategic instruction has an emerging research base for educating students with disabilities. Strategic

247

instruction can mean a lot of different things and can be applied in different ways to teaching and supporting students in social studies. For example, one aspect of strategic instruction is helping students to understand text structure, which can be particularly important in social studies because of its above-grade reading levels and expository structure (often not as familiar to younger students; Armbruster & Anderson, 1984; Bakken, Mastropieri, & Scruggs, 1997). Compare-contrast, problem-solution, explanation, sequence, description, and cause-effect are the most common text structures in social studies textbooks (Anderson & Armbruster, 1984), and clue words are the most common way of helping students understand text structure (Williams et al., 2007). Teachers can explicitly teach students to identify common clue words connected to the different types of structures: *because, therefore,* and *thus* for cause-effect; *likewise, on the other hand,* and *similarly* for compare-and-contrast; *before, after,* and *finally* for sequence; and *produces* and *causes* for explanation.

Similar to the clue-word approach to identifying text structure is the use of mnemonics to assist students in retaining and recalling factual information such as the factual knowledge level of learning social studies as identified by Scruggs et al. (2008). Use of mnemonics has a strong research base for helping students with disabilities (Fontana, Scruggs, & Mastropieri, 2007; Scruggs & Mastropieri, 2000). Mnemonics in social studies occur in three different representations: first-letter strategy (e.g., HOMES for remembering the Great Lakes—Huron, Ontario, Michigan, Erie, and Superior); the keyword strategy, which involves pairing an image with a word (e.g., Fontana et al., 2007 paired a picture of an ant on a government building to teach the word *anarchist*); and the pegword strategy, which focuses on images to remember order such as bun for one, shoe for two, and tree for three (e.g., images of a bun with sugar, a stamp with a shoe, and a tea pot with a tree to remember the order of the three major acts from the British government that contributed to the Boston Tea Party; The Access Center, n.d.; Scruggs & Mastropieri, 2000).

In addition to social studies content strategies, research supports two specific literacy strategies applicable for Tier III interventions (Englert & Mariage, 1991; Englert et al., 1988). POSSE is a reading strategy and stands for Predict, Organize, Search, Summarize, and Evaluate. Students are explicitly taught to approach their reading (e.g., text, passage) by making predictions about it from its title, headings, and images (Englert & Mariage, 1991). Next, students are taught to organize ideas and concepts from the reading through use of a semantic map and then identify the structure of the reading (e.g., main idea, details). Students then focus on summarizing the passage and asking themselves higher order thinking questions to elicit further understanding (e.g., asking what will happen next or if there was something they did not understand). Finally, students evaluate what they have read. POWER (Plan, Organize, Write, Edit, Revise), on the other hand, is a writing strategy (Englert et al., 1988). Through use of think sheets, students are guided through each step of the writing progress from planning to organizing, writing, evaluating, and revising. Teachers can color-code the procedural facilitators to provide students additional support in applying this scaffolded writing progress.

For older students, teachers can also employ the Strategic Instruction Model (SIM; Center for Research on Learning, 2009c). SIM includes Content Enhancement Routines (CER) and Learning Strategies, and while they have slightly different audiences and approaches, both provide multiple strategies and organizers (Center for Research on Learning, 2009a, 2009b, 2009c). SIM is in depth and often implemented with specific professional development. SIM can benefit students, and we encourage readers to explore CER and Learning Strategies at http://www.ku-crl.org.

Within the emerging research base of technology, social studies, and students with disabilities, two different approaches appear: technology-based strategic instruction (e.g., computer-based concept maps; Blankenship, Ayers, & Langone, 2005; Boon, Burke, Fore, & Spencer, 2006), and a web-based history learning environment (e.g., the Virtual History Museum [VHM]; Bouck, Courtad, Okolo, Englert, & Heutsche, 2009; Okolo, Englert, Bouck, Heutsche, & Wang, in press). In terms of computer-based concept maps, teachers can use purchased software (e.g., Inspiration or Kidspiration) or free online applications (e.g., Webspiration, C-Map) to allow students to represent their thinking of a concept. Use of computer-based concept maps can be done while students are reading to make sense of how things work together, at the end as a review or assessment, or even prior to writing to organize students' thinking.

On the other hand, the VHM (see http://vhm.msu.edu) focuses on exposing students to primary and secondary sources using text that is more considerate and at an appropriate reading level. With VHM, teachers can create appropriate text about a particular topic for students as well as access supplemental materials (e.g., images, documents, videos, music). Further, VHM focuses on students representing their understanding of the material presented through charts and maps (e.g., descriptive chart, compare and contrast, a Venn diagram), essays (e.g., compare and contrast, persuasive, descriptive, a position statement), or answering questions (e.g., short answer, multiple choice). Additionally, VHM has built in scaffolds to support students such as activities that come with individualized scaffolds to further support students in writing an essay or creating a chart (see Bouck et al., 2009; Okolo et al., in press, for additional information regarding VHM).

Finally, accommodations are an appropriate and evidence-based approach for providing instruction to students with disabilities at a level playing field (Fuchs & Fuchs, 1999; Fuchs, Fuchs, & Capizzi, 2005). The most common types of accommodations are characterized by presentation (e.g., reading aloud directions), equipment and materials (e.g., books on tape), response (e.g., scribe), scheduling and timing (e.g., extended time), and setting (i.e., different location; Thurlow, Lazarus, Thompson, & Morse, 2005). Accommodations are often provided at the individual student level through students' IEPs; however, teachers can also consider applying the principle of Universal Design for Learning (UDL; Council for Exceptional Children [CEC], 2005) as an alternative means of providing individual accommodations for students with disabilities. UDL involves developing curricula, lesson plans, and other educational programming to address the diverse range of learners in a classroom beforehand, reducing the need to individually accommodate students to provide them access and improved opportunity for achievement (CEC, 2005). Simply put, teachers wishing to implement UDL can consider providing students with multiple means of presenting a concept (i.e., the teacher teaches through multiple means—lecture, inquiry, videos, text, simulations); multiple means of engagement (i.e., students have multiple opportunities in which to address their learning and interact with a concept); and multiple means of expression (i.e., students have multiple opportunities to express their learning—written paper, oral responses, or developing a video). For a more complete discussion of UDL in general, please see CEC, 2005, and for an example of UDL in social studies, please see Bouck et al., 2009.

Collecting appropriate data. Similar to Tiers I and II, Tier III data collection involves the use of progress monitoring to determine students' success with the intervention, and CBMs provide an excellent resource for progress monitoring. Progress monitoring in Tier III should be more frequent than the progress monitoring in Tier I and even Tier II (i.e., weekly or even twice a week; Stecker, Fuchs et al., 2008). However, when students are placed into Tier III, we also need to seriously consider that these students possess significant challenges to access, participation, and achievement in social studies. Hence, similar to the consideration of effective teaching and strategies, data collection should include the use of accommodations. In other words, in Tier III, students should be provided access to accommodations to use when taking the CBM, thus ensuring a more accurate picture of what students know and their progress.

Case Study

Mr. Nowak is a fifth-grade teacher at Saranac Elementary. He teaches 30 students in reading, writing, mathematics, science, and social studies. Mr. Nowak's school started implementing RtI in the previous school year, and he is preparing for the current year to better apply RtI in the core content areas of social studies and science.

In social studies, Mr. Nowak thinks about the curriculum across the school year. In fifth grade, the social studies curriculum in Mr. Nowak's state and school is United States history. In particular, Mr. Nowak teaches students about the arrival of explorers through the adoption of the Bill of Rights in 1791. In thinking about RtI, Mr. Nowak pulls out the big ideas across the year's curriculum such as freedom, government, and exploration and conquest. Next, Mr. Nowak develops two types of CBMs—one based on vocabulary matching (see Espin et al., 2001; Espin et al., 2005) and one based on content and involving short-answer questions focused on the big ideas. He plans on assessing students every week and develops CBMs to be given weekly, alternating between the vocabulary matching and short-answer ones. Once Mr. Nowak develops the questions and randomly places them on the set number of assessments, he then randomly places the assessments in order by type.

As Mr. Nowak implements the CBMs in class, he records all of his students' progress. He begins to monitor students who are consistently struggling on the weekly CBMs—in both vocabulary matching and higher order open-ended content. After 8 weeks, Mr. Nowak refers six of his 30 students for Tier II services based on their performance. Although Tier II services can be handled in multiple ways, at Mr. Nowak's school, Tier II services for social studies are provided by general education teachers with support from a trained paraprofessional. (A specially trained individual provides Tier II services for reading, mathematics, and behavior.)

For his Tier II services, Mr. Nowak focuses both on students' struggles with the abstract cognitive processes associated with social studies as well as improving students' literacy in the content areas. Working in a small group, the students are provided specific strategies to approach both reading and writing in the content areas as well as thinking skills. For example, Mr. Nowak and his paraprofessional focus on teaching the students to be strategic readers; using strategies such as previewing the text; making predictions and confirming those predictions; making connections from the current text to previous texts, other information learned, and students' own lives; retelling and summarizing; and discussing the text. Mr. Nowak teaches the students how to use graphic organizers to organize the reading as well as all of the information presented for a particular topic or unit. Mr. Nowak also allows the students to have time to work together to discuss the information and then check in with himself or the trained paraprofessional. In terms of supporting the students with the abstract cognitive processes, Mr. Nowak explicitly teaches the students to think aloud when posed with an abstract problem, and the small group works together to model an example each week during social studies instructional time.

After 20 weeks of Tier II service and continual progress monitoring with the CBMs, four of the six students are determined to have responded to the more intensive instruction; two of the six are referred to Tier III services. The two students deemed to need Tier III support are referred to the special education department, and in addition to the evidenced-based, high-quality social studies instruction they receive in Mr. Nowak's class, they receive supplemental support instruction in the special education classroom by a trained special education teacher. In particular, the special education teacher makes recommendations for appropriate accommodations to be made in the general education classroom for daily class activities as well as for assessments that would benefit the individual students in social studies. Further, the special education teacher provides more intensive strategic instruction such as teaching the students to employ the POSSE strategy for reading the required content and the POWER strategy when asked for written expression assignments. Further, the students are taught how to apply mnemonics to encode and retrieve information, understand clue words connected to text structure, and use technology to supplement more traditional social studies instruction.

Conclusion

Social studies has received relatively little attention in RtI research thus far. The lack of attention may be due to the complex, multidisciplinary nature of social studies; the current legislative focus (e.g., NCLB) on mathematics and language arts; the little time spent on social studies in schools; or the frequently assumed role of RtI—identifying students with LD, which is typically focused on literacy or mathematics (Bailey et al., 2006; Fuchs,

Fuchs et al., 2007; Lintner, 2006; Lintner & Schweder, 2008; Vaughn et al., 2010). RtI, as applied to social studies, is best understood as prevention and intervention (Barnes & Harlacher, 2008), or in other words, an "innovative approach to service delivery" (Legere & Conca, 2010, p. 33). This approach still involves three tiers, focused on providing high-quality, research-based social studies instructional practices to *all* students as well as additional interventions for students who fail to respond to said instruction. In particular, Tier I social studies instruction should be high-quality, evidence-based, focused on "big ideas" and strategic thinking skills, and provided to all students. Tier II and III interventions must also meet the quality standards of RtI, but may focus on the thinking skills needed in social studies, on content-area reading, or on a variety of learning tasks spanning the higher and lower level thinking needed for social studies achievement. Although there is still little empirical research on RtI in the social studies classroom, the principles of RtI may still be used to provide high-quality, effective social studies instruction to *all* learners, helping fulfill the promise of equal access to education.

References

The Access Center. (n.d.). *Using mnemonic instruction to facilitate access to the general education curriculum.* Retrieved from http://www.k8accesscenter.org/training_resources/Mnemonics.asp

Anderson, T. H., & Ambruster, B. B. (1984). Content area textbooks. In R. C. Anderson, J. Osborn, & R. J. Tierney (Eds.), *Learning to read in American schools: Basal readers and content texts* (pp. 193–224). Hillsdale, NJ: Lawrence Erlbaum.

Armbruster, B. B., & Anderson, T. H. (1984). Structures of explanations in history textbooks, or so what if Governor Stanford missed the spike and hit the rail? *Journal of Curriculum Studies, 16,* 247–274.

Bailey, G., Shaw, E. L., & Hollifield, D. (2006). The devaluation of social studies in the elementary grades. *Journal of Social Studies Research, 30*(2), 18–30.

Baker, S., Gersten, R., & Graham, S. (2003). Teaching expressive writing to students with learning disabilities: Research-based applications and examples. *Journal of Learning Disabilities, 36,* 109–115.

Bakken, J. P., Mastropieri, M. A., & Scruggs, T. E. (1997). Reading comprehension of expository science material and students with learning disabilities: A comparison of strategies. *The Journal of Special Education, 31,* 300–324.

Barnes, A. C., & Harlarcher, J. E. (2008). Clearing the confusion: Response to Intervention as a set of principles. *Education and Treatment of Children, 31,* 417–431.

Beyer, B. K. (2008a). How to teach thinking skills in social studies and history. *The Social Studies, 99,* 196–201.

Beyer, B. K. (2008b). What research tells us about teaching thinking skills. *The Social Studies, 99,* 223–232.

Blankenship, T. L., Ayers, K. M., & Langone, J. (2005). Effects of computer-based cognitive mapping on reading comprehension for students with emotional behavioral disorders. *Journal of Special Education Technology, 20*(2), 15–23.

Boon, R. T., Burke, M. D., Fore, C., & Spencer, V. G. (2006). The impact of cognitive organizers and technology-based practices on student success in secondary social studies classrooms. *Journal of Special Education Technology, 21*(1), 5–15.

Boon, R. T., Fore, C., Blankenship, T., & Chalk, J. (2007). Technology-based practices in social studies instruction for students with high-incidence disabilities: A review of the literature. *Journal of Special Education Technology, 22*(4), 41–56.

Bouck, E. C., Courtad, C. A., Okolo, C., Englert, C. S., & Heutsche, A. (2009). The virtual history museum: Helping bring UDL to social studies instruction. *Teaching Exceptional Children, 42*(2), 14–21.

Canter, A., Klotz, M. B., & Cowan, K. (2008). Response to Intervention: The future for secondary schools. *Principal Leadership, 8*(6), 12–15.

Center for Research on Learning. (2009a). *Content enhancement.* Retrieved from http://www.ku-crl.org/sim/content.shtml

Center for Research on Learning. (2009b). *Learning strategies.* Retrieved from http://www.ku-crl.org/sim/strategies.shtml

Center for Research on Learning. (2009c). *Strategic instruction model.* Retrieved from http://www.ku-crl.org/sim

Checkley, K. (2008). *The essentials of social studies, grades K–8: Effective curriculum, instruction, and assessment.* Alexandria, VA: ASCD.

Council for Exceptional Children. (2005). *Universal design for learning: A guide for teachers and education professionals.* Boston, MA: Pearson.

Crawford, D. B., Carnine, D. W., Harniss, M. K., Hollenbeck, K. L., & Miller, S. K. (2011). Effective strategies for teaching social studies. In M. D. Coyne, E. J. Kame'enui, & D. W. Carnine (Eds.). *Effective teach-*

ing strategies that accommodate diverse learners (4th ed., pp. 213–242). Boston, MA: Pearson.

Cuban, L. (2003). *Why is it so hard to get good schools?* New York, NY: Teachers College Press.

De La Paz, S. (2005). Effects of historical reasoning instruction and writing strategy mastery in culturally and academically diverse middle school classrooms. *Journal of Educational Psychology, 97,* 139–156.

De La Paz, S., & Graham, S. (1997). Effects of dictation and advanced planning instruction on the composing of students with writing and learning problems. *Journal of Educational Psychology, 89,* 203–222.

Englert, C. S., & Mariage, T. (1991). Making students partners in the comprehension process: Send for the reading POSSE. *Learning Disability Quarterly, 14,* 123–138.

Englert, C. S., Raphael, T. E., Anderson, L. M., Anthony, H. M., Fear, K. L., & Gregg, S. L. (1988). A case for writing intervention: Strategies for writing informational text. *Learning Disabilities Focus, 3,* 98–113.

Espin, C. A., Busch, T. W., Shin, J., & Kruschwitz, R. (2001). Curriculum-based measurement in the content areas: Validity of vocabulary-matching as an indicator of performance in social studies. *Learning Disabilities Research & Practice, 16,* 142–151.

Espin, C. A., & Deno, S. L. (1993). Performance in reading from content-area text as an indicator of achievement. *Remedial and Special Education, 14*(6), 47–59.

Espin, C. A., & Deno, S. L. (1995). Curriculum-based measures for secondary students: Utility and task specificity of text-based reading and vocabulary measures for predicting performance in content-area tasks. *Diagnostique, 20,* 121–142.

Espin, C. A., & Foegen, A. (1996). Validity of three general outcome measures for predicting secondary students' performance on content-area tasks. *Exceptional Children, 62,* 497–514.

Espin, C. A., Shin, J., & Busch, T. W. (2005). Curriculum-based measurement in the content areas: Vocabulary matching as an indicator of progress in social studies learning. *Journal of Learning Disabilities, 38,* 353–363.

Fairbanks, S., Sugai, G., Guardino, D., & Lathrop, M. (2007). Response to Intervention: Examining classroom behavior support in second grade. *Exceptional Children, 73,* 288–310.

Ferretti, R. P., MacArthur, C. D., & Okolo, C. M. (2001). Teaching for historical understanding in inclusive classrooms. *Learning Disability Quarterly, 24,* 59–71.

Fontana, J. L., Scruggs, T., & Mastropieri, M. A. (2007). Mnemonic strategy instruction in inclusive secondary social studies classes. *Remedial and Special Education, 28,* 345–355.

Fuchs, D., & Deshler, D. D. (2007). What we need to know about Responsiveness to Intervention (and shouldn't be afraid to ask). *Learning Disabilities Research & Practice, 22,* 129–136.

Fuchs, D., Fuchs, L., Hintze, J., & Lembke, E. (2007). *Using curriculum-based measurement to determine Response to Intervention (RTI).* Retrieved from http://www.studentprogress.org/summer_institute/default.asp#RTI

Fuchs, D., & Fuchs, L. S. (2006). Introduction to Response to Intervention: What, why, and how valid is it? *Reading Research Quarterly, 41,* 93–99.

Fuchs, L. S., & Fuchs, D. (1999). Fair and unfair testing accommodations. *School Administrator, 10*(56), 24–29.

Fuchs, L. S., Fuchs, D., & Capizzi, A. M. (2005). Identifying appropriate test accommodations for students with learning disabilities. *Focus on Exceptional Children, 37*(6), 1–8.

Fuchs, L. S., Fuchs, D., Compton, D. L., Bryant, J. D., Hamlett, C. L., & Seethlater, P. M. (2007). Mathematics screening and progress monitoring at first grade: Implications for Responsiveness to Intervention. *Exceptional Children, 73,* 311–330.

Fuchs, D., Mock, D., Morgan, P. L., & Young, C. L. (2003). Responsiveness-to-Intervention: Definitions, evidence, and implications for the learning disabilities construct. *Learning Disabilities Research & Practice, 18,* 157–171.

Gresham, F. M. (2005). Response to Intervention: An alternative means of identifying students as emotionally disturbed. *Education and Treatment of Children, 28,* 328–344.

Harniss, M. K., Dickson, S. V., Kinder, D., & Hollenbeck, K. L. (2001). Textual problems and instructional strategies: Strategies for enhancing learning from published history textbooks. *Reading and Writing Quarterly: Overcoming Learning Difficulties, 17,* 127–150.

Hedin, L. R., & Conderman, G. (2010). Teaching students to comprehend informational text through rereading. *The Reading Teacher, 63,* 556–565.

Key, L., Bradley, J. A., & Bradley, K. S. (2010). Stimulating instruction in social studies. *The Social Studies, 101,* 117–120.

Legere, E. J., & Conca, L. M. (2010). Response to Intervention by a child with severe reading disability: A case study. *Teaching Exceptional Children, 43*(1), 32–41.

Leinhardt, G., & Young, K. M. (1996). Two texts, three readers: Distance and expertise in reading history. *Cognition and Instruction, 14,* 441–486.

Lintner, T. (2006). Social studies (still) on the back burner: Perceptions and practices of K–5 social studies instruction. *Journal of Social Studies Research, 30*(1), 3–8.

Lintner, T., & Schweder, W. (2008). Social studies in special education classrooms: A glimpse behind closed doors. *Journal of Social Studies Research, 32*(1), 3–9.

Marston, D. (2005). Tiers of intervention in Responsiveness to Intervention: Prevention outcomes and learning disabilities identification patterns. *Journal of Learning Disabilities, 38,* 539–544.

Martin, D., & Wineburg, S. (2008). Seeing thinking on the web. *The History Teacher, 4,* 305–319.

McCall, A. L., Janssen, B., & Riederer, K. (2008). More time for powerful social studies: When university social studies methods faculty and classroom teachers collaborate. *The Social Studies, 99,* 135–141.

McMaster, K., & Espin, C. (2007). Technical features of curriculum-based measurement in writing: A literature review. *The Journal of Special Education, 42,* 68–84.

Memory, D. M., Yoder, C. A., Bolinger, K. B., & Warren, W. J. (2004). Creating thinking and inquiry tasks that reflect the concerns and interests of adolescents. *The Social Studies, 95,* 147–154.

National Council for the Social Studies. (2008). *Expectations of excellence: Curriculum standards for social studies* (Draft Revision). Retrieved from http://www.socialstudies.org/standards/taskforce/fall2008draft

No Child Left Behind Act of 2001, 20 U.S.C § 6301 et seq. (2002).

O'Connor, R. E., Fulmer, D., & Harty, K. (2003, December). *Tiers of intervention in kindergarten through third grade.* Paper presented at the National Research Center on Learning Disabilities Responsiveness-to-Intervention Symposium, Kansas City, MO.

Okolo, C. M., Englert, C. S., Bouck, E. C., Heutsche, A. M., & Wang, H. (in press). The virtual history museum: Learning U.S. history in diverse eighth grade classrooms. *Remedial and Special Education.*

Okolo, C. M., & Ferretti, R. P. (1996a). Knowledge acquisition and multimedia design projects in the social studies for students with learning disabilities. *Journal of Special Education Technology, 13,* 91–103.

Okolo, C. M., & Ferretti, R. P. (1996b). The impact of multimedia design projects on the knowledge, attitudes, and collaboration of students in inclusive classrooms. *Journal of Computing in Childhood Education, 7,* 223–251.

Patton, J., Polloway, E., & Cronin, M. (1987). Social studies instruction for handicapped students: A review of current practices. *The Social Studies, 78,* 131–135.

Paxton, R. J. (1997). "Someone with like a life write it": The effects of a visible author on high school history students. *Journal of Educational Psychology, 89,* 235–250.

Schell, E., & Fisher, D. (2007). *Teaching social studies: A literacy-based approach.* Upper Saddle River, NJ: Pearson.

Scruggs, T. E., & Mastropieri, M. A. (2000). The effectiveness of mnemonic instruction for students with learning and behavior problems: An update and research synthesis. *Journal of Behavioral Education, 10,* 163–173.

Scruggs, T. E., Mastropieri, M. A., & Okolo, C. M. (2008). Science and social studies for students with disabilities. *Focus on Exceptional Children, 41*(2), 1–24.

Slater, W. H., & Horstman, F. R. (2002). Teaching reading and writing to struggling middle school and high school students: The case for reciprocal teaching. *Preventing School Failure, 46,* 163–166.

Stecker, P. M., Fuchs, D., & Fuchs, L. S. (2008). Progress monitoring as essential practice within Response to Intervention. *Rural Special Education Quarterly, 27*(4), 10–17.

Stecker, P. M., Lembke, E. S., & Foegen, A. (2008). Using progress-monitoring data to improve instructional decision making. *Preventing School Failure, 52*(2), 48–58.

Steele, M. M. (2008). Teaching social studies to middle school students with learning problems. *The Clearing House, 81,* 197–200.

Thurlow, M. L., Lazarus, S. S., Thompson, S. J., & Morse, A. B. (2005). State policies on assessment participation and accommodations for students with disabilities. *Journal of Special Education, 38,* 232–240.

Tilly, W. D. (2003, December). *How many tiers are needed for successful prevention and early intervention? Heartland area education agency's evolution from four to three tiers.* Paper presented at the National Research Center on Learning Disabilities Responsiveness-to-Intervention Symposium, Kansas City, MO.

Torgesen, J. K. (2000). Individual differences in response to early interventions in reading: The lingering problem of treatment resisters. *Learning Disabilities Research & Practice, 15,* 55–64.

VanFossen, P. J. (2005). "Reading and math take so much time . . .": An overview of social studies instruction in elementary classrooms in Indiana. *Theory and Research in Social Education, 33,* 376–403.

Vaughn, S. (2003, December). *How many tiers are needed for Response to Intervention to achieve acceptable prevention outcomes?* Paper presented at the National Research Center on Learning Disabilities Responsiveness-to-Intervention Symposium, Kansas City, MO.

Vaughn, S., Cirino, P. T., Wanzek, J., Wexler, J., Fletcher, J. M., Denton, C. D., Barth, A., . . . & Francis, D. J. (2010). Response to Intervention for middle school students with reading difficulties: Effects of a primary and secondary intervention. *School Psychology Review, 39,* 3–21.

Ward-Lonergan, J. M., Liles, B. Z., & Anderson, A. M. (1999). Verbal retelling abilities in adolescents with and without language-learning disabilities for social studies lectures. *Journal of Learning Disabilities, 32,* 213–222.

Wiggins, G., & McTighe, J. (1998). *Understanding by design.* Alexandria, VA: ASCD.

Williams, J. P., Nubla-Kung, A. M., Polloni, S., Stafford, K. B., Garcia, A., & Snyder, A. E. (2007). Teaching cause-effect text structure through social studies content to at-risk second graders. *Journal of Learning Disabilities, 40,* 111–120.

CHAPTER 13

Data-Based
Decision Making Across a
Multitiered System of Support

Gary L. Cates

This book has provided a unique contribution to the field of education, given the current spirit of educational legislation (e.g., NCLB, IDEA) in the United States centered on accountability and student outcomes. In addition, Response to Intervention (RtI) seems to be at the forefront of much of the current discussion related to accountability and student outcomes. Although a variety of discussion topics related to RtI, such as a call for a demonstration of efficacy of RtI (e.g. Reynolds & Shaywitz, 2009), the functional utility of screening instruments (e.g. Goodman, 2006; Hall, 2006), and what constitutes adequate progress (e.g., Fuchs, 2003), have been presented, it is clear that a common thread among these discussions is related to how best to provide educational services to all students. Because there are numerous philosophical differences and thus practices within the field of education, it may behoove the field to address these differences in the context of empirical justification of practice. The focus of this chapter is to provide a model for data-based decision making in schools implementing RtI by focusing on common RtI practices. First, the reader will be provided with a description of six common components of RtI models as presented in Cates, Blum, and Swerdlik (2011). Second, the chapter will discuss how adequate yearly progress (AYP) can be used as anchoring context for making data-based decisions related to the implementation of these common practice components. Finally, the reader will be provided with specific empirical examples of how to: (a) determine cut scores for local benchmarking assessments, (b) determine levels of support needed for all students within a school across all tiers, (c) make definitive decisions with regard to moving students within and across tiers, and (d) determine educational goals for all students.

Common Components in the Implementation of RtI

Figure 13.1 represents a flow chart of common components provided in RtI. The components include: (a) core instruction, (b) universal screening, (c) standard protocol intervention, (d) individualized intervention, (e) special education and (f) progress monitoring throughout the RtI process. It is at each independent component that a data-based decision must be made. The shaded boxes represent assessment components that must be evaluated, while the nonshaded boxes represent intervention components that must be evaluated.

Figure 13.2 displays the five questions that may be routinely asked at each component respectively. These questions include: (a) Is the core instruction effective? (b) Does the universal screening measure adequately predict student performance on state standards? (c) Is Tier II support effective? (d) Is Tier III support effective? and (e) Is special education support effective?

The questions related to the effectiveness of Tiers II and III and special education can be asked at both the individual student level and at the overall tier level. Specifically, these questions are: (a) Are the practices effective in general? and (b) Are the practices effective for individual students? In posing these questions, school personnel may more clearly identify specific areas in need of development. It should be pointed out that in designing an RtI model around these questions, implementation of and changes to the system should be addressed in the order in which the questions are posed.

Question 1: Is the Core Instruction Effective?

The evidence of outcomes that is available for all public schools is the school report card. The school report card provides empirical data related to a school's performance relative to national expectations. In addition to empirical data, the school report card provides a descriptor of whether the school is making AYP. To make AYP for the 2010–2011 school year in the state of Illinois, a school must have met (a) the 95% participation rate on state assessments, in the aggregate and for all subgroups; (b) the target of 85% meeting or exceeding state standards (reading and mathematics only); and (c) the 91% attendance rate for elementary and middle schools and a

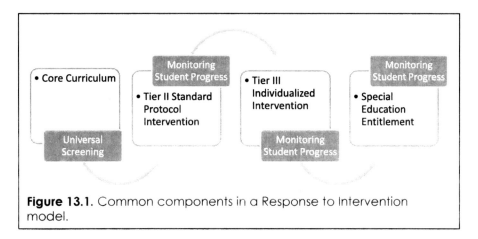

Figure 13.1. Common components in a Response to Intervention model.

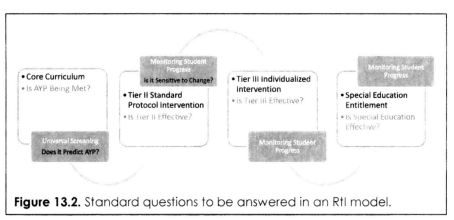

Figure 13.2. Standard questions to be answered in an RtI model.

82% graduation rate for high schools (Illinois State Board of Education, n.d.). If a school is not making AYP, then changes need to be made to ensure that AYP occurs in the future. It is important to point out that making AYP means that disaggregated subgroups (e.g., free and reduced lunch, minorities, English Language Learners) are also meeting state standards. It is therefore important to analyze school data across these groups in addition to overall school-level analysis.

Question 2: Does the Universal Screening Measure Adequately Predict Student Performance on State Standards?

A universal screening measure is a variable or group of variables for which data are collected across all students. This variable(s) generally requires a brief administration of some tool to obtain and adequately predict student performance on state standards as measured by high-stakes assessments. For example, Oral Reading Fluency (ORF) is how fast and accurately a student can read for one minute (e.g., Roehrig, Petscher, Nettles, Hudson, & Torgesen, 2008). Although the variable is not intended to be an assessment of specific reading achievement, research (e.g., Hixson & McGlinchey, 2004) has suggested that ORF can adequately identify students who may be at risk for not meeting expectations (i.e., individual student AYP). Being able to adequately predict which students may not meet standards is particularly helpful to a school that is focused on making AYP because it allows schools to provide these students with supplemental instruction aimed at improving performance prior to the administration of the high-stakes assessment tests. It is important to point out, however, that the universal screening measure must adequately predict student performance. If the measure is an inadequate predictor, then it can either predict that some students would meet expectations who actually do not (false negatives) or predict that some students would not meet expectations who actually do (false positives). Both of these outcomes would improperly guide decision making. Therefore school personnel should determine the correlation between the universal screening measure and the high-stakes test used to measure student performance on state standards.

Cut scores. One data-based decision-making question that is often posed is "What should be used as the cut score for providing Tier II supplemental support?" In consulting with schools, the author has discovered that a lot of variability exists across schools with regard to a cut score. Some cut scores have included local norms (e.g., a specific percentile score), while others have focused on national norms provided by companies such as AIMSweb (published by Pearson) or DIBELS (University of Oregon Center on Teaching and Learning, 2008). Depending on what norms (national or local) and what percentile cut point is used (e.g., 25th, 10th, etc.), students may or may not be provided services in one school over another (e.g., Fuchs, 2003). In addition, percentile scores have a major flaw with regard to identification in general. A percentile rank method will always identify students regardless of performance. Because of the nature of the percentile rank, 25% of the students will be at or below the 25th percentile. Therefore, despite solid evidence-based practices that may improve student performance substantially, using a 25th-percentile cut score will result in 25% of students being identified for support.

It is thus recommended that schools rely on the correlation between the universal screening measure and the high-stakes test (e.g., Fuchs, 2003). A universal screening measure that adequately predicts student performance can afford school personnel the opportunity to make more precise decisions on which students to provide supplemental support to as well as a method for determining when to begin to fade out such supports. This is accomplished through deriving a cut score. This cut score is determined through the correlation that school personnel calculated when determining the adequacy of the universal screening measure(s). Using simple slope-y intercept calculations, school personnel can identify what score, x, is needed on the universal screening measure to meet expectation, y, on the high-stakes test. This cut score is then used (a) to identify students in need of additional support and (b) as the point at which support is faded. The major advantage of using the correlation-derived cut score is that it will only identify students who are at risk for not meeting expectations on the high-stakes test regardless of percentile rank. Figure 13.3 represents the relationship between a high-stakes test taken by a group of students during their third-grade year (represented on the y axis) and their respective Oral Reading Fluency scores in the fall of the second grade (presented on the x axis). The horizontal line represents the level of performance specified by the state as "meeting expectations." The vertical line represents the ORF cut score that captures the majority of students who are likely to not meet expectations. You may note that a few students are captured who do not necessarily need additional support (false positives) as well as students who should have received support but did not (false negatives). The stronger the correlation between the universal screening measure and the high-stakes outcome measure, the fewer false positives and false negatives will be found (e.g., Hinkle, Wiersma, & Jurs, 2003).

Question 3: Are the Core Curriculum and Instruction Effective?

Core instruction is the instruction that is provided to all students. It is the universal grade-level instruction. This is the Tier I level foundation of instruction on which all other instructional decisions are made. It is therefore highly important to have sound evidence-based curriculum and instruction. There are two ways of determining if core curriculum and instruction are effective. One way to determine if the core curriculum and instruction are effective is to apply the 80% successful criterion (e.g., Brown-Chidsey & Steege, 2005). That is, if 80% of students are success-ful at meeting or exceeding state standards, then the universal curriculum is effective. If not, then a change is needed. A second, more liberal way of determining if core curriculum and instruction are effective may be adopted by those schools beginning the RtI implementation process. This

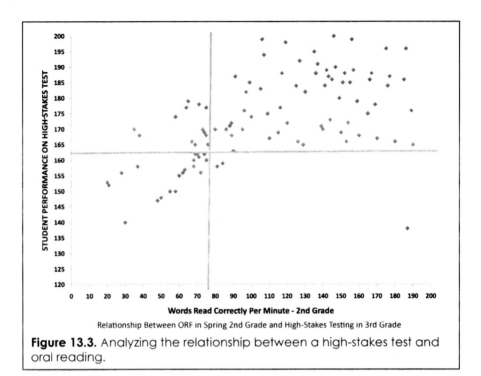

Figure 13.3. Analyzing the relationship between a high-stakes test and oral reading.

second method focuses on an AYP rule of thumb. The AYP rule-of-thumb method suggests that if the school is making AYP, then the curriculum is sufficient. However, it should be pointed out that AYP will increase over time, and therefore some slight intensification/modification of current curriculum and/or instruction may be warranted to maintain the meeting of AYP. Therefore, if a school is meeting AYP, it should consider working toward the 80% rule of thumb. Being somewhere between AYP and 80% is ideal for those schools in the beginning stages of implementing RtI.

Question 4: Is Tier II Support Effective?

When students fail to meet expectations and/or they are found to be at risk of not meeting state standards through the universal screening measure, additional instructional support is provided to target specific academic areas. The effectiveness of this Tier II instructional support should be evaluated in two ways. First, the overall effectiveness of Tier II support should be evaluated for all students as a group who receive such support. One way to evaluate the overall effectiveness is to determine if the number of students needing Tier II support is increasing above, decreasing below, or staying at the level of the 10% rule of thumb. That is, no more than 10% of students should be receiving Tier II supplemental support. If more than 10% require such support, then changes to the core curriculum and/or instruction are needed.

The second way that the effectiveness of Tier II instructional support should be evaluated is for each individual student receiving such support. At this level of evaluation, school personnel should evaluate whether (a) the support resulted in the student meeting performance criteria upon a prespecified date or (b) the support is currently facilitating performance such that the data suggest that the student is likely to meet cut score criteria upon the prespecified evaluation date. The prespecified date is nothing more than the date at which school personnel have agreed to evaluate the final outcome of the support. For many this may be a benchmarking period, at the end of a quarter, after a specified amount of time has passed as suggested by an intervention manual, school teams, or a school board. If a student meets the cut score criterion at the end of the prespecified evaluation period, then the intervention support is considered effective. If a student does not meet the cut score criterion at the end of a full round evaluation period, then the intervention support is considered ineffective and either (a) the intervention should be intensified, (b) a new intervention should implemented at the same intensity level, or (c) a new intervention should be implemented at a higher intensity level.

Sometimes, however, progress-monitoring data may suggest that the student is not on track to meet the criterion at the end of the prespecified evaluation period. In this case an intervention may be tweaked. A tweak is a subtle change in the intervention/support that does not constitute a "change" in the actual intervention. Rather, a tweak is a slight change based on both data and a hypothesis that the tweak may increase the probability of the student meeting the criterion at the end of the prespecified evaluation period. Tweaks may include such modifications as placement of materials, font sizes, seating arrangements, and volume. These decisions are generally made via visual inspection of data displayed in graphs. How to determine the trajectory is discussed in the section titled "Making Decisions Across and Within Tiers for Individual Students."

Question 5: Is Tier III Support Effective?

When students receiving services at the Tier II level do not meet the criterion at the end of the prespecified evaluation period, then Tier III intervention support may be warranted. Like Tier II evaluation, Tier III support requires the same evaluation process with the same decision rules. First, Tier III support should be evaluated for all of the students as a whole.

It is suggested that no more than 5% of students receive Tier III support. If more than 5% of students are receiving Tier III support, then school personnel should consider revising Tiers I and/or II to reduce this percentage. Second, Tier III support should be evaluated for each individual student receiving such support. Again, the evaluation should seek to answer (a) Did the intervention result in the student meeting criterion by the end of the prespecified full evaluation period? or (b) Is the student making adequate progress toward the goal such that the student is likely to meet the criterion by the end of the prespecified evaluation period?

Question 6: Is Special Education Support Effective?

When students either (a) fail to meet criterion by the end of the prespecified evaluation period of Tier III or (b) need intervention/support that requires an inordinate amount of resources, then special education entitlement is warranted. Like Tiers II and III, special education support should be evaluated using the same evaluation procedures and decision rules. It is suggested that no more than 5% of students be receiving special education services.

Making Decisions Across and Within Tiers for Individual Students

As mentioned previously, school personnel need to determine whether an intervention/support is effective at the end of the prespecified evaluation period. In addition, school personnel also need to determine whether a student is making sufficient progress toward meeting the criterion during the evaluation period. Although both levels of evaluation examine effectiveness, each serves a different purpose related to measuring outcomes. Evaluation at the end of the prespecified period determines whether a student moves toward more intensive tier support, moves toward less intensive support, or continues receiving support at his current level of support (i.e., moving between tiers). Evaluating during the evaluation period (i.e., progress monitoring) determines whether a tweak should be made within the current level of support.

Across-Tier Decision Making: Changes

Because data are used in making decisions related to evaluation, it is important to specify how data will be used to determine when and if a student moves to a different level of support (i.e., moving toward a different tier). To make these decisions specific, goals should be set for each tier. If students are not meeting those goals, then more intensive service is needed. If a student is surpassing the goal, then less intensive service is needed.

Tier I. To move from Tier I core instruction to more intensive Tier II support, a student should score below the correlation-derived cut score that suggests she is at risk for not meeting expectations.

Tier II and III. To move from Tier II or Tier III to less intensive support, after receiving the Tier II service a student must meet the cut score criterion that suggests that she is no longer at risk for not meeting expectations. It should be pointed out, however, that the full level of support should not be discontinued at once. Instead, a systematic fading of the support should take place. For example, if Tier II support is provided 3 days per week for 30 minutes a day and the student reaches criterion at the end of the prespecified evaluation period (e.g., 8–12 weeks), then services are not fully discontinued at this point. Instead, the level of service should decrease to between Tier I and Tier II support (e.g., 2 days per week for 30 minutes a day followed by 1 day per week for 30 minutes a day). Following a systematic fading procedure may ensure that students are not leaving one level of support to another only to return back very soon (Kazdin, 2001).

Special education. To move from special education toward less intensive Tier III level support, after receiving special education a student must meet the cut score criterion that suggests that he is no longer at risk for not meeting expectations and the level of support can be faded to an acceptable level that does not require an inordinate amount of resources. It should be noted that Individual Education Programs (IEP) are written such that their goals allow for an evaluation and decision-making process.

Within-Tier Decision Making: Tweaks

In order to know whether a student is making adequate progress toward a goal, three things need to be determined beforehand. First, the student's present level of performance should be known. That is, a student's performance should be measured using the universal screening measure. Second, the cut score should be established (this is the goal). Third, the outcome evaluation date should be specified (this is the prespecified evaluation period). Knowing these three things, school personnel can monitor progress and determine if the student is on track to meet the final goal (i.e., the cut score). Figures 13.4, 13.5, and 13.6 display three different hypothetical scenarios. Each scenario represents a student's performance at a

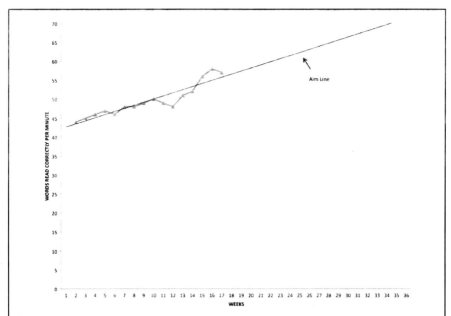

Figure 13.4. Data-based decision making, scenario 1, of a student's performance under Tier II level of support.

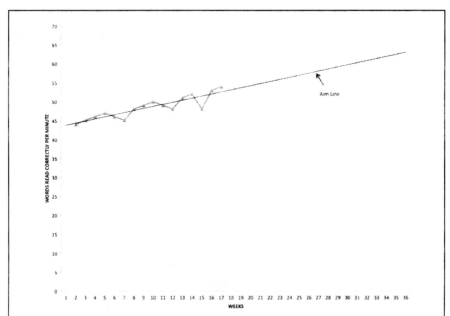

Figure 13.5. Data-based decision making, scenario 2, of a student's performance under Tier II level of support.

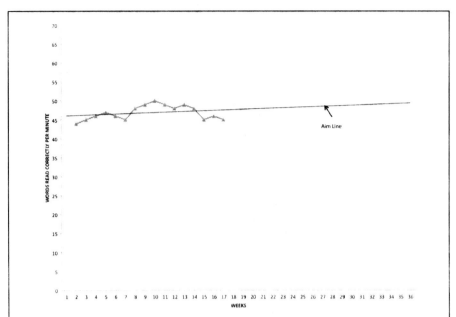

Figure 13.6. Data-based decision making, scenario 3, of a student's performance under Tier II level of support.

Tier II level of intensity. The first three data points in each scenario are the student's initial level performance before the Tier II level of support (i.e., baseline). The final data point in each scenario is the criterion that predicts success on the high-stakes state outcome measure. By simply drawing a line between the median data point during baseline and the correlation-derived cut score at the prespecified evaluation period, a natural expected growth rate is obtained. As data are collected through progress monitoring, a decision as to whether the student is meeting the growth rate can be made by comparing the data plotted over time to the growth line (sometimes referred to as an aimline).

To make a decision as to whether the student is on track to meet the criterion by the prespecified evaluation period, visual inspection of the last three data points is required. However, at least six data points should be collected prior to analyzing these last three data points (Kazdin, 1982). If any of the three points are at or above expected levels, then no tweaks should be made. If all three points are below the expected levels, then a tweak may be made. In scenario 1, Figure 13.4, all three of the last three data points are above the expected level of growth. Therefore, no tweak should be made. The student is above pace to meet the criterion by the prespecified evaluation date. In scenario 2, Figure 13.5, the student's last three data points are variable (above and below the expected growth rate);

271

therefore, no tweak should be made. Finally, in scenario 3, Figure 13.6, the last three data points are all below the expected rate of growth, and therefore a tweak may be made.

Conclusion

This chapter presents a model for making data-based decisions across a multitiered system of support. Specifically, six questions were provided that can govern the data-based decision-making process. All questions have the common theme of attempting to ensure that all students are making AYP. The perspective of this data-based decision-making model is to consider RtI as a continuum of support. It is then the responsibility of school personnel to determine where each child is on the continuum and provide the appropriate level of support to ensure adequate progress. When progress is not being made, then a change should take place at the end of prespecified evaluation periods, and/or tweaks should be made during the progress monitoring of the support implementation. In following a systematic set of decision-making processes, school personnel will be better informed as to (a) their probability of meeting AYP standards and (b) what level of support is needed for meeting these standards for all students in their schools.

References

Brown-Chidsey, R., & Steege, M. W. (2005). *Response to Intervention: Principles and strategies for effective practice.* New York, NY: Guilford Press.

Cates, G. L., Blum, C., & Swerdlik, M. E. (2011). *Effective RTI training and practices: Helping school and district teams improve academic performance and social behavior.* Champaign, IL: Research Press.

Fuchs, L. (2003). Assessing intervention responsiveness. *Learning Disability Research & Practice, 18,* 172–186.

Goodman, K. S. (2006). *The truth about DIBELS.* Portsmouth, NH: Heinemann.

Hall, S. (2006). *I've DIBEL'd, now what?* Frederick, CO: Sopris West.

Hinkle, D., Wiersma, W., & Jurs, S. (2003). *Applied statistics for the behavioral sciences.* Boston, MA: Houghton Mifflin.

Hixson, M. D., & McGlinchey, M. T. (2004). The relationship between race, income, and oral reading fluency and performance on two reading comprehension measures. *Journal of Psychoeducational Assessment,* *22,* 351–364.

Illinois State Board of Education. (n.d.). *No Child Left Behind/Adequate yearly progress.* Retrieved from http://www.isbe.net/ayp/htmls/faq.htm

Kazdin, A. E. (1982). *Single case research design: Methods for applied and clinical settings.* Columbus, OH: Oxford Press.

Kazdin, A. E. (2001). *Behavior modification in applied settings* (6th ed.). Belmont, CA: Wadsworth.

Reynolds, C. R., & Shaywitz, S. E. (2009). Response to Intervention: Ready or not? Or, from wait-to-fail to watch them fail. *School Psychology Quarterly, 24,* 130–145.

Roehrig, A. D., Petscher, Y., Nettles, S. M., Hudson, R. F., & Torgesen, J. K. (2008). Accuracy of the DIBELS oral reading fluency measure for predicting third grade reading comprehension outcomes. *Journal of School Psychology, 46,* 343–366.

University of Oregon Center on Teaching and Learning. (2008). *DIBELS data system.* Retrieved from https://dibels.uoregon.edu

About
the Editor

Jeffrey P. Bakken, Ph.D., is professor and Interim Associate Dean for Research, Graduate Studies, and International Education in the College of Education at Illinois State University. He has a bachelor's degree in Elementary Education from the University of Wisconsin-LaCrosse and graduate degrees in the area of Special Education-Learning Disabilities from Purdue University. Dr. Bakken is a teacher, consultant, and scholar. His specific areas of interest include RtI, collaboration, transition, teacher effectiveness, assessment, learning strategies, and technology. He has written more than 120 academic publications, including books, journal articles, chapters, monographs, reports, and proceedings; has made more than 220 presentations at local, state, regional, national, and international levels; and has received more than $1 million in external funding. Currently, he serves as an external evaluator on a federally funded RtI Network grant project focusing on the implementation of RtI in the state of Illinois.

Dr. Bakken has received the College of Education and the University Research Initiative Award, the College of Education Outstanding College Researcher Award, the College of Education Outstanding College Teacher Award, and the Outstanding University Teacher Award from Illinois State University. Additionally, he is on the editorial boards of many scholarly publications, including *Remedial and Special Education* and *Exceptional Children*, and is the managing editor of *Multicultural Learning and Teaching*, as well as the coeditor for *Advances in Special Education*, published by the Emerald Group. Through his work, he has committed himself to improving teachers' knowledge and techniques as well as services for students with exceptionalities and their families.

About
the Authors

Kristie Asaro-Saddler is an assistant professor in the Division of Special Education at the University at Albany in Albany, NY. Dr. Asaro-Saddler is a former special education teacher for children with autism spectrum disorders (ASD) and developmental disabilities. She currently teaches master's-level special education students and conducts research on writing and the self-regulation of writing with children with ASD. She has published articles and presented across the country on this topic.

Emily C. Bouck is an associate professor of educational studies in the special education program at Purdue University. Her research focuses on the in-school and postschool outcomes of students with high-incidence disabilities with particular attention to issues of academic and functional curriculum and the technology.

Frederick J. Brigham earned his Ph.D. from Purdue University in 1992. Before that, he was a special education and elementary education teacher, a program consultant, and a director of special education. He is an associate professor of special education and research methodology at George Mason University in Fairfax, VA. His research interests include content learning strategies, visual-spatial learning, and assessment.

Brian R. Bryant lives and works in Austin, TX. He is currently a research professor in the Department of Special Education and fellow with the Mathematics Institute for Learning Disabilities and Difficulties in The Meadows Center for Preventing Educational Risk in the College of Education at The University of Texas at Austin. His research interests include mathematics and literacy assessments and interventions for students with learning disabilities and support provisions for individuals with intellectual and developmental disabilities, as well as assistive technology supports for individuals with varying disabilities. He has written and published numerous tests, interventions, articles, books, and book chapters.

Diane Pedrotty Bryant is a professor in the Department of Special Education and the Project Director of the Mathematics Institute for Learning Disabilities and Difficulties in The Meadows Center for Preventing Educational Risk in the College of Education at The University of Texas at Austin. She serves as the principal investigator for several grants that focus on developing and validating supplemental mathematics interventions for struggling students. She has published numerous articles on instructional strategies for students with learning disabilities and is the coauthor of several textbooks and tests.

Gary L. Cates earned his Ph.D. from Mississippi State University and is currently associate professor of psychology at Illinois State University. Dr. Cates has authored and coauthored numerous research studies and national presentations including a new coauthored book titled *Effective Training and Practices in RTI: Helping Schools and District Teams Improve Academic Performance and Social Behavior*. His primary research interests include the prevention and remediation of academic skills deficits. He also currently serves as an external evaluator on a federally funded RtI Network grant project, focusing on the implementation of RtI in the state of Illinois. His current consultation work primarily focuses on the implementation and evaluation of Response to Intervention models with strong emphasis on data-based decision making.

Yojanna Cuenca-Sanchez is an assistant professor in the Special Education Department at Illinois State University. She received her Ph.D. from George Mason University in VA. Her current research focuses on writing instruction for children and adolescents with emotional and behavioral disorders (EBD) and how to incorporate self-determination skills within the content areas.

Karen H. Douglas is an assistant professor at Illinois State University, where she teaches curriculum development and communication strategies. Her research interests include technology, literacy, and transition for students with significant cognitive disabilities. Her two primary foci are on the use of everyday technology to support functional life skills and electronic text supports to aide comprehension of learners with intellectual disabilities.

Barbara M. Fulk is a professor in the Special Education Department at Illinois State University. She received her Ph.D. from Purdue University in Indiana. Besides teaching and conducting research, she also serves as the coordinator of the Master's and Graduate Certificate Programs in the Department of Special Education. Her current research interests are related to learning disabilities (LD), methods for adapting instruction, and collaborating with professionals and families.

Daniel L. Gadke is a doctoral candidate in the school psychology program at Illinois State University. During his time at Illinois State University, he worked on topics surrounding the development and implementation of a Response to Intervention (RtI) model. As a graduate student, he was afforded a number of opportunities to collaborate with schools regarding RtI and has given various presentations on the topic at both local and state levels. His clinical focus involves working with children with autism spectrum disorders for the Autism Program's Illinois State University affiliate site. Currently, he is completing his predoctoral internship in the Applied Behavioral Sciences sequence at the Kennedy Krieger Institute with the Johns Hopkins School of Medicine.

Melissa C. Jenkins has been a special education teacher serving students in kindergarten through fifth grade for the last 9 years. She is a currently a student at George Mason University, pursuing a Ph.D. in Special Education and Education Leadership. Her research interests include behavioral and math interventions for students with high-incidence disabilities.

Nancy Johnson Emanuel graduated from Bridgewater State College, Bridgewater, MA, with a bachelor's degree in History and Secondary Education. She went on to serve in the US Navy for 9 years as a Russian linguist and has taught at both the secondary and elementary levels of public education. She received her master's degree in Special Education from the University of Virginia and is currently a doctoral student in

Special Education and Education Leadership at George Mason University in Fairfax, VA. Nancy is the department supervisor of special education at Osbourn High School in Manassas City, VA.

Sarah R. Jones is an assistant professor of Special Education at Indiana Wesleyan University and a doctoral student in special education at Purdue University. Her research focuses on high-quality inclusive instruction for secondary students with mild disabilities, with particular attention to inclusive language arts instruction.

Kullaya Kosuwan is a lecturer in the Special Education Program, Faculty of Education, Songkhla Rajabhat University, Songkhla, Thailand. Her research interests include intervention strategies for children with learning disabilities, autism spectrum disorders, and intellectual and developmental disabilities, as well as positive behavior support and self-determination.

Valerie Mazzotti received her doctorate in special education from the University of North Carolina at Charlotte. She is currently in her second year as an assistant professor of Special Education at Western Carolina University. Dr. Mazzotti's current research interests include interventions for students at risk for or with mild to moderate disabilities, evidence-based practices, self-determination, secondary transition, and positive behavior support.

Michelle J. McCollin is an associate professor of special education at Slippery Rock University of Pennsylvania. Her research interests include multicultural special education, culturally sensitive literacy instruction, teacher quality, and disproportionality in general and special education. She has presented papers at the local, state, national, and international levels. She also serves in several leadership positions, including as president of the Pennsylvania Association of the Council for Exceptional Children.

April Mustian is currently in her second year as assistant professor of special education at Illinois State University. Dr. Mustian's current research interests include academic and behavioral interventions for students with and at risk for mild to moderate disabilities with emphasis on Emotional Disturbance (ED), Response to Intervention (RtI), disproportionality, applied behavior analysis, and positive behavior support.

Festus E. Obiakor is professor, Department of Exceptional Education, School of Education, University of Wisconsin-Milwaukee. His research interests are in self-concept development, multicultural psychology and special education, educational reform and innovation, and international special education. He has consistently advocated the comprehensive support model (CSM) to bring together the energies of students, families, educational professionals, communities, and government agencies. He is the author of more than 150 publications, including books, chapters, and articles, and he is a frequently invited speaker to many institutions, organizations, and conferences. He serves on the editorial boards of many reputable refereed journals, including *Multicultural Learning and Teaching*, for which he currently serves as cofounding and coexecutive editor.

Bruce Saddler is an associate professor in the Division of Special Education at the University at Albany in Albany, NY. A former K–12 special education teacher and teacher of the year, he currently conducts and publishes empirical research and provides professional workshops concerning writing and the remediation of writing difficulties. Of particular interest to Dr. Saddler is sentence combining, a writing technique he has spent a decade investigating, teaching, and discussing.

Elizabeth A. Skinner is assistant professor in the Department of Curriculum & Instruction at Illinois State University, where she teaches bilingual education courses and serves as the faculty liaison for the Chicago Professional Development School. Elizabeth was a bilingual teacher at a dual language school in the Chicago Public Schools system for 7 years prior to earning her Ph.D. in Curriculum Studies at the University of Illinois Chicago.

Gia Super has been teaching bilingual students in public schools for 11 years and currently teaches second grade at a dual language school in Chicago. She is a doctoral student in the Department of Educational Policy Studies at the University of Illinois Chicago.

Mark E. Swerdlik is a professor of psychology, coordinator of graduate programs in school psychology, and a clinical supervisor in the Psychological Services Center at Illinois State University, where he has been involved in the training of school psychologists for more than 30 years. Dr. Swerdlik is a fellow of the American Psychological Association-Division of School Psychology and has been awarded a Diplomate in

School Psychology from the American Board of Professional Psychology, and a Diplomate in Assessment Psychology from the American Board of Assessment Psychology. Dr. Swerdlik has provided training to a number of Illinois and Midwestern school districts in implementing all components of a Response to Intervention model, has presented papers at national and state conferences, and has coauthored a book and a variety of book chapters and articles on this topic.

Sarah Urbanc is passionate about researching and implementing best practice reading instruction in her classroom. She has a master's degree in reading from Illinois State University as well as a Reading Specialist certificate. For the past 7 years, Sarah has taught third grade at Wilder-Waite Grade School in the Dunlap School District in Peoria, IL.

Jennifer Walker is currently a behavior specialist and social skills curriculum trainer supporting kindergarten through 12th-grade teachers. She is currently pursuing a Ph.D. at George Mason University in Special Education and Education Leadership. Her research interests include behavioral and written language interventions for students with emotional and behavioral disabilities.

Linda Wedwick is an associate professor in the Mary and Jean Borg Center for Reading and Literacy at Illinois State University and a former middle school teacher of language arts. Her current projects involve research into students' self-selection of texts for independent reading and middle school students' attitudes about reading. Her publications have appeared in *The Reading Teacher*, *Voices from the Middle*, and *Illinois Reading Council Journal*.

CPSIA information can be obtained at www.ICGtesting.com
Printed in the USA
LVOW11s1611081215

465893LV00007B/69/P